15

SOLDIERS IN A NARROW LAND

SOLDIERS IN A NARROW LAND

The Pinochet Regime in Chile

MARY HELEN SPOONER

UNIVERSITY OF CALIFORNIA PRESS
BERKELEY   LOS ANGELES   LONDON

University of California Press
Berkeley and Los Angeles, California

University of California Press, Ltd.
London, England

First Paperback Printing 1999

© 1994 by
The Regents of the University of California

Library of Congress Cataloging-in-Publication Data

Spooner, Mary Helen.
    Soldiers in a narrow land : the Pinochet regime in Chile /
Mary Helen Spooner.
        p.   cm.
    Includes bibliographical references (p.) and index.
    ISBN 0-520-22169-9 (pbk. : alk. paper)
    1. Chile—Politics and government—1973–1988.   2. Pi-
nochet Ugarte, Augusto.   3. Military government—Chile—
History.   4. Human rights—Chile—History.   I. Title.
F3100.S66   1994
320.983—dc20   93-9910
                                                              CIP

Printed in the United States of America
08 07 06 05 04 03 02 01
9 8 7 6 5 4 3 2

The paper used in this publication meets the minimum require-
ments of ANSI/NISO Z39.48-1992 (R 1997) (*Permanence of
Paper*). ∞

For Alan, Daniel, and Alexandra,
la familia que me dió Chile

A soldier's training begins with the prohibition of many things permitted to ordinary people; and heavy penalties are attached to the smallest transgression. Everyone is made aware in childhood of a sphere of prohibited things, but the soldier's is immensely larger. Wall after wall is erected around him; they are illuminated for him, so that he sees them growing. They are as high and strong as they are clearly outlined. They are continually spoken of, so that he cannot pretend not to know them. He begins to move as though he always felt them around him. The angularity of his body is an echo of their hardness and smoothness; he comes to resemble a stereometric figure.

In the vast desert of prohibitions surrounding the soldier a command comes as salvation: the stereometric figure comes to life and starts moving.

—Elias Canetti, *Crowds and Power*

Contents

Preface to the Paperback Edition

He is something of an anachronism, this aging former dictator whose pleasant visit to Great Britain suddenly turned ugly. For months he was under house arrest, first at a hospital where he had undergone back surgery and later at a private estate southeast of London. Augusto Pinochet Ugarte, former army commander, junta member, president of Chile for seventeen years, and senator for life (this last title bestowed according to the terms of a constitution his regime drafted) never imagined himself in detention in a foreign land. A Spanish judge requested his extradition to Spain on charges of genocide and torture; Pinochet claimed he enjoyed diplomatic immunity as a former head of state. After turning over his office to an elected president in March 1990, Pinochet spent eight more years as Chile's army commander and continued to cast a long shadow over the country's newly restored democratic institutions. Then in his seventies and well past the age when most senior army officers retired, Pinochet controlled the institution as rigidly as ever, occasionally hinting that the army would rise up if civilian officials attempted to reduce the military's power or bring to justice any officers accused of human rights abuses. On March 11, 1998, he took his permanent seat in the Chilean Senate, an institution his regime had shut down shortly after coming to power. His opponents mounted different legal challenges to his Senate seat, which according to the terms of the constitution is given to any past president who has served at least six years in office. Pinochet had not been elected president and therefore had no right to a Senate seat, they argued, and managed to pass a nonbinding resolution rejecting him as senator, by a vote of 56–26.

Outside the National Congress building, thousands of Chilean protesters demonstrated against Pinochet, hurling rocks as police tried to
control the crowd with tear gas. More than five hundred people were
arrested and thirty-four injured in this and similar demonstrations
around the country that day. Inside the Senate, several legislators carried photographs of the military regime's victims, including former army
commander Carlos Prats and diplomat Orlando Letelier. Both men
were killed by Pinochet's secret police while living outside Chile.

If Pinochet seemed to be enjoying a multitude of privileges, with little fear of retribution by Chilean authorities, officials in other countries
were taking a decidedly less benevolent view of his career. In July 1996
a group of Spanish jurists filed a suit charging him with "international
terrorism, genocide, and crimes against humanity." A Spanish magistrate ruled that his court had jurisdiction in the case inasmuch as the
charges dealt with crimes covered under international law. The following year the European parliament passed a unanimous resolution supporting the Spanish court's investigation. A second Spanish judge began
an inquiry into the disappearances of Spanish citizens in Argentina,
whose own military authorities had cooperated with their Chilean counterparts in hunting down and killing suspected leftists.

Pinochet and his supporters appeared not to take the Spanish investi-
gations seriously, perhaps dismissing the case as just another example of
Marxist propaganda. In 1997 he even proposed a visit to Spain, only to
be warned by Chile's civilian government that such a trip was "not rec-
ommended." He had traveled to Great Britain in the past (once as a
guest of Royal Ordnance) and had been received by Margaret Thatcher
and other conservative leaders. The usually xenophobic Pinochet had
come to view that country as a friendly haven in a world that seemed
bent on maligning him, and a stay in a London hotel was a most civi-
lized pleasure.

On September 23, 1998, Pinochet, carrying a diplomatic passport,
flew to London. He had tea with Lady Thatcher and enjoyed shopping
at Harrods (where he was pleased to be recognized by a store clerk)
before checking into a private hospital for an operation to repair a her-
niated disk on October 9. On October 16, 1998, he was placed under
arrest by British police, who were acting on a request from Spanish
judge Baltasar Garzon to have the former dictator extradited and prose-

cuted for the crimes of torture and murder. For at least a week the eighty-three-year-old Pinochet was unaware of his detention, believing that his extended stay at the London clinic was due to medical reasons. When he was finally informed of what was happening, he began to suffer "a very great stress which caused psychological complications," according to his wife, Lucia. A few days later he was transferred, under heavy guard, to a hospital on the outskirts of London where he remained a few more weeks before being moved to an estate where he was kept under house arrest.

At first, the former dictator's arrest sparked an uproar. At a mass demonstration in an affluent Santiago suburb, his supporters demanded his release; a similar number of his opponents celebrated his arrest in one of the Chilean capital's biggest parks. The government of President Eduardo Frei formally protested Pinochet's arrest, arguing that the diplomatic passport he carried should have been respected. This was a matter for Chileans to decide, not a foreign court, so the argument went, and if Pinochet were to be put on trial anywhere, it should be in Chile. But behind the Frei government's public position on Pinochet's arrest, the smirking was evident. One high government official was heard to say that he needed to wear an orthopedic neck brace to prevent himself from grinning. Pinochet's supporters launched a well-organized campaign in his defense, with a group of Chilean businessmen agreeing to pay more than $3 million in legal fees. A former regime cabinet minister organized a telemarketing fund-raiser, with a recorded message phoned to hundreds of thousands of homes requesting donations for Pinochet to be sent in along with phone bill payments. A Web site showed photos of Pinochet under house arrest, wearing a well-tailored suit and holding his cane, his gray hair neatly combed—the very image of the patient elder statesman his supporters wanted to present to the world. The accompanying text proclaimed that Pinochet had "stopped a Cuban-backed Marxist dictatorship" in Chile in the early 1970s and had "brought back democracy."

The Pinochet Foundation also set up toll-free hot lines and sold compact discs and wine to raise money to pay for the former dictator's mounting legal bills and the cost of his rented mansion. A Cabernet Sauvignon bearing the label *Capital General,* a reference to Pinochet's army rank, was marketed for $25 a bottle. The foundation did not reveal how much money these fund-raising efforts produced but did say it had already paid $600,000 to Pinochet's British lawyers and was facing another $340,000 payment in March 1999.

The first few weeks of Pinochet's arrest appeared to raise the country's political temperature, and the British government even issued a warning that Britons should avoid nonessential travel to Chile, for fear of reprisals. There were dire warnings from Pinochet supporters that his continued detention posed a danger to the country's democratic future, hinting strongly that the Chilean armed forces might take some action against the civilian government in reprisal for Pinochet's arrest. The country's leading tabloid newspaper, *La Tercera,* published daily reports on Pinochet's arrest, with a photograph of the former dictator on the front page. But despite the avalanche of publicity about the case, polls showed that most Chileans were unaffected by Pinochet's arrest. A survey by the British-based Market Opinion Research International (MORI) indicated that 45 percent of those polled thought Pinochet's arrest was "bad," 44 percent, "good." In answer to other questions, 71 percent said that the case had had no effect on their daily lives; 57 percent said that if Pinochet were to return to Chile, he should be put on trial; 63 percent said they believed he was guilty of having committed crimes during his regime; and 66 percent said his arrest did not endanger Chile's democracy. If the poll's soundings accurately reflect Chilean opinion, then the survey suggested that the majority of Chileans wanted to move on, putting Pinochet and the military regime behind them.

The longer Pinochet remained under house arrest in Great Britain, the less important he seemed to Chilean public life. National elections scheduled for December 8, 1999, were fast approaching, the third since Pinochet had lost a one-man presidential plebiscite more than a decade earlier. If the Chilean armed forces were disgruntled by their former leader's arrest in a foreign country, they seemed well aware that his situation was out of their hands and were hardly inclined to rattle sabres. The 1973 military coup that ousted socialist president Salvador Allende's government was an anomaly in modern Chilean history, occurring against the background of the Cold War. Since the Pinochet regime grudgingly relinquished power in 1990, Chile, like the rest of the world, has changed profoundly. The fall of communist governments may not have deterred Pinochet's most die-hard supporters from invoking the threat of Marxism, but a new generation of young Chilean voters, with only the vaguest childhood memories of the Allende and Pinochet years, has come of age and seems little inclined to dwell on the past. The passage of time has allowed older Chileans to look back on the Pinochet regime with greater critical detachment. The former dictator's arrest may have raised uncomfortable questions about the efficacy of Chile's legal system and about the appropriateness of prosecuting him abroad for crimes committed largely within the country. But it also allowed Chileans to take another hard look at their nation's history.

Acknowledgments

My first and most heartfelt thanks go to the Chileans who agreed to be interviewed for this book and who showed their trust by patiently recounting experiences that were often bitter or painful. Some requested anonymity, and one day I hope to be able to thank them publicly.

My next debt of gratitude is to Deborah Schneider, a literary agent who believed in this book from its beginnings as an unsolicited query landing on her desk in New York. For two years she searched for the right home for this book, never giving up hope and always lending this first-time author the encouragement needed to keep going.

Naomi Schneider, my editor, carefully guided me and the manuscript through the long, hard process of critique, review, and revision. Enrique Hermosilla of FLACSO in Santiago and Margarita Ortiz of INFO-South in Miami helped me locate papers, articles, and documents. Herminia Astudillo and Edith Barra provided help in Santiago.

Finally, I must thank my husband, Alan Stephens, for his patience and support, and our children, Daniel and Alexandra, for their pride in "Mommy's book."

Prologue

Chilean Voices

"We did not make the coup in order to establish a one-man dictatorship. We could not have imagined, fifteen years ago, what would eventually come about in Chile." The retired air force general sat across the table in his apartment in eastern Santiago and looked at me somewhat suspiciously. During the first few years after he left the regime, he rarely if ever spoke of his experiences outside a closed circle of family and trusted friends, a precautionary habit shared by many Chileans. But of late he had been known to speak to the occasional journalist.

"As a rule I never speak to the foreign press," he said. "Anything I have to say should be said in Chile and not to the outside world." I explained that I was not as interested in his opinions on current issues as I was in his experiences, the events he had witnessed from within the regime, though I understood if he wanted to keep certain things to himself. He looked at me for a moment, and paused before speaking. "Ask me," he said.

I came to Santiago in early 1980, with a trunk, a manual typewriter, and a small grant from the Inter American Press Association, which each year sends four or five young American and Canadian journalists to Latin America and an equal number of their Latin American counterparts to North America. I had already spent three years working in Guatemala, Venezuela, and Colombia, but no story, no country had ever fascinated me as much as Chile and its military regime. As a graduate student at the University of Missouri, I had written my master's thesis on newsmagazine coverage of Chile during Salvador Allende's ill-fated socialist government, coverage that did not reveal the U.S. role in its destabilization. This factor, whose importance is still being debated, had not been revealed until after the bloody 1973 coup. I wanted to examine the extent to which the U.S. role had contributed to General Augusto Pinochet's permanence in power; I was unaware at the time that his own role in the coup was minimal and that his consolidation of power over the years was in many ways a strictly Chilean affair. And I hoped to witness the first stirrings of a democratic transition, a process far slower and more excruciating than most outside observers could ever imagine. Once set in place, the regime proved durable and resistant to outside influences, with diplomatic brickbats sometimes carrying all the weight of a paper airplane hurled against an armored tank.

Chile, extending for more than 3,000 miles along South America's western coast, is not on the way to anywhere, and it is a rare traveler who arrives either by accident or en route to some other destination. "Night, snow, and sand make up the form of my thin country, all silence lies in its long line," wrote Pablo Neruda, one of two Nobel Prize–winning poets Chile has given the world.[1] The territory begins in the north with the Atacama desert, then temperate valley continuing southward into a lake district that would resemble Switzerland were it not for the volcanoes incongruously dotting the landscape. The lakes expand as the traveler continues south, until the land mass finally disintegrates into an archipelago of hundreds of islands and islets, some sparsely populated, others barren, still others rising out of the South Pacific only at low tides.

"Maybe because we live between the Andes and the sea, our geography has isolated us. We have come to understand many things much later than the rest of the world," Hernol Flores, president of the country's civil service employees union, told me. "We Chileans were ignorant of what a dictatorship involved. We had lived for 163 years under a constitutional system, and democracy was like air to us, a central condition of being Chilean."

En los tiempos de la república, in the time of the republic, he recalled, Chileans swelled with pride when cadets from the military academy marched by. As schoolboys, Flores said, he and his classmates would pledge "a soldier's word" when asked to swear the truth.

The Chilean military, Latin America's most professional armed forces, were seen as honest, invincible defenders of the constitution, "a force for freedom and democracy."

For many Chileans, who had never lived under military rule and did not fully understand what military government would involve, the belated realization came brutally. Flores's predecessor as president of the public employees' union, Tucapél Jiménez, an early backer of the new regime, was found murdered in 1982, the victim of a right-wing death squad that had menaced him and his union for years. A few weeks after his death, Chilean police announced that an unemployed construction worker had hanged himself after writing a suicide note confessing to the murder. This assertion did not convince even regime supporters, but it was accompanied by a wave of officially inspired rumors to the effect that a dispute involving Jiménez's personal life rather than his union activities had motivated his killers. An official investigation into the killing eventually showed that the hapless construction worker had been murdered, but it failed, not surprisingly, to find the guilty parties in either killing.

Coming to Chile to work as a journalist held obvious risks, for the regime had a blacklist of foreign reporters banned from entering the country and I did not yet enjoy the backing of a large news organization. But after a few months' residence I was reporting for ABC radio, the *Financial Times,* the *Economist, Newsweek,* and other publications. What was supposed to have been a stay of roughly twelve months stretched to over nine years in a country I came to love.

Chile, even under a dictatorship, can cast a spell on visitors. I met many other foreigners who had come to the country for a visit or a temporary posting and had ended up as permanent residents. It was in Chile that I met my husband, who had initially come for a three-month job assignment, and where our children, Daniel and Alexandra, were adopted. What made Chile special was not only its physical beauty, but the Chileans themselves, who have an unusual mixture of Latin warmth and an almost English reserve and formality.

But friendship is not easy to come by in an atmosphere of political polarization and repression. Even the most superficial encounters were sometimes tense as each party in a two-way exchange attempted to guess the sympathies of the other, for reasons having as much to do with self-defense as with curiosity.

A woman I met at a reception shortly after I arrived in Santiago is a case in point. After exchanging the usual pleasantries she looked me in the eye and said carefully, "My husband was a cabinet official—with the former government." When she saw that my reaction was not hostile, we began a more animated conversation in lowered voices. Then there was the Chilean businessman with good contacts in the regime, who would speak off the record, always in English and with a radio playing in the background to thwart any hidden microphones the regime's security forces might have planted in his office. From such encounters it might be argued that the regime had unintentionally drawn attention to the importance of free discourse, but the practical effect of such intimidation was to discourage people from making new acquaintances and contacts.

If Chile's geography encourages insularity, years of dictatorship made its society even more inward-looking. Many if not all Chileans who supported the regime were openly hostile, even abusive, to foreign reporters, and to avoid such confrontations I eventually adopted the habit of not mentioning my work to strangers unless I was actively engaged in it. And like many Chileans I acquired the defensive habit of sizing up a person I had just met, looking carefully for any clues to their acceptance or opposition of the regime before deciding whether to reveal my profession. I told a Chilean doctor with a beard, darker coloring, and an irreverent manner; but talking to a smartly dressed middle-aged housewife residing in Santiago's *barrio alto*, the upper-income suburbs in the eastern part of the city, I limited myself to a statement of my husband's profession.

The Chilean capital's English-speaking community, which like many expatriate enclaves is small, gossipy, and cliquish, offered no relief. One evening I was at an embassy cocktail party, talking to a Chilean lawyer working with the Catholic Church's human rights department, when I turned briefly to say hello to a woman I knew distantly. When I saw her later, she awkwardly told me what her husband—whom I'd never met—had said to her after they passed me: "Why are you talking to her? She's a journalist and her husband is a communist." The Chilean lawyer with whom I was conversing was neither my husband nor a Communist Party member, I assured her, but then I realized that my work was at least as offensive to them as the supposed political affiliation of my imaginary spouse. Such incidents were not uncommon, for many expatriates saw Chile through the prism of company contracts that included housing in an affluent area and membership in Santiago's Prince of Wales Country Club, where proregime sentiment ran high. And yet, whenever I found myself berating the society that the Pinochet regime had produced (or was it the other way around?) I had to remind myself that I was there voluntarily and that Chileans who found this atmosphere toxic usually had no alternative.

"Social life was destroyed," a Jesuit priest who worked in a poor neighborhood in central Santiago commented to me. "We Chileans used to be a very sociable people; we like to have fiestas, to invite the whole neighborhood." His parishioners, he said, now tended to lock themselves up in their modest homes after dark, visiting only relatives and a few trusted friends. The same social restrictions seem to operate in the upper-middle-class neighborhood where my husband and I rented a house. For the first few months after we moved in, our only contact with the other families living on our street consisted of a visit by a young woman from Opus Dei, a secretive ultra-traditionalist Catholic group, and an inquiry from the man next door who asked rather nicely if we needed any help. But by then I had taken on the bristle-like caution so sadly common under the dictatorship and did not follow up this all-too-rare gesture of neighborliness. When I learned that my neighbor had a son who was an army officer, I suspected I had taken the wiser course, and two years later we had yet to encounter our neighbor on the street, much less have the sort of conversation in which my status as a foreign journalist would have been revealed.

But then their housekeeper, whose habitual discretion had perhaps been shattered by grief, happened to tell us that our neighbors' two-year-old granddaughter had died after drowning in her parents' swimming pool. I wrote my neighbors a brief, formal note of condolence and attached it to a bouquet of flowers, but I hesitated even before undertaking this most ordinary gesture, fearing that it might elicit a hostile reaction if my neighbor and his wife had somehow learned I was a journalist. After seven years in Chile I had become, to my own disgust, as wary and mistrustful as any Chilean. As it turned out, however, my neighbors' initial reaction was surprise. A few days later the husband came to our house to thank us for the flowers. We spoke for a while, and he mentioned that he and his family had lived for a time in Venezuela, an experience that he said had caused them to have an outlook somewhat different from that of many Chileans, "who might not have known how to respond to your flowers."

In early 1980 when I arrived, Chile was in the midst of an economic boom of sorts that gave Santiago's downtown area and its upper-income suburbs a feeling of unprecedented affluence. The Pinochet regime's civilian economic team, dubbed the Chicago Boys because several members of the group had taken postgraduate degrees at the University of Chicago, had engineered what *Time* described as "An Odd Free Market Success," boosted by high copper prices and record levels of foreign investment.[2] Yet the aura of prosperity did not translate into improved living conditions for poor Chileans or a more relaxed political environment.

At times, political repression manifested itself in bizarre ways. A civilian official at the state copper corporation, CODELCO, whom I had interviewed on the subject of molybdenum (a copper byproduct that had become Chile's second largest export), attempted to get my press credential revoked. In the interview he had told me how CODELCO planned to begin direct sales of molybdenum to its clients abroad. But his comment irked the U.S. firm that still had a distribution contract with CODELCO, and the official reacted by calling the regime's communications office, DINACOS, which accredits foreign journalists in Chile, claiming that I had failed to keep a supposed promise to let him read and approve the story before filing it. The CODELCO executive was not the only Chilean functionary who sought to censor his own statements, and over the years I encountered several civilian officials who ended our interviews with a request to review my story before it was filed, even when the subject was so seemingly neutral as economic projections. The authoritarian atmosphere was so pervasive and so arbitrary that Chilean officials were terrified of accidentally uttering something not strictly in line with what their own superiors would have them say. To be quoted at all in the foreign press was a risky undertaking for Chileans outside the government, even for those with proregime sympathies. This was the case for the then-president of Chile's National Agricultural Society, who accepted an invitation to have lunch with Santiago's foreign press club on an off-the-record basis, but who was so fearful of having his innocuous views made public that he said almost nothing about the situation of Chilean farmers.

Chileans opposed to the regime seemed alternately heartened by the outside world's interest and irritated by foreign reporters' requests for interviews, which might expose them to the risk of arrest, prosecution by a military court, or expulsion from the country. In 1981 I interviewed Jaime Castillo, a Christian Democrat who was president of the Chilean human rights commission. He spoke about the regime's new constitution, the different human rights policies of the Carter and Reagan administrations, and about Central America and his own Christian Democratic party.

"Don't forget that I live in a dictatorship," he said as I picked up my bag and was preparing to leave. He meant that I had to take every care in reproducing his statements, cautious as they were and punctuated with qualifying phrases such as "it is not for me to say." The interview appeared on the back page of *Newsweek*'s international edition of March 30, 1981. Several weeks later Castillo and three other Chilean opposition figures were arrested in their homes, transported to the Argentine border, and expelled from the country. More than two years passed before he was allowed back into Chile, and in a subsequent conversation Castillo told me that the *Newsweek* interview had influenced the regime's decision to send him into exile. "But it was not your fault," he kindly hastened to add, when I must have blanched. Perhaps not, but a sense of guilt accompanied my more logical feeling of indignation.

If I had to let the Chileans I approached gauge the risks themselves, something at which they were far more adept than I was, the insinuation of responsibility nevertheless cropped up again and again. Ita Ford, one of four American churchwomen murdered in El Salvador in 1980, had worked for years in Chile before moving to Central America, and slum dwellers she had known in Santiago were preparing a memorial service on the anniversary of her death. When I telephoned a Maryknoll missionary to ask about the service, she somewhat nervously said she would call me back after talking to its organizers. When she did call back, she told me they had asked if there was any way to read what I wrote before it was published. No, I said, there wasn't, and I ended up not visiting this particular poor neighborhood and feeling dissatisfied and frustrated by the entire episode.

The direct censorship imposed by the regime after the coup gave way to a form of self-censorship in which Chilean journalists attempted to ward off official sanctions by second-guessing the authorities' reaction and discreetly toning down or eliminating material deemed likely to incur official displeasure. Foreign journalists were not necessarily expected to play along with this game, but those Santiago-based correspondents whose dispatches offended the regime could expect to be called on the carpet at DINACOS, the government communications office, or issued an indirect expulsion threat through an intermediary, often a Chilean journalist sympathetic to the regime.

In 1981 I wrote a story for the *London Observer*'s syndication service on the country's Roman Catholic bishops issuing excommunication orders against "he who tortures or is an accomplice to torture; he who orders it, solicits or incites torture; or he who is able to stop torture and fails to do so."[3] My copy of the story, filed in the morning through Reuters's network, had disappeared from my box at the news agency when I returned that afternoon. A Chilean reporter who at the time worked for Reuters and who staunchly supported Pinochet was standing near the mailboxes, along with the office secretary. Both looked uncomfortable when I commented that my file was missing; the reporter indicated that there had been some mix-up and to come back the following day. The next morning my box was still empty, and when I asked a young Reuters office assistant what had happened, he insisted that he personally had placed a copy of my file in my box after transmitting it the previous morning.

Since the story of the bishops' excommunication orders had been covered in Chile's progovernment press, it did not occur to me that Chilean officialdom might have taken issue with my report. I assumed the file had been innocently mislaid, and I thought no more about the incident until a few weeks later, when I learned that another proregime journalist had told several colleagues that I was about to be arrested and expelled from the country. When I confronted the journalist, who worked at United Press International as director of the agency's Chilean service, he said he had been at a cocktail party a few days earlier where "someone very close to the interior ministry" had asked him if he knew me. The interior ministry official had then pulled a copy of the excommunication story from his pocket, showed it to him, and announced that "this girl has to go." The Chilean journalist refused to tell me the name of the official and, somewhat embarrassed, said that the threat had really been a warning.

In other cases it was difficult to tell where official pressures ended and proregime sympathies began. *El Mercurio*, the country's rightwing and most influential newspaper—and according to a U.S. Senate investigation, a recipient of Central Intelligence Agency funds during the Allende years—occasionally printed very brief human-rights-related stories, usually pegged to a court suit filed in behalf of a Chilean who had undergone *apremios ilegítimos*, illegitimate pressures at the hands of unidentified captors. The articles were usually written in such an oblique way that only the most discerning reader could understand the real story behind the *El Mercurio* item and grasp that "illegitimate pressures" really meant torture. At least two editors at other publications, neither a regime supporter, defended the use of the euphemism by telling me that *tortura* was too strong a word for general newspaper readers.

A bestselling book in Santiago during this period was *El Día Decisivo* (The crucial day), an extended question-and-answer session with Pinochet by an interviewer who for some unexplained reason chose to remain anonymous; in fact Pinochet himself is flatteringly listed as the author. The book, which was translated into English and other languages for distribution by Chilean embassies abroad, offers a revised account of the 1973 coup in which Pinochet greatly magnifies his own role. In the introduction the publisher writes:

In the past, whenever the country needed to overcome affliction, her children arose like heroes, leaders, or statesmen to help her successfully out of her predicament. Later, in the calm that follows the storm, when the historian's pen describes those events for posterity, the life of each hero, leader, or statesman is found to be the culmination of a process of human and cultural formation, a disciplined, rigorous process, almost prescient of the call that the country was to make.

The life of President Pinochet, the protagonist of the events of September 11, 1973, is a case in point. As a young Army officer he very early realized the perils associated with international Marxism. He studied its doctrine and methods, and became conversant with the procedures of the Communist Party in Chilean politics.[4]

But retired Chilean military officers directly involved in the events up to and after September 11, 1973, tell a very different story, of a vacillating general who had become army commander barely three weeks earlier, who repeatedly warned his colleagues of the dire consequences in store for them if the coup plans were leaked. Dictatorships often attempt to rewrite history, and one oft-repeated claim by the Pinochet regime and its adherents was that Chile had never had a "real democracy," but rather a long succession of governments nominally led by civilians representing narrow sectarian interests. In order to establish a solid base for a future democracy, according to this argument, the Chilean armed forces must remain in power while the necessary restructuring of the country's entire legal and political framework was undertaken.

The regime's attempts to rewrite history and alter events to fit its own ever-changing propaganda needs were evident on many levels. A clerk at the newspaper archives in the Biblioteca Nacional abruptly told me I could not read the September 1973 back issues of *El Mercurio* or *La Tercera,* a leading Chilean tabloid, because the copies were all "in very bad condition." How this came to be was not explained. A request to look at the newspapers under the supervision of a library guard was rejected, but the clerk suggested I might want to see copies of *La Nación,* the official government newspaper, from that period. (I returned a few months later and asked for *La Nación's* September 1973 issues, and was told curtly that this volume could no longer be lent, for it, too, was "in very bad condition.")

The bound volume I received contained a gap dating from September 12, the day after the coup, to September 21, which might be explained in part by the upheaval in the newspaper's personnel as Allende government staff members either fled or were fired and editorial content was adjusted to the new military regime. The issue for September 11, 1973, prepared the day before, had the unintentionally ironic headline, "The Armed Forces Depart," referring to the resignation of three military officers who had served in the Allende cabinet.

La Nación's next issue, September 21, 1973, bore a front-page photograph of overworked Chilean barbers cutting the locks of long-haired young men as a crowd of customers with similar hairstyles waited their turn. The accompanying story described a sudden, unexplained change in preferred hair length following the coup. After another four-issue gap in the bound library volume, the September 26 issue reports that the junta has ordered the arrest of thirteen Chilean leftists whose photographs appear on the front page. The next issue states that the junta has offered a cash reward for the capture of any fleeing Marxists.

Even Pinochet's own public statements were subject to cosmetic revision in the Chilean press. On August 16, 1984, I attended a rare press conference Pinochet gave for foreign journalists at the La Moneda presidential palace. A presidential aide informed us that the session was to be off the record and instructed us to leave our tape recorders outside the dining room. Pinochet entered the room, looking vigorous and in good spirits, and one of the reporters asked him if the meeting was in fact going to be off the record. He shrugged, smiled, and said that no, he had probably said most of what he would tell us that day on previous occasions. We looked around awkwardly, wanting to get up from the table and retrieve our tape recorders and yet not wanting to offend our host. A DINACOS official said that they were already recording the press conference and would make a copy available afterward. "Unfortunately some foreign news media have misinterpreted some of his declarations in the past," the functionary said. Pinochet fielded questions for slightly more than an hour, and appeared to enjoy the exchange, though most of the questions were not posed as assertively as they might have been under normal circumstances. He ended the session by shaking everyone's hand (and kissing me, inquiring where I was from).

We filed our stories from handwritten notes, and that afternoon I picked up a copy of the official transcript of the press conference. The document, bearing the seal of the presidential press secretary's office, was markedly different from what Pinochet had actually said. Not only was the text incomplete, but it included questions that had not been asked and remarks that Pinochet had not made. A correspondent from the Italian news agency ANSA had asked him if he would be willing to meet with youths from the Christian Democratic Party. Pinochet had answered, "No, because they are as putrid as the rest. I speak only with wholesome youth." The official text had been softened to read,

"No, because I only talk to non-politicized youth." Discussion of the controversy surrounding the construction of Pinochet's country home outside Santiago and relations with the United States and the Catholic Church were either eliminated or else markedly changed. When asked about his plans after leaving the presidency, Pinochet said, according to the official transcript, "Now, what happens with me, history will tell." His real response had been more apocalyptic: "Now, when I finish they can kill me as I expect. I'm a soldier and I'm ready."

An enterprising correspondent who had brought along a second tape recorder and used it after Pinochet indicated the session would be on the record was able to substantiate the foreign press club's subsequent protest to DINACOS, but an official there offered the following justification: when covering the president of Chile, "You should know what is on the record and off the record."

Most of what was reported about Pinochet and his activities came from a small group of progovernment Chilean reporters with access to La Moneda, yet the regime did not always trust even this carefully selected group. At the occasional press conference Pinochet held for the domestic media, censorship was the norm; in several cases the reporters were not even allowed to take notes, but were limited to asking questions. The Chilean government television station, Channel 7, the only one that reached the entire country, routinely broadcast camera footage of Pinochet's own speeches without the original sound; instead the announcer's voiceover paraphrased the general's words.

Memory, collective and individual, fades with time, a process often accelerated by trauma. In Gabriel García Marquez's *One Hundred Years of Solitude,* an entire town suffers mass amnesia in the wake of a banana company's massacre of six hundred workers. In a dictatorship those who do remember must weigh the benefits of speaking the truth against the dangers of official reaction. Alejandro Rios, a retired professor of geography and history at Chile's military academy, where Pinochet had been a cadet, told an interviewer that Pinochet had been a poor student. For this recollection the country's military courts prosecuted him on charges of insulting the president and the armed forces. More than two years after his words appeared in print, the eighty-eight-year-old Rios was still forced to come before a military judge each month.

Locating information on Pinochet's life and career, as well as on the internal workings of the military regime, was a bit like trying to put together a jigsaw puzzle with most of the pieces missing. Many former government officials with whom I spoke felt themselves to be in a more delicate position even than Chileans openly opposed to the regime. Often, the most obvious witnesses to events were the hardest to locate, such as ex-conscripts who had done their military service at the time of the coup. The old saying about there being all kinds of men in the army except rich men's sons is particularly true in Chile, and conversations with people who had supported the coup often lapsed into an uncomfortable silence when I asked if they knew anyone who had actually fought on September 11, 1973.

Few if any of the Chileans interviewed for this book were eager to talk, which lent more credibility to their accounts, since liars are often suspiciously forthcoming with their versions of events. To a journalist seeking accuracy, understatement is far preferable to exaggeration, and the flattened monotone of people describing the horrors they had witnessed lent chilling conviction to their accounts. A handful of retired military officers spoke, some on the record, some on background. A former Chilean police prefect, now employed as the security chief for the Sheraton Hotel in Santiago, also spoke, on the record. His boss had forbidden him to talk about anything remotely "political," but with a conspiratorial grin he said he saw no reason he could not talk to a foreign journalist about his extraordinary dealings with the regime's security forces. Former civilian officials of the regime were sometimes willing to talk, depending on their current relationship with the government and the direction of the prevailing political winds. And there was the testimony of a half dozen or so former security agents who, conscience-stricken, had left the regime's intelligence services and fled into exile outside Chile, where they told their stories to human rights groups. Although the jigsaw puzzle is still incomplete, their accounts, taken together, present much of the Pinochet regime's true face.

"If there are any doubts about what really went on under the regime, well, I had it straight from the horse's mouth," said Mariana

Callejas, a former agent for the regime's secret police organization, the DINA. "These army people, the captains, the majors, when they talked about assassinations it was as if they were talking about the last movie they saw." For other Chilean military officers, knowledge of such atrocities was painful and a matter of deep shame. "I am still trying to understand what happened to our institution, how officials I knew and respected came to commit the acts they did," said a retired army officer, who spoke on the condition that his name not be used. He had left the service before the coup and from his retirement had watched events unfold with a mixture of resignation and horror. There was the general, a onetime friend, who had ordered executions of political detainees already tried and serving prison sentences. There were the two young officers with promising careers he had once known who were recruited into the DINA. They came into public view a few years later, when U.S. authorities sought their extradition in connection with the 1976 car-bomb assassination in Washington of Chilean exile leader Orlando Letelier and his American coworker, Ronni Moffitt.

In telling his story, this retired army officer felt himself to be wading into more precarious straits even than Chileans who had been politically persecuted, for he had known many of the guilty parties personally and had good reason to fear reprisals. But as the Pinochet regime was drawing to an end, his concern for the truth overcame his fear.

Part One

The Dictator's Rise

Chapter One

Coup Plotting

*This is surely the last time I will address you. My words are
not spoken in bitterness, but in disappointment.*

*There will be a moral judgment against those who be-
trayed the oath they took as soldiers of Chile, legitimately
designated as commanders in chief. . . . Long live Chile!
Long live the people! Long live the workers! These are my
last words. And I am convinced my sacrifice will not be in
vain. I am certain that this sacrifice will be a moral lesson
that will punish cowardice, treachery, and treason.*

—Chilean president Salvador Allende, in his final
radio broadcast from the La Moneda presidential
palace during the September 11, 1973, coup

The grave of the world's first freely elected socialist president was left
unmarked at the time of his burial, and for years anyone seeking its
location did so at a certain risk. Guards at the Santa Ines cemetery in
Viña del Mar, a coastal resort town northwest of Santiago, habitually
denied that Salvador Allende was even buried there or else feigned ignorance of the grave's site.

With some misgivings, I visited the cemetery in 1985 and was almost immediately confronted by a guard who tried to discourage me
from even looking for the grave. When I insisted, the cemetery ad-
ministrator reluctantly directed me to one of the plots of the Grove
family, Allende's relatives, while demanding to know my name, occupation, and reason for coming. The site itself, a dark brown patch of
earth, was quite ordinary save for the fact that it appeared to be the
only grave in the cemetery without flowers.

"A lot of foreign people come here," the cemetery guard who had
followed me to the site said, shaking his head and scowling. There was
no headstone for the former president of Chile; yet outside his own
country the man in the unmarked grave had become a revolutionary

martyr, taking his place alongside Che Guevara, Leon Trotsky, and other folk heroes of the Left.

The funeral was a hasty affair, the body moved by the army from the La Moneda presidential palace the day of the coup and buried September 12 without ceremony.[1] Barely three weeks earlier, Allende had sworn in as Chilean army commander Augusto Pinochet Ugarte, a general whom few officials in the left-wing government or other military officers would have envisioned as the country's future military strongman. Pinochet was, a retired Chilean army general told me, "a man in the second row, a man you did not notice." Some found him mediocre, an unlikely officer to reach the rank of general, much less become head of state. A former Allende cabinet official recalled Pinochet as the most deferential of military officers, always saying, "Yes, minister," and "At your service, minister." The official curriculum vitae supplied by the regime's communications office is rather sketchy, offering the barest outline of Pinochet's military career, and in some places there are even contradictions between the chronology of dates and Pinochet's own version of events. The inconsistencies can be partially resolved from interviews with those who knew him before the coup and from comparing his own public statements—which in many cases were softened by presidential aides before they appeared in print—to other accounts of the same incidents.

Pinochet was born on November 25, 1915, in Valparaiso, Chile's principal port city, which is located about eighty miles northwest of Santiago. (Coincidentally, Allende was born there as well.) The Pinochet family traced its origins to a Breton immigrant who came to Chile in the eighteenth century; though his descendants hardly formed part of the country's aristocracy, their lack of Indian blood assured them a place in the Chilean middle class. Pinochet, the eldest of six children, was named after his father, who worked as a customs clerk and an insurance salesman. This latter job took him away from home a great deal, and the fragmentary information available suggests he did not play a major role in his children's upbringing. That task fell to his mother, Avelina Ugarte, who later told a Chilean journalist she had always favored her eldest son.[2]

By most accounts Avelina Ugarte was a stern matriarch who made certain her children observed a rigid code of manners and paid attention to outward appearances. While Pinochet was growing up the country's middle class was still small, clinging precariously to the rung of the social ladder just below an even tinier aristocratic elite whose customs and lifestyle were slavishly imitated. Below the middle class were the vast majority of Chileans, a poor and largely rural mestizo underclass whose chances for social and economic advancement were virtually nil.

The country's middle class expanded over the next few decades, not so much as a result of poor Chileans improving their lot but by the assimilation of second-generation European immigrants who arrived at the end of the century.[3] Chilean sociologists readily acknowledge the country's extreme class consciousness, a bias often shared even by those professing progressive views. This attitude carries with it a strong racist element; most Chileans tend to assume that a person with European features belongs to the country's middle or upper class and that anyone with darker coloring is part of the lower class. In Isabel Allende's novel *The House of the Spirits*, Blanca is offended by her French suitor's suggestion that she take advantage of the foreign market for South American crafts to export some of her ceramic pieces, saying that "neither she nor her work contained a drop of Indian blood."[4] The Spanish word *indio* is almost an insult, and many upper- and middle-class Chileans consider themselves transplanted Europeans.[5]

Valparaiso, founded in 1536, resembles a tattered version of San Francisco. It is a city of hills clustering around a bay, with a maze of steep and winding streets whose wooden houses seem to defy gravity. The Chilean navy has its headquarters here, and a statue in the city's principal plaza commemorates a victory over the Peruvian navy during the 1879 War of the Pacific. In this war the smaller but more disciplined Chilean military managed to defeat its Peruvian and Bolivian counterparts and conquer some of their territory, including Bolivia's sea outlet. In a continent not noted for military professionalism, the Chilean armed forces stood out as a rare exception; the country could boast that its military had never suffered defeat. Adding to this pride was the fact that the Chilean military had kept almost completely out of government since independence, leaving the business of running the country to civilians.

The Chilean army academy where Pinochet studied and the army staff school where he later served as deputy director were founded a few years after this war by Emil Korner, a Prussian army captain. Korner came to Chile in 1886 and eventually became a citizen and a commissioned officer in the army he helped to reorganize.[6] Gray uniforms, the goose step, a rigid hierarchical order, and political neutrality were part of the Prussian military legacy.

The historic exception came in 1924, when a liberal president beset by confrontations with a conservative congress resigned and left a military junta to govern in his stead. The original junta was overthrown four months later by a triumvirate of officers who proclaimed their regime the Socialist Republic of Chile. The group invited President Arturo Alessandri back into government, where he subsequently ruled by decree, without a congress, until new elections were held.

Pinochet entered the military academy in 1933, during Alessandri's second administration. His mother claimed to have predicted then that her son would one day be commander of the Chilean army. His academic record, however, offered little basis for such a belief. His grades at Valparaiso's Sagrados Corazones school were poor, with failing marks in English and several other subjects. It was only after his third application to the academy that Pinochet was admitted.[7]

In *The Crucial Day*, Pinochet said that his first two applications to the military academy were rejected because he was either "too young or too weak as a result of very rapid growth in those years."[8] The real reason almost certainly had to do with Pinochet's academic record, for when he finally did begin his studies at the academy, he was nearly two years older than most of his classmates, many of whom came from military families and thus enjoyed the additional moral support of their fathers' army careers. Pinochet's own father, he said in *The Crucial Day*, wanted him to become a doctor; if this is true, it would not have been a very realistic ambition.

Although Pinochet's former professor at the academy, Alejandro Rios, recalled Pinochet as a poor student who had to struggle to keep up with his younger classmates, the instructors and professors nevertheless liked him and seemed touched by the sheer effort Pinochet put into his work. His conduct was good, he did not participate in pranks or carousing, and he attended Mass regularly at the academy chapel.

In 1936 Pinochet graduated from the academy, fifth or sixth from the bottom of his class, and entered the army infantry school for a year, leaving with the rank of second lieutenant. He said that because few of his fellow junior officers discussed political matters, he came to believe that the subject was an unpleasant one. "I think the officers of the Chilean army were cloistered in their barracks, which were like airtight compartments isolating them from all contact with the outside world," he said in *The Crucial Day*. This isolation may refer to the Chilean military's tradition of political neutrality, but it also reflects his own ignorance of nonmilitary subjects, for he later said,

Whenever we were involved in discussions with civilians we appeared lacking in culture, and when we were asked in conversation, with good or malicious intent, about our political views, we avoided the subject and thought we put an end to the matter by saying simply, "Sorry, we are apolitical and don't like to discuss such matters." It was a poor excuse but it served to evade the issue and explain our ignorance.[9]

At age twenty-eight, while assigned to an army base in San Bernardo, a town south of Santiago, Pinochet met and married Lucía Hiriart, ten years his junior. The pretty daughter of a centrist politician, Lucía Hiriart de Pinochet would prove to be as strong-willed and demanding as her mother-in-law, and would later relish the role of First Lady. The marriage produced two sons and three daughters, one of whom joined the reformist Christian Democratic party for a time prior to the coup. Indeed, if Pinochet had any ideological leanings during his early career they were likely leftward rather than right.

In 1948 the government of President Gabriel González Videla banned Chile's Communist Party, and persecution of party members began. Augusto Pinochet, now an army captain assigned to the Iquique garrison in northern Chile, was placed in charge of moving five hundred "communist agitators" detained by the civilian police to a makeshift prison camp in the nearby fishing town of Pisagua. When a group of left-wing Chilean members of congress—including Salvador Allende, then a senator—attempted to visit the prisoners, their caravan was stopped on the road leading to Pisagua by carabineros, members of Chile's paramilitary national police force. According to Pinochet, the carabineros telephoned his command post for instructions, and he ordered that the congressmen be denied entry. "As they insisted they would pass, permit or no permit, I had them advised that if they did they would be fired on on the road," he related in his memoir.[10]

This story was no doubt intended to retroactively establish Pinochet's hard-line anticommunist credentials, but it is probably not true. A surviving member of the González Videla government told me it was highly unlikely that a Chilean army officer would have felt free to rebuff and threaten a congressional delegation in this manner, and if Pinochet had done so he would almost certainly have been punished. At the time the Chilean armed forces were still subject to the authority of a civilian president. When *The Crucial Day's* anonymous interviewer asked if Allende had ever reminded him of this incident, Pinochet said no and commented that perhaps the socialist president confused him with another officer with the same surname.

Pinochet's only posting abroad was as an instructor at the Ecuadorean military academy in Quito from 1956 to 1959, where he had poor relations with Chilean embassy officials. This experience likely contributed to Pinochet's later suspicion of all diplomats. He returned to Santiago to become deputy director of Chile's war academy, the army staff school founded by Emil Korner. While in this post he published two books, the first of which, *La Guerra del Pacífico*, is about the 1879 war with Peru and Bolivia.

According to Chilean army sources, the book is really a compilation of papers submitted by Pinochet's students; the chapters of the finished project vary noticeably in length and are written in different styles.[11] The other book, *Geopolítica*, concerns the science, or pseudo-science, of geopolitics, which conceives geographical location as a prime determinant of political identity and action. This concept, with its view of nations inevitably struggling with each other over territory, formed the basis of the Nazis' rhetoric of conquest. Geopolitics can be said, however, to have its own argument in South America, a continent marked by often bitter territorial disputes. According to Chilean academic sources Pinochet contributed little of his own material to *Geopolítica*. Several sections of the book are near-verbatim reproductions of lectures given at the war academy in 1950 by a Chilean army historian, Gregorio Rodríguez, which Pinochet attended.[12]

If his intellectual credentials were less than distinguished, the younger Pinochet nonetheless proved himself a competent enough official to move up through the ranks, becoming a lieutenant colonel in 1960. It was a time of increased U.S. interest in the region, for the Cuban revolution one year earlier had in effect brought the Cold War to

Latin America. The United States stepped up its military assistance programs to Latin America, as well as economic aid, in an effort to ward off the spread of Marxism. This effort marked a crucial change in the way the region's armed forces viewed their role.

"Before, our armies didn't fight guerrillas, they had only fought neighboring countries in border disputes," said Horacio Toro, a retired Chilean general who worked with the Pinochet regime during its first two years. "Che Guevara, with his small band of ragtag men, Bolivians who didn't really want to fight under him, was hardly a big military threat, but he was presented as the biggest danger ever to the region's security. His case confirmed what so many officials had been taught in their courses in the United States, so military officers became convinced that their real mission was to destroy Marxism, and in attempting to do so they ended up destroying democracy."[13]

But Pinochet was not among those Chilean officers selected for special training courses at the U.S. Army School of the Americas in Panama or military bases in the United States, though he did go to Washington in 1956 as part of a visiting Chilean military delegation. "His big stumbling block was English," one of Pinochet's former classmates, who requested anonymity, told me. "He could never master enough of the language, and in any case he never really felt comfortable outside Chile."

In 1964, the year Pinochet became deputy directory of the war academy, a reform-minded Christian Democrat, Eduardo Frei, was elected president of Chile. The other two candidates were Julio Duran, a right-wing politician, and Salvador Allende, the socialist senator. When it appeared that Allende would win a three-way race, the Chilean right threw its support to Frei, who received 56.1 percent of the vote. Allende received 38.9 percent. An unseen, though ultimately not decisive, factor in this election was the United States, which channeled $2.6 million into the Frei campaign. Under the Frei government Chile became one of the largest recipients of U.S. aid in Latin America, accounting for 10 percent of economic and military assistance to the region.

But a colonial economy, largely dependent on a single export—copper—cannot be restructured overnight, and the Frei government was faced with rapidly rising social expectations from one side and a backlash from wealthy influential Chileans on the other. By Frei's second year in office industrial production was falling while inflation was climbing, and the price of copper, which accounted for 80 percent of the country's exports, had declined as well. In addition, a small left-wing guerrilla organization, the Movement of the Revolutionary Left (MIR), had formed, giving Chile its first taste of Marxist violence.

By 1969, the year Pinochet was promoted to the rank of brigadier general, the country's inflation had reached 30 percent annually, and the Frei government was facing problems with the military, who were demanding a pay hike. The military pay raise was backed by Frei's right-wing opponents in the Chilean congress as well as Salvador Allende's Socialist party, which issued a statement supporting their demands. One general decided to try and force the issue by staging a short-lived revolt. Although this rebellion consisted only of troops quartering themselves in one artillery regiment in Santiago in a kind of labor stoppage, it marked the beginning of visible unrest within the military.

Brigadier General Augusto Pinochet did not take part in this rebellion or in the coup plotting that followed. He was then commanding the Chilean army's Sixth Division in Santiago, and was considered a "constitutionalist" general, that is, an officer who believed in and adhered strictly to the neutral role assigned to the country's armed forces.

On September 4, 1970, Salvador Allende, in his third bid for the Chilean presidency, won a 36.2 percent plurality of votes, narrowly defeating a rightist former president, Jorge Alessandri (34.7 percent), and a left-leaning Christian Democrat, Radomiro Tomic (27.8 percent). In his memoir Pinochet said he listened "with bitterness" to the election returns and later met with other officers at army headquarters where he warned his colleagues that Allende's victory meant that Chile would eventually become a satellite of the Soviet Union.[14] Again, Pinochet almost certainly embellished this version of events. However he viewed Allende—and his ignorance of politics and general reluctance to venture outside the sphere of military affairs makes it unlikely he felt strongly one way or another—his actions over the next three years were hardly those of a staunch anticommunist.

Even if his ideology was not offended, however, Pinochet's soldierly sense of order would have been disturbed by many of the events that followed Allende's election. The U.S. role in attempting to undermine

Allende has been extensively documented elsewhere, and rather than reproduce this material it is more instructive to examine those specific incidents likely to have influenced Pinochet. One of the first was a far-fetched plan by right-wing extremists to provoke a coup that resulted in the killing of Pinochet's army commander, General René Schneider. The plan was to kidnap Schneider, who like Pinochet was considered an apolitical, constitutionalist officer, somehow make the kidnapping appear to be the work of the far Left, and thus prompt the military to take over the government.

The plotters were a clumsy lot. Their first attempt was foiled when General Schneider left a reception in a private car rather than his official limousine, and the second when the abductors somehow lost him in traffic. But on October 22, 1970, as Schneider was being driven to his office at the Chilean defense ministry, his automobile was struck by a second vehicle, whose occupants leapt out and began smashing the windows of the general's car. Schneider reportedly pulled out his service revolver; his attackers drew their guns and fired at him, wounding him critically. He died in a hospital three days later, on the day the Chilean congress ratified Allende's election by a vote of 153 to 35, with 7 abstentions.

There are conflicting accounts of how the plot to kidnap General Schneider was hatched and the extent of U.S. involvement. The 1975 Senate document *Covert Action in Chile* has only this to say about the Schneider killing: "A rather disorganized coup attempt did begin on October 22, but aborted following the shooting of General Schneider."[15] Seymour Hersh, in *The Price of Power*, suggests that U.S. officials were much closer to Schneider's would-be kidnappers than the Senate report indicated. Hersh interviewed Colonel Paul Wimert, the army attaché at the U.S. embassy in Santiago, who said that after the first two kidnapping attempts failed, a different Chilean coup plotter, General Camilo Valenzuela, was encouraged to try. Wimert said that as an incentive he passed $50,000 to Valenzuela and another $50,000 to a Chilean naval admiral working with him. After Schneider's shooting, the American official decided to retrieve the money. The admiral returned his share willingly, but Valenzuela handed his over only after Wimert drew his gun and struck him.[16]

Whatever the true involvement of the U.S. in this plot, it produced the opposite effect to what had been intended. Valenzuela and an-

other general were arrested, and the subsequent outrage over Schneider's killing put a temporary end to any serious discussion within the
military of a coup. General Carlos Prats, a man to whom Augusto Pinochet professed complete loyalty, became commander of the Chilean
army, and Salvador Allende was sworn in as president of Chile.

Allende's first year in office was relatively calm, U.S. hostility notwithstanding. According to Chilean military sources I consulted,
there was virtually no discussion of a coup during this period, partly
because of the aftershock of the Schneider assassination. But in late
1971 right-wing political groups in Chile resumed their efforts to get
the military to act. A retired army general serving in Santiago at the
time described a kind of grassroots campaign in which military officers
received a steady stream of telephone calls and visits from civilians,
including friends and relatives, urging a coup. Each campaigner encouraged the officer to "do the right thing," or "act in the nation's interest." One retired army officer, who requested anonymity, described
to me how an envelope containing a chicken feather arrived at his
home, implying that he and other military officials reluctant to join
the coup plotting were cowards.

These efforts were aided by a disinformation campaign in Chile's
right-wing press, most notably in *El Mercurio,* the country's largest
newspaper. Another right-wing newspaper, *Tribuna,* attacked the
armed forces for what it considered their support of the Allende government, saying the military had sold out for the good salaries, housing, and other benefits afforded its officers. This particular report
prompted the commander of the Chilean army's Santiago garrison,
General Augusto Pinochet, to announce on December 5, 1971, that
the military would sue *Tribuna* for "grave offenses to the dignity of
the armed forces." In announcing the measure, Pinochet asked those
Chilean journalists present to cut back the sensationalist tone of so
much of the country's press, to reduce tensions.

"What do they want? A civil war?" he asked rhetorically. "Because
coups d'état do not happen in Chile." But the tensions continued to
increase. The CIA spent $8 million in Chile in an effort to create the
conditions for a coup, while the United States cut off most bilateral aid
(military assistance being a notable exception) and lobbied against
loans from multilateral lending institutions to Chile.[17] Terror from

the country's far right, often dressed up to look like the work of left-wing guerrillas, continued, but so did armed actions by the guerrilla group MIR. Though neither group posed a genuine military threat to the country, the series of bombings and farm takeovers in the countryside horrified most Chileans.

In 1971 the Chilean army discovered a guerrilla training center in Chaihuen, a tiny hamlet in southern Chile. The camp consisted of a few makeshift buildings where MIR had held meetings and "trained" for its actions with exercise sessions. The quantity of weapons seized in raids such as this tended to be paltry, according to a former army intelligence official who visited the site. This same official recalled asking Allende's Interior Minister José Tohá why, if Chile now had a socialist government, did so many youths continue to join MIR? What was the point?

"We did not expect to win the election," Tohá told him. "We weren't really prepared, and some of our kids feel frustrated." Allende did not fit many Chileans' idea of a socialist: he was an extravagant dresser, enjoyed Chivas Regal whiskey and the country's fine wines, and had installed his personal secretary and mistress, Miria Contreras, in a big house in eastern Santiago while his wife, Hortensia Bussi de Allende, lived as Chile's official First Lady a few miles away.

On January 6, 1972, the Chilean congress, concerned by what it viewed as Interior Minister José Tohá's tolerance of the MIR guerrillas and other constitutional violations, voted 80 to 59 to impeach Tohá. Allende responded by transferring Tohá to the defense ministry, a maneuver of dubious legality that Chileans compared to the "castle" move in chess where the rook is moved to protect the king. A few months later the dean of the University of Chile Law School and two other jurists, worried about the apparent lack of respect for the country's constitution, decided to offer a seminar on constitutional law to the Chilean military. It was the military, after all, that according to tradition was sworn to uphold the constitution.

The offer was well received by the Chilean navy and air force, but when the jurists approached the army's second-ranking officer at the time, General Augusto Pinochet, his reaction was unexpectedly hostile.[18] "You are the coup plotters! How dare you come to the army with such a proposal!" Pinochet did not seem to understand that the jurists were merely offering a seminar, that they as legal scholars deeply respected the democratic process and did not support coup plots. To Pinochet it appeared that the world of intellectuals and politics, which he had never grasped, was trying to edge in on his beloved army. Shouting, Pinochet ordered the stunned academics out of his office. The entire encounter had lasted no longer than ten minutes.

In September 1972 Pinochet visited Mexico City to attend the Mexican independence day celebrations on the sixteenth of the month. The official invitation had been extended first to his commander, General Carlos Prats, but Prats, beset by political pressures, did not think it an opportune time to leave the country. Besides, he had to attend Chile's own national holiday festivities, including the traditional military parade on September 19, which commemorates the victories of the Chilean army. So he passed the invitation on to Pinochet, who was happy to travel as Chile's official representative. While in Mexico City Pinochet was interviewed by Televisa, the Mexican national television network, and asked about the likelihood of a military coup in Chile. Pinochet angrily told his interviewer that the Chilean armed forces were sworn to protect the constitution and did not mount coups. Back in Santiago, as army troops marched past the crowd of spectators in O'Higgins Park, right-wing Chileans threw chicken feed at the passing soldiers. They were too chicken, the message indicated, to act.

Meanwhile, Chile's new defense minister, José Tohá, had thrown himself wholeheartedly into his new job, believing that one of the problems underlying the country's political crisis was that Chilean civilians and the country's military simply did not know each other. Tohá made an effort to get to know the generals, their views, and their concerns, and to learn how they saw their role in Chile. He and his wife Moy often entertained Chilean officers and their wives, and among their most frequent guests were Augusto Pinochet and his wife, Lucía.

After a reception or some official function the Pinochets often went back to the Tohás' house for drinks or coffee, and even if the relationship could not be described as intimate, it was certainly friendly.[19]

The Tohá children, Carolina and José, called Pinochet "Uncle"; the general even brought them tin soldiers, the same toys he played with as a boy.

Lucía Hiriart de Pinochet had mostly domestic interests such as how to prepare a certain recipe or how to find enough time to organize a big Sunday dinner with her children's and grandchildren's favorite dishes. Augusto Pinochet seemed to have trouble with social conversation: he could talk about military business and family affairs easily enough, but when the subject turned to current or cultural events he seemed lost. His sentences did not make sense; his thoughts seemed unconnected. He was perhaps the least cultured of the Chilean army generals, but he compensated for this shortcoming with his great personal warmth. He seemed to like this tall, bearded socialist who had befriended him, and when Tohá left the cabinet a year later Pinochet was seen blinking back the tears at the defense ministry farewell ceremony. A letter from Pinochet and his wife to José Tohá and his wife Moy, dated July 10, 1973, reads:

Lucía and Augusto Pinochet Ugarte, division general, send attentive greetings to their distinguished friends Dr. José Tohá and Señora Victoria (Moy) E. Morales de Tohá and in a very heartfelt sense thank them for the noble gesture of friendship upon their leaving the defense ministry.

Lucía and Augusto express the affection they have for the Tohá-Morales couple and ask that you continue to consider them your friends.

Two weeks earlier Santiago witnessed the first real attempt at a military coup by a faction of the Chilean army egged on by a right-wing extremist group, Patria y Libertad. A group of tanks and armored vehicles surrounded the La Moneda presidential palace and nearby defense ministry, firing indiscriminately. But General Prats, the army commander, telephoned military installations in the city and secured their support in putting down the uprising within a matter of hours. Aiding him in this task was his chief of staff, General Augusto Pinochet, who expressed indignation at the uprising.

That afternoon a group of Chilean navy admirals arrived in Santiago from Valparaiso, seeking a meeting with their air force counterparts. The air force commander, César Ruiz, agreed, but said that only five of his generals should participate. According to one of the officers present, the air force and navy officials spoke more or less openly about the situation in the country, about how things could not and should not continue as they had been. One of the admirals voiced the concern that a successful military takeover would trigger a bloody civil war in Chile. An air force general asked him how many people the admiral estimated would be killed in a coup: ten thousand? twenty thousand? thirty thousand? "Twenty thousand," he replied. "And is the country's fate worth twenty thousand dead?" the air force general wanted to know. "Of course," the admiral replied. It was the first time the two branches of the Chilean armed forces had broached the subject of a coup, for the mini-uprisings by factions of the army never had any real chance of success without the backing of the other services.

The navy and air force commanders then approached General Prats, the army commander, for a meeting with his generals. Prats authorized five of his generals, including Augusto Pinochet, to attend the meeting, which was set for 6 P.M. at the defense ministry a few days later. When Allende learned of this, he ordered Prats and the two other service commanders to a meeting at 6:30 P.M. at his house that day, in an effort to hold off the coup plotting. But the generals and admirals gathered at the defense ministry anyway, to wait for their commanders to finish at Allende's house.

The meeting began with one of the admirals inviting Pinochet to speak, as he was one of the most senior officers present. Pinochet looked uncomfortable. "We cannot talk about politics, because that is against the constitution," he told them.

"But that is precisely why we are gathered here, and General Prats knows it," the admiral said.

"We can talk about economics," Pinochet said. One of the younger officials present, an air force general, then took the floor.

"Excuse me, general, but if we talk about economics we are going to end up talking about politics anyway. Given the situation in the country, we have a certain responsibility." Pinochet took off his glasses in a gesture of forced emphasis and told the air force general, "Look, my friend, I think the same way you do."

The discussion began, but it was obvious that Pinochet had not wanted it to happen, perhaps because he not only did not support a coup but also did not want to reveal his difficulties with nonmilitary matters to his comrades in arms. And of all the interservice planning sessions by the Chilean military prior to the coup, it was the only one he would attend. General Prats, in his own attempt to pour oil on troubled waters, asked each branch of the armed forces to draw up a memorandum that described their points of disagreement with the Allende government and then for the three branches to combine the memoranda into a final report. The officers were later outraged to learn that Prats had leaked the air force's preliminary memorandum to Allende and Defense Minister José Tohá before the final report was delivered.[20]

The wave of strikes and shortages continued in Chile, with inflation approaching 300 percent over the previous year.[21] Allende reshuffled his cabinet yet again, asking the navy, army, and air force to each nominate two of their officers as ministers. This move was designed to placate the military and also to offer the country a new cabinet with seemingly neutral officials. The military balked, then reluctantly agreed to release one officer each. General Carlos Prats took over the defense ministry from José Tohá, and the air force commander, General César Ruiz, became minister of public works and transport. The situation became somewhat calmer, albeit only temporarily.

On July 26, 1973, Allende's navy aide-de-camp, Commander Arturo Araya, was shot as he stood on the balcony of his home. He was not killed outright but died in the hospital shortly afterward. It was the first time a Chilean military official had been killed since the death of former army commander René Schneider, and immediately the country's left and right wings began trading accusations. The Chilean right maintained that Araya was killed by MIR guerrillas at the behest of Allende's Cuban son-in-law, for a supposed affair the naval attaché was having with his wife, Allende's daughter. Leftists insisted that Araya was killed by right-wing extremists wanting to provoke a military coup by making it appear as though left-wing terrorists had begun targeting the armed forces.

Allende appointed the defense ministry's deputy chief of staff, Nicanor Díaz, an air force general, to investigate. As the official in charge of coordinating the different armed forces' intelligence services, he was an obvious candidate for the job (though he ran into some resentment from Chile's civilian detective police). Díaz was also one of the five air force generals taking part in the coup plotting whose interservice meetings had now moved from the defense ministry to private homes in eastern Santiago. One of their hosts, a Christian Democratic politician, was happy to lend his house to the coup plotters. He received the military officers at the door, and after having a servant prepare them coffee and snacks he left them to their planning sessions.

But General Díaz was also taking the Araya assassination case seriously, and he soon found that of the two sides exchanging accusations, the Left was closer to the truth. Araya's killers were from a splinter group that had broken off from the extremist Patria y Libertad movement; they were led by a civilian with fascist leanings who had once worked for the army's intelligence service. This splinter group had argued that Patria y Libertad was not sufficiently active in the fight against Allende. Díaz found this ironic, for it was a time when Patria y Libertad was setting fuel tanks on fire and planting bombs in Santiago and other cities. But even if he and other military officers were outraged by the tactics of Patria y Libertad and its various offshoots, they did not view the country's mainstream right-wing political parties in the same light.

The investigation into the Araya killing brought Díaz into almost daily contact with Allende, whom he found alternately pompous and conciliatory.[22] When he wanted to, Allende could be the nicest guy in the world, Díaz thought, for just when a discussion seemed to be reaching the boiling point, he would stop suddenly and say, "Excuse me, you must be tired, may I offer you a drink?" The two men had some violent exchanges when discussing the course of the investigation, and Díaz complained that he was being followed. He was going to give orders to his men to shoot first and ask questions later, he told Allende, because one murdered military officer was enough.

The surveillance stopped. Díaz managed to identify the man who ordered the killing of Araya and the man who pulled the trigger. But the Chilean navy, engrossed in its own coup plans while trying to ferret out any would-be Allende loyalists, seemed unconcerned about this murder of one of its own. The navy, whose officers tend to come from more affluent social backgrounds than do officers from other branches of the armed forces, had been the first branch of the military targeted by the political Right's campaign for a coup.

The Chilean navy's high command was already actively planning a coup, and any officers suspected of pro-Allende leanings had to be silenced. A purge within the service began on August 6, 1973, with the arrest of a handful of lower-ranking officers accused of being leftist infiltrators. Their treatment at the hands of their superiors was a grim forerunner of things to come. One chief petty officer testified:

They hung me from a wooden cross with my hands and arms tied with a rope. It is difficult to explain. . . . They placed me like a cross, but with my legs so far apart as if they intended me to do the splits. They started to beat me all over my body, especially the genitals.

I was taken there with orders that I should confess to everything they told me. I said nothing. During the meeting with the prosecutor I said that I had once again been beaten up. I was told that I had disobeyed the orders they had given me to confess that I was guilty. From that moment onward they did not allow me to sleep. Every fifteen minutes they woke me up for some more blows. I spent the whole of Sunday night this way.

All the people who beat me up were officers of the navy. There were no soldiers. On Monday, August 13, they took me to the prosecutor Jiménez to jail me with some other sailors. I said only that we were opposed to the coup and that we would not support anyone who committed it.[23]

Tensions were also rising in the Chilean air force, where commander César Ruiz told his generals that if he was not able to resolve the truckers' strike that was about to paralyze the country, he would resign as cabinet minister in eight days. This self-imposed deadline passed; General Ruiz felt his hands were tied by the public works and transport ministry's bureaucracy. The truckers' strike had thrown a monkey wrench into Chile's distribution system: gasoline was being rationed to 2.5 gallons per automobile per week, and heating fuel was becoming scarce at a time when the Chilean winter would last for at least another month. Periodic food shortages had always been a problem during the Allende government, as price controls prompted producers to cut back their output and retailers to sell what goods were available on the black market; now the shortages were becoming acute.

Ruiz took a letter of resignation to President Allende, who advised him that if he planned to quit the cabinet he should resign as air force commander as well. He balked at this, and Allende called the air force's second-ranking officer, General Gustavo Leigh, to appoint him commander. Leigh declined, as did the general below him. Allende said he knew the air force generals had agreed to decline an appointment in Ruiz's stead, but if they did not cooperate he would name his own air force aide-de-camp, a junior officer, as their commander.

Ruiz and Leigh went to the El Bosque air force base in south Santiago to talk to the other officers. There was applause for Ruiz from officials who supported him unconditionally and who were understandably disturbed at what was happening to their institution. Leigh told the officers that he would not assume the post of commander if Ruiz did not formally hand it over to him. Some of them applauded. General Prats telephoned the base frequently to inquire what was going on and if there was anything he might do to help. The officials there curtly told him it was the Chilean air force's business.

Ruiz asked for a meeting of all the air force generals, a gathering that according to one of the participants dissolved into an angry exchange. Two of the generals insisted Ruiz had to go, others were neutral, and still others said he should remain. But by then César Ruiz was worn out. He was, according to one officer, no longer the smiling and confident general they had known, but a man wracked with tension.

"General Leigh, I will hand over this post at the hour you state," he said finally. The air force generals moved to the defense ministry, where Gustavo Leigh, future member of the Chilean junta, was sworn in. Although not every officer supported a coup, most of the air force was furious with Allende over this incident. On the same day that General Leigh assumed command of the institution, a small group of air force officials requisitioned a helicopter from the El Bosque air force base and flew to intercept Allende, who was returning from a trip to Chillán, about three hundred miles south of the capital. Their plan was to force Allende's plane down at the air force base and hold him hostage. The plan did not succeed, of course, but it served as one more rehearsal for the coup.

Coup plans were continuing in the air force, in the navy, and even within the defense ministry, where the Chilean defense minister and army commander, General Carlos Prats, was being assured by his subordinates that they were studying national defense plans. But Prats knew, and some of his generals in the army knew he knew. A core group of five or six army generals backed a coup; to ensure its success they wanted Prats out of the way, and perhaps his loyal number two man, Augusto Pinochet, as well.[24] Meanwhile, the military was already making periodic raids on suspected arms caches owned by the Chilean left that turned up illegal weapons, but far fewer raids on right-wing extremist groups. The double standard irked some members of the Allende government. The amounts and types of weapons seized were never published, but the mere suggestion of a parallel militia provided the armed forces with yet another pretext for a coup.

The day after the air force commander, César Ruiz, resigned, about three hundred Chilean women, mostly military wives, gathered outside General Carlos Prats's official army residence on Presidente Errazuriz Street in eastern Santiago. In the group were the spouses of six procoup army generals, who gave the guard a letter addressed to Prats's wife, Sofía, asking that she persuade her husband to resign. It was about 5 P.M., and General Prats happened to be in bed with the flu. The demonstration was broken up by carabineros, but the women returned a few hours later, this time accompanied by right-wing youths. There were scuffles and shouting, and the carabineros decided to use tear gas.

The fracas outside his residence, along with the idea that his subordinates would resort to sending their wives to demonstrate for his resignation, pushed Prats to near breaking point. Early the following morning he spoke with Pinochet on the telephone, saying that he was willing to forget the "sad episode" outside his house if the other army generals were willing to publicly express their support for him. If not, Prats said he had no other choice but to resign. Pinochet, according to Chilean army sources and the account contained in Prats's own memoirs, professed his loyalty to his commander and assured him he would do everything possible to secure this expression of support.[25]

Pinochet's effort failed. Only two of the generals present backed Prats, and they were officers who themselves wanted to resign. One alternative might have been to fire the recalcitrant officers, or at least those generals clearly identified with coup plotting. But that might have sparked a military rebellion giving way to the very coup Prats was trying desperately to avoid.

On August 23, Prats formally resigned as both army commander and defense minister. Pinochet was sworn in as army commander, and Orlando Letelier, formerly Allende's foreign minister, became defense minister. Prats returned to the official army commander's residence, which he would soon turn over to Pinochet.

Pinochet's version of his appointment as Chile's army commander makes no mention of any efforts to rally support for Prats among the other army generals, and in his memoir he expresses wonder at why Allende would appoint him army commander "when he could have counted on others who were his friends."[26] The next day Pinochet held a meeting of all the army generals, asking for their resignation en masse in order to leave their new commander free to make new appointments and promotions. The unstated plan, obviously, was to disguise as much as possible the ouster of the coup plotters, hiding their departures in a smokescreen of new assignments and promotions. But the other army generals refused, in an act of defiance Pinochet would not forget. Pinochet, in *The Crucial Day*, claimed that the corps of generals handed over their resignations as soon as he became commander, but that he rejected them, save for those of two officers known to oppose a coup.

On the evening Prats resigned, Pinochet and his wife paid Prats and his family a visit, and according to Prats's daughters they seemed the most sympathetic of guests. Nevertheless, from that day until shortly after the coup, Prats had almost no contact with his once loyal subordinate: he tried calling him at the defense ministry, at the army headquarters, and at the official army commander's residence that he had turned over to Pinochet, but Pinochet was not available and messages that he left did not seem to get through. Perhaps Pinochet, faced with a group of defiant generals busily plotting the coup, did not want to be seen in contact with Prats, and no doubt the fate of his murdered predecessor, General René Schneider, weighed on his mind as well. In order to maintain his rather tenuous hold on his new post, Pinochet would have to tread very carefully indeed.

About two weeks after Prats resigned, Moy de Tohá, the wife of the former Allende cabinet minister who had befriended Pinochet and his wife, telephoned Pinochet to invite him to a farewell party she wanted to have for Prats. It wouldn't be a big gathering, she told Pinochet, just the former army commander, his wife, the current defense minister, Orlando Letelier, and his wife, and the foreign minister, Clodomiro Almeyda, and his wife.

That would be fine, Pinochet said, but his wife Lucía had become so upset about the truckers' strike that he had sent her and his two youngest children to the mountains for a few days. But he promised Moy de Tohá that they would get together when she returned the following week.[27] Lucía Hiriart de Pinochet and her two younger children, Marco and Jacqueline, had gone to the Chilean army's mountaineering school, located north of Santiago, near the Argentine border. The school's director, Colonel René Cantuarias, had been known to oppose a coup.[28] Why Pinochet would send his wife and children there is open to speculation. However, if the coup had failed, it would have given him two alternative courses of action: he could take an army helicopter from Santiago, pick up his family at the school, and flee across the border to Argentina, or use the site as a base from which to amass forces loyal to the Allende government.[29]

On Saturday, September 8, 1973, General Sergio Arellano Stark, one of the coup's backers in the army, went to Pinochet to inform him of the army's plans for the coup. Pinochet's reaction was one of "surprise and irritation."[30] He was told he need only approve the already drawn up plans, in order that the other military commanders begin coordinating their actions, and that the air force commander, General Gustavo Leigh, was waiting to hear from him. Pinochet said he would give his approval, but asked for a few moments to reflect on the situation.

The Chilean air force commander did not hear from Pinochet that day, however, and did not find him at home when he went to the army commander's residence the following morning, September 9. When he returned at around 5 P.M. he found two navy admirals and a captain who had brought Pinochet a letter from Chile's navy commander, Admiral José Merino. The letter, addressed to Pinochet and to Leigh, asked that the two generals merely sign the missive in order that the Chilean navy put its coup plans into effect. Leigh signed and after some hesitation so did Pinochet, who warned of the dire consequences for them if the plans failed.

Pinochet called a meeting of some army generals the following day at lunchtime, announced that the coup would take place, and ordered them to make preparations. How specific Pinochet was in issuing these orders is not known, but the record shows that at least some army generals based in the provinces were not even informed of the coup plans. Much of the preparation on this last day before the coup was undertaken by the general in charge of the Chilean army's second division, who hurriedly called a meeting of all the force's unit commanders. The lights remained on at the defense ministry all night.

What Pinochet himself did to prepare on the eve of the coup is unclear. In *The Crucial Day* he said he spent the evening, "the longest night of my life," at his official residence, rather than at the Chilean defense ministry or at any of the army's installations. "My main concern was the fear of betrayal by some infiltrated individual or that some column commanding officer might move his troops ahead of time and trigger a response from the government, whose paramilitary forces, once mobilized, could even contain the action by building barricades of heavy vehicles across roads to the city."[31] Even if the unlikely threat of a leftist paramilitary force genuinely disturbed Pinochet, it certainly did not prompt him to hasten to his post on the morning of September 11, 1973.

He said that he awoke at 5:30 A.M., showered, and started to dress, a process still not completed when Allende tried to telephone him an hour later. Feigning sleepiness, Pinochet said he answered the phone abruptly and the operator told him the president would call back later. He then "finished dressing quickly." At 7 A.M. an army vehicle arrived at his residence to drive him to the army telecommunications center; Pinochet said he left the house ten minutes later but then made the driver stop at the home of one of his grown children:

There I stayed for a while looking down at my little grandchildren, who were unaware of what was about to happen, and thought how the significant resolution adopted was crucial for their future, for their freedom, as my wife had told me sometime before.

I got in the car and ordered the driver to go to the telecommunications center, where the command post of the commander of the army was located. I arrived there twenty minutes before eight o'clock. When I drove into the yard General Oscar Bonilla came to meet me, very worried at my delay.[32]

Pinochet was, in the words of former U.S. ambassador Nathaniel Davis, the last of the principal actors to take his place that day.

Along Avenida Colón in eastern Santiago, housewives hoping to buy fresh bread at the local bakery formed a line extending at least three blocks. It was about 7:30 A.M. when they saw Salvador Allende's motorcade speed past on its way to the La Moneda presidential palace downtown.[33]

The coup began with a predawn uprising by the Chilean navy in the port of Valparaiso. Allende had been advised of this in his home in eastern Santiago and immediately began telephoning his officials. He put in a call to the Chilean defense ministry and spoke to Hernán Brady, commander of the army's Second Division, who had spent the night there frantically trying to organize the army's actions for the coup. Brady, whom Allende and former defense minister José Tohá considered a friend, was visibly worried when the ministry's deputy chief of staff, air force general Nicanor Díaz, arrived at 6 A.M.

"Allende called me," Brady told Díaz.[34] The Chilean president had telephoned a short time before to inquire about the naval uprising in Valparaiso, then demanded to know what he was doing at the defense ministry at such an early hour. Brady told Allende there was a seizure of illegal armaments under way and feigned ignorance of the navy uprising. Allende asked him what he planned to do.

"What my commander tells me to do."

"And where is your commander?" Allende asked him. Pinochet was not answering his telephone at his army commander's residence, and was not at his post, either. Pinochet later arrived at the army's telecommunications center, where his command post was located.

On the other side of Santiago's main avenue, some of Allende's closest advisers and friends were gathering at the La Moneda presidential palace, across the street from the Chilean defense ministry. Dr. Patricio Guijón, a surgeon who was one of a half-dozen physicians serving on the presidential medical team, arrived there shortly after 8:00 A.M. One of the other doctors had telephoned him that morning, telling him to get down to La Moneda as soon as possible. Guijón did not know that a coup was under way, but it was not his habit to ask too many questions. The Chilean physician dropped his sons off at school before he left, and as he drove through the streets of eastern Santiago the traffic seemed more or less normal. But as he approached the center of the capital and the presidential palace, he saw policemen setting up barriers to block traffic. It was then Guijón sensed what was about to happen.[35]

The main entrance to La Moneda was closed, and Guijón had to show his identification to a palace guard at a side door in order to enter. He found the other doctors on the medical staff waiting in one of the offices, listening to the radio. The Chilean doctors talked, but not about medical matters, for they knew that it would be impossible to treat any wounded in La Moneda. They were there only out of loyalty to the president. They spent the next few hours waiting, watching people come and go as the officials in La Moneda sparred on the telephone with the officials in the defense ministry.

Allende appeared in an army helmet and told the carabineros guarding La Moneda that they could leave if they wished, but they would have to leave their weapons behind. The doctors watched nervously as guns were piled up on the floor. The telephone in the office where they were gathered rang, and Allende took the call in their presence.[36] It was Admiral Carvajal at the defense ministry, trying to negotiate Allende's resignation, with the offer of a Chilean air force plane to take him and his family out of the country. Allende angrily refused.[37] Then the doctors heard on the radio that La Moneda was going to be bombarded. The doctors looked at each other in disbelief.

Back at the Chilean defense ministry, things were operating with less than military precision. Many of the officers were tired, not everyone had been told what was going to happen, and there were telephone calls from a number of generals and colonels who had not even know the coup was going to take place that day. Not every military officer had been trusted to go along with the uprising.

Sergio Arellano Iturriaga, whose father, Sergio Arellano Stark, was one of the Chilean army's chief coup plotters, had been recruited to set up a radio network to broadcast the military's announcements that day. The younger Arellano, a lawyer and member of the Christian Democratic party, was assigned to a room on the fifth floor of the defense ministry, where he discreetly observed the soldiers' movements.[38] From his window he had no view of La Moneda, but he could see a small contingent of troops advancing slowly in that direction. There were leftist snipers hiding on the roofs of the surrounding government buildings, and when they fired the teenage soldiers crouched behind and under cars parked along the street. Some of them took cover and stayed there.

A group of younger army officials belonging to an elite, Ranger-type squadron arrived on Arellano's floor. They all looked enthusiastic as they left on their mission—to occupy the buildings around La Moneda where the snipers were operating. The squadron returned that afternoon missing some of its men. The survivors looked enraged, murderous.

When the Chilean air force dispatched its Hawker Hunters to bombard La Moneda, Arellano and some other civilian and military officials moved to Admiral Carvajal's unoccupied office to watch. The small group stared at the spectacle. "What stupidity," an army captain muttered, and it was difficult to tell if he was referring to the bombardment or to Allende's stubborn determination to hold onto the Chilean presidency at all costs. The La Moneda presidential palace, the symbol of Chilean democracy, was being destroyed.

Dr. Guijón and his medical colleagues had no experience of a combat situation, and images of World War II films flickered through his mind, the ones where a bomb falls on a building and leaves nothing behind but an enormous crater. The women remaining in La Moneda began leaving the building, all except Allende's secretary and mistress Miria Contreras, nicknamed La Payita, who stayed almost to the end. They all moved to a small cellar containing office equipment. When the first hit came, there was a tremendous noise, but no explosion. Guijón and the others looked around at each other, surprised to find themselves still alive, and laughed nervously.[39]

The incendiary rockets launched by the Hawker Hunters set one side of La Moneda on fire, and hit the palace approximately every ten minutes. When the bombardment stopped, tanks pulled up outside the building and began firing tear gas. The group inside La Moneda moved from the cellar to the second floor, then Guijón and the other doctors were called back downstairs to treat the group's first casualty.

Augusto Olivares, a journalist who had worked in Allende's press office, was slumped on a bench with a pistol at his side. There was nothing the Chilean doctors could do; he had died instantly after shooting himself. They moved back to the second floor, and at this point Guijón's field of vision seemed to narrow. In situations of extreme danger, a psychiatrist friend later explained to him, one is reduced to such basic survival movements as sidestepping holes in the ground and avoiding beams and rafters crashing down.

The lights went off in the second-floor hallway where the group was huddled, and the smoke and tear gas grew thicker. Someone passed out gas masks in olive green cases marked, ironically, U.S. Army.

Then they heard Allende's voice. "This is a massacre! Give yourselves up! La Payita goes out first, I'll go out last."[40] They needed a white flag to show the soldiers outside. Someone found a broom, and Guijón obligingly offered up his white doctor's coat. Thinking it would make him seem less threatening to the soldiers waiting outside, Guijón also discarded his U.S. Army gas mask. The group began moving down the hall, down the stairs.

Then, Guijón recalled, he got one of those odd ideas which sometimes pops into the heads of people in critical situations: This is the first time you're in a war, and you're not bringing your sons any souvenir. He decided to go back for his U.S. Army gas mask, pushing past the others climbing down the stairs in the opposite direction, back to the hall on the darkened second floor. There was apparently no one else around, but then Guijón noticed a light coming from one of the rooms. He looked inside.

As Guijón watched, Salvador Allende, seated on a sofa in the Red Salon, placed a rifle under his chin and pulled the trigger. The force of the shot seemed to lift him off the sofa for a split second. Already numb from the bombardment, the tear gas, and the tension, Guijón walked over to Allende's body and reflexively took his pulse. The president's cranium was destroyed, his face was unrecognizable; in fact there was nothing past his eyebrows.

The rifle was still positioned between the cadaver's legs. Guijón moved it to one side, found a footstool and sat down beside the dead Chilean president. If I could not accompany him in life, the least I can do is accompany him in the hour of his death, he thought. He waited for the soldiers to find him, the body, and the rifle with Allende's and his fingerprints.[41]

At the Chilean defense ministry, the news of Allende's death passed through the different offices by word of mouth. Some of the officers seemed stunned, and one officer who had been Allende's army aide-de-camp, Sergio Badiola, had tears in his eyes.[42]

Later Dr. Guijón could not remember how much time elapsed from the moment he sat down to wait by the dead president and the moment when two young soldiers entered the Red Salon, gripping their rifles and peering around the room for snipers. Guijón raised his hands in the air and told them as best he could what had happened. General Javier Palacios then arrived, and the doctor repeated his story—that he was a member of the presidential medical staff and had happened to be there when Allende killed himself. The general, much to Guijón's relief, did not react violently.

After several hours and countless photographs of the Red Salon and Allende's corpse, Palacios took Guijón downstairs and out of La Moneda. There, lying face down on the street, were the other officials and personal friends who had been with Allende during his final hours. The other five doctors on the presidential medical staff were there, and Guijón decided to try to take advantage of the relative goodwill he perceived in General Palacios to ask that his fellow physicians be released.

"Have them stand up," Palacios said, and inspected their Chilean identity cards. He told four of the physicians they should be prepared to testify at any time, but for the moment they could go. The fifth doctor, Arturo Jirón, Allende's health minister, had to stay, as did Guijón, and the two men were escorted across the street to the defense ministry.

Once again, Guijón had to tell his story, but this time in the most minutely detailed, point-by-point official statement, beginning with where he had parked his automobile that morning, where he had been at such-and-such a moment, his wife's name and profession, and his children's names and ages. The officials kept him there until about 11 P.M., then drove Guijón and Health Minister Arturo Jirón to the military academy in eastern Santiago. They and other Allende government officials were kept there for three days before they were sent to a concentration camp in Chile's extreme south.

Allende's body was finally removed from La Moneda early that evening, covered with a blanket and carried out by Chilean firemen who had arrived to put out fires inside the palace caused by the Hawker Hunter's incendiary rockets. The body was taken to the military hospital for an autopsy.

The bombardment caused more damage to the inside of Chile's presidential palace than to the outside of the building, which was cordoned off by the military after Allende's body was moved. On Saturday, September 15, Sergio Arellano Iturriaga was assigned to escort a group of Chilean and foreign journalists to La Moneda. The staircase leading to the second floor had been partially destroyed, and it wasn't clear that the floor would support the group's weight. Some of the journalists were reluctant to go on, but after a brief discussion everyone proceeded up the stairs and down the hallway to the Red Salon where Allende had died.[43]

It was not a pleasant sight. Above the sofa where Allende had sat, a bloodstained tapestry showed the bullet's trajectory; the sofa upholstery, too, was bloody. Photographs of the room, which had been untouched since the day of the coup, appeared all over the world, showing the Allende government's grisly end. An army captain who accompanied the group picked up a lamp that had fallen by the sofa and found Allende's dried blood on his hand. The visit lasted perhaps an hour.

What was Pinochet's reaction to the news of Allende's death? *The Crucial Day* offers few clues; it merely reprints General Palacios's report on what his patrol had encountered in La Moneda. Pinochet recalled that it became "urgently necessary" that an official medical team examine the body, "to avoid subsequent accusations that the armed forces murdered him."[44] Ousting Allende from La Moneda, rather than fighting the ineffectual resistance posed by scattered leftist groups, was the Chilean military's real objective that day.

"Our limited ability to defend the Allende government in the face of a massive military onslaught was all too evident," recalled Guillermo Norambuena, a former socialist youth leader from Santiago. "We were supposed to have thousands of Chileans, mostly young people, in the street." But this was not to be. The would-be coup resisters found that telephones didn't always work, and many of their contacts did not answer in any case; some had already gone into hiding. A few hours after Norambuena left the Socialist party youth offices, located in an old colonial building in downtown Santiago, carabineros raided the abandoned edifice, riddling it with bullets.[45]

The use of brute military force, especially the spectacular bombardment of La Moneda, may have dissuaded many Allende sympathizers from further action. The Chilean air force also strafed some slum areas where residents appeared to be gathering to protest the coup. General Nicanor Díaz, then the defense ministry's chief of staff, recalled one incident in which a Chilean air force B-26 plane equipped with sixteen machine guns flew over Santiago that day, and, after descending over a procession of slum residents moving toward the center of the capital, fired a burst of ammunition about fifty meters ahead of the crowd. He claimed that the action killed no one but was effective in dispersing the demonstrators. "It wasn't that these people were cowards. You just cannot fight modern armaments with slaps of the hand," he said.[46]

There are few reliable estimates of the fatalities that day; the death toll quickly climbed into the thousands in the next few weeks during the coup's bloody aftermath. In some worker-controlled factories on the outskirts of Santiago, leftist labor leaders had stockpiled some small arms and set up barricades in a desperate attempt to hold off the military takeover, but these efforts hardly constituted a serious challenge to the coup. In *The Crucial Day* Pinochet admitted that the Chilean military had not encountered "the attacks we had been expecting" from the industrial sites taken over by left-wing trade unionists on the outskirts of the capital.

By 6 P.M. that day, when Dr. Guijón was being taken from La Moneda to the defense ministry and Allende's death was officially recorded, Pinochet and the other military commanders felt secure enough to leave their posts and go to the military academy several miles away to be sworn in as a junta, the country's new de facto rulers. The day's events had not constituted much of a challenge for the Chilean military. Pinochet ended his revisionist account of the coup by saying, "I recall that at the time of Chile's liberation, of the liberation of our conscience and overburdening thoughts, with a lump in my throat I could only say, '¡Viva Chile!' "[47]

And what of Carlos Prats, Pinochet's predecessor as army commander, the man to whom he once professed unswerving loyalty? At seven o'clock that morning a right-wing congresswoman, Silvia Alessandri, who had served on the Chilean congress's defense committee and who had been a friend of the former army commander, received a phone call at her home. It was another right-wing Chilean politician, who warned her, "Take care of your friend the general—they're going to kill him."[48] The former Chilean army commander, who had tried to prevent his institution from being dragged into the country's political polarization, had become the target of far-right extremists, possibly the same group behind the 1970 killing of his predecessor, General René Schneider. The congresswoman, who supported the coup, passed the warning on to Prats.

The following day Prats, who had heard other rumors that an ultrarightist group wanted him dead, telephoned the defense ministry and asked to speak to Pinochet. Once again, Prats was told that Pinochet was not available to take his call. Prats left a message that he wished to leave the country, and could Pinochet secure him the necessary safe conduct pass? Prats received no response for two days.

On September 14, Pinochet received word from the army general staff that "certain points" of Prats's actions while army commander had to be cleared up before he would be allowed to leave Chile. Had Prats known that Marxists were preparing to destroy the country's armed forces? Did he know that government funds had found their way into the hands of "extremist individuals and political bodies"? What about the presence of "Marxist aliens" in the country who were organizing leftist paramilitary forces? Had he known of illegal armed groups operating from within the Allende government? All these questions were contained in a document handed to Pinochet by his own subordinates in the army, questions he must have known were based on ridiculous assumptions. But rumors were still flying in Santiago about Prats's position; one story, inspired more by leftist wishful thinking than by fact, was that Prats was leading pro-Allende troops from the south to fight against the new regime.[49]

It had been barely three weeks since Pinochet unsuccessfully tried to secure a show of support for Prats among the army corps of generals and since Prats's subsequent resignation. Even less time had elapsed since Pinochet tried to remove the five or six putschist generals from the force by asking for—and being bluntly refused—a mass resignation of the army's top officers in order that he, their new commander, could make new assignments. Prats posed a very tricky problem for Pinochet, who finally telephoned him to say that he knew the rumor about Prats leading a countercoup was unfounded, for since he left the army Prats had been virtually isolated. But would he be willing to go on Chilean television to clarify his position?

A military patrol took Prats to the offices of the Chilean army chaplain, where he was filmed making a brief statement that he was not directing a resistance movement and that he had no wish to contribute to further bloodshed. He wanted only to leave the country, something he had been trying to do since leaving the army. He said he hoped Chile's new government authorities would grant him the necessary safe conduct pass and safeguards.

Early the next morning a military vehicle arrived at the apartment where Prats, his wife, and one of his daughters were staying and drove him to a Chilean air force base. From there the former commander of the Chilean army was flown to a town near the Argentine border, and then driven to the border. Prats was met by an Argentine official acting on orders of that country's army commander, who escorted him to Mendoza, a city in the Argentine Andes. Prats had left Pinochet a letter, a copy of which he kept. "The future will tell who was wrong. If what you did brings overall well-being to the nation and the people really feel that true social justice reigns, I shall be glad to say I was wrong in so strongly seeking a political solution that would avoid the coup."[50]

Prats later proceeded to Buenos Aires and was joined by his wife, Sofía. He began to write his memoirs, whose publication proved embarrassing to Pinochet and to the new regime. He also kept in contact, through letters, to a few of the remaining sympathetic officers in the Chilean army.

Prats received death threats in Buenos Aires, and he wanted to move to Spain, where he had once been military attaché at the Chilean embassy and where he still had many friends. The Chilean embassy in Buenos Aires, however, stalled at issuing him a passport. Just before midnight on September 29, 1974, a bomb placed under Prats's car exploded as he and his wife were pulling into the garage of their apartment building in Buenos Aires. The force of the explosion blew Prats's right leg and arm off; his wife, Sofía, was burned to death.[51]

There were no military honors for the former Chilean army commander's coffin when it arrived a few days later in Santiago, just as there had been no ceremonial farewell when he left Chile. The news of his death caused sufficient stir, however, to prompt the regime to issue a communiqué lamenting Prats's death and stating that the circumstances of his killing "justify the security measures the government has adopted and will adopt to ensure tranquility and protect the lives of all Chile's inhabitants." A regime spokesman told reporters that the authorities had no objection to Prats's burial in Santiago but that they did not plan to investigate his assassination (which would have implicated the regime's own security forces).[52]

Prats was dead, but not easily forgotten. Like Banquo's ghost, his phantom presence lingered in the Chilean army commander's residence, where Pinochet and his wife now lived. Lucía Hiriart de Pinochet was irked by the constant reminders of Prats and his wife, Sofía. The elderly butler, who had worked for Prats, kept confusing her with Prats's wife. "Sí, Señora Sofía," he would say in response to her instructions. She would correct him indignantly, but without effect. When the butler made this mistake once too often he was fired, although some suspected he had deliberately provoked his own dismissal.[53]

To exorcise these ghosts, the Pinochets ordered the residence torn down and a much larger house constructed on the same site. The new army commander's residence was a white colonial-style edifice with columns and a high protective wall built around the edges of the property. It was a residence more in keeping with the Chilean army commander's expanded powers, and Lucía Hiriart de Pinochet was not going to make the mistake Sofía de Prats had made in being too accessible to other army wives.

Chapter Two

The Aftermath

*The first cadavers began to arrive at the clandestine ceme-
tery in November of 1973, a few months after the military coup. The first executed prisoners were from the
National Stadium. In the early hours of the morning the army's Ford, Toyota, or Mack trucks would transfer their
loads, covered with canvas, to the military installations in
San Bernardo.*

*While some stood guard with their machine guns in
hand, other soldiers dug the graves. At first, due to the
quantity of dead that were arriving, the graves were one
meter deep. Later they gave orders that the graves be at
least four meters deep.*

> —Ricardo Guzmán Bousquet, former agent in
> the regime's security forces, during testimony to
> human rights groups and the press in Spain,
> March 1988

Shortly before the 6 P.M. curfew on September 12, 1973, Marta
Gabriela Cortés walked the last few blocks to her home in a working-
class section of eastern Santiago carrying a suitcase and her two-day-
old daughter. On the eve of the coup, the nineteen-year-old housewife
had given birth to her first child at Salvador Hospital, about ten miles
away. When the military takeover occurred, much of the hospital's
medical staff fled and Cortés and three other patients found themselves alone in the maternity ward where they listened, terrified, to
the sounds of gunfire and the Chilean air force planes thunder-
ing overhead.

She had no telephone, no way of contacting her husband or family,
but ventured to ask a hospital orderly if he knew what the situation
was in her neighborhood, located about ten blocks from Salvador
Allende's home. "Oh, no," he said. "That whole area has been
bombed."

The next day, when no physician came to examine her or her baby
and the hospital filled up with army troops, Marta Cortés decided to
leave.[1] Bluffing her way past soldiers who demanded to see her discharge papers, she met an older couple who offered to take her part of
the way home in their car. It was an hour before curfew, but the drive
took longer than usual, with military checkpoints at every major in-
tersection. The young mother got out with her baby at a corner a few
blocks from her home, and discovered, thankfully, that her neighborhood was still standing. But as she walked toward home she found a
blackened hole in the pavement about two feet wide and over three
feet deep. The Chilean Hawker Hunters had strafed Allende's house
prior to the bombardment of La Moneda, and one of the incendiary
rockets had fallen wide of the target, blasting the ground at the corner
of Harris and La Escuela Streets.

Hortensia Bussi de Allende had taken refuge in the Mexican embassy in Santiago after her husband's painfully brief funeral in Viña
del Mar. She asked her friend, Moy de Tohá, wife of Allende's former
cabinet minister, if she could draw on some of her old military contacts
to get permission to enter the Allende house and retrieve some of
Hortensia's things.

Chile has no official presidential residence; presidents traditionally
live in their own private homes. And yet the military had taken over
the Allende family's home, positioning armed soldiers at the entrance.
Permission for Moy de Tohá to enter finally came two days later, when
General Nicanor Díaz, the chief of staff of the defense ministry, called
to tell her a car was on its way to take her to the Allende residence.
Accompanied by an officer in civilian dress, Moy de Tohá arrived at
the house, only to be told by the officer guarding the residence that
she could not go inside.[2]

An argument ensued, lasting at least an hour, as the official who had
brought her insisted that they were acting on orders of the defense
ministry. The officer guarding the house balked, claiming there was
nothing inside but if Moy de Tohá would tell him exactly what she
wanted, he would look for it.

Allende's house looked as though it had been abandoned for thirty years rather than for just three days. The incendiary rockets had shattered a row of newly planted rosebushes just about to bud, leaving dried stems and flowers scattered on the ground. Soldiers had vandalized the interior of the residence, ripping apart works by Chilean painter Roberto Matta and Ecuadorean artist Osvaldo Guayasamin with their bayonets. Upstairs on the landing two suits of armor were strewn across the floor. And in Allende's bedroom, a half-dressed soldier who had discovered the family's liquor supply lay sprawled across the late president's bed. Moy de Tohá managed to find two suitcases. She threw in a few items of clothing, some photos, and medicines and left as soon as she could.

From her refuge in the Mexican embassy, Hortensia Bussi de Allende seemed at first to accept the story of her husband's suicide. "Yes, he did it with a submachine gun given to him by his friend Fidel Castro," she told a Mexican television interviewer who had telephoned the embassy. "He always said he would never abandon La Moneda as president and would kill himself rather than betray his ideals."[3] In Paris, François Mitterrand substantiated Hortensia Bussi de Allende's story. He recalled that during his visit to Santiago two years earlier his Chilean host had shown him a bust of José Manuel Balmaceda, a Chilean president who had killed himself in 1891 in the midst of a civil war. "If I am overthrown one day, I will do the same," Mitterrand quoted Allende as saying.[4]

Three days after she arrived in Mexico City as an exile, Hortensia Bussi de Allende retracted her earlier statement and asserted that on the basis of new information she now believed Allende had been murdered by the military storming La Moneda. Contradicting her previous statement, she said her husband had once told her that "the only way I shall leave La Moneda is dead, but fighting. I shall not commit suicide like Balmaceda."[5] The revised version of Allende's death offered more comfort to his supporters, especially those outside Chile. Among members of Allende's own Socialist party the subject was a bitter one, and even those who believed he had committed suicide were willing to let the matter drop, perhaps out of deference to Hortensia Bussi de Allende. (In later years Allende's widow seemed to acknowledge her husband's suicide, saying in her infrequent press conferences and interviews that she did not want to talk about "the past.")

I am writing these quick lines for my memoirs only three days after the unspeakable events took my great comrade, President Allende, to his death. His assassination was hushed up, he was buried secretly, and only his widow was allowed to accompany that immortal body. The aggressors' version is that they found signs of suicide on his lifeless body. The version published abroad is different. Immediately after the aerial bombardment, the tanks went into action, many tanks, fighting heroically against a single man: the president of the Republic of Chile, Salvador Allende, who was waiting for them in his office, with no other company than his great heart, surrounded by smoke and flames.

They couldn't pass up such a beautiful occasion. He had to be machine-gunned because he would never resign from office. That body was buried secretly, in an inconspicuous spot. That corpse, followed to its grave only by a woman who carried with her the grief of the world, that glorious dead figure, was riddled and ripped to pieces by the machine guns of Chile's soldiers, who had betrayed Chile once more.

—Pablo Neruda, *Memoirs: Confieso Que He Vivido*[6]

Chile's Nobel Prize–winning poet was dying of cancer, though doctors thought he might live another one to three years. When the coup came he was at his home in Isla Negra, on Chile's Pacific coast. He died twelve days later, in Santiago's Clínica Indisa, heartbroken by learning that so many of his fellow Chilean Communist Party members had been arrested and killed.

Since so many of his surviving friends were in hiding, Neruda had had few visitors at the hospital other than his wife, Matilde, his sister, his secretary, and Nemesio Antunez, a respected painter and political independent who had been director of the Museo de Bellas Artes. Antunez had his own difficulties with the new regime. Shortly after the coup, the military, acting on a report that armed leftists were inside the museum, had sent three tanks to the building and begun firing indiscriminately.

There was no one inside the museum except one guard, who did not even have a service revolver. He notified Antunez of what was happening, and the painter called the police to tell them that he had only left the building half an hour earlier, that there were no armed leftists inside. The bullets pockmarked the walls and left holes in some of the paintings, including two nineteenth-century portraits. The shooting also riddled several walls that only a few days before held an exhibition of works by major Mexican artists, including Diego Rivera. The paintings, on loan from Mexico, had been hung the day before the coup, but fortunately taken down immediately afterward. To shoot up a museum was a completely criminal act, Antunez believed, and he resigned from his job as director.[7]

The painter and the poet talked of Mexico, which had offered Neruda political asylum immediately after the coup. "You come with me," Antunez recalled him saying. "We'll go to Cuernavaca. You can paint there and I'll write . . . about what is going on here. . . . You're not going to be able to stay on here. This place is going to become a black hole for culture." Neruda had been in Spain under Franco, had seen the bombardments during the Spanish Civil War, and had few illusions about Chile's new military government. "These generals," he said, "they're going to start kissing babies in the streets, presenting themselves as upstanding citizens."

"We have to leave, we have to leave," Neruda kept saying. But Chile's Nobel laureate died on September 23, 1973. When his coffin was brought from the hospital to his home in Santiago, his widow and friends found the house had been ransacked. The windows were broken, leaving shards of glass over the floors. The rubble had also clogged a gutter outside, causing water to back up into the dining room. When Antunez and the other pallbearers carried Neruda's coffin inside, the broken glass crunched under their feet. There was a long-case clock that looked as if it had been smashed with a rifle butt, and a painting whose glass covering bore a star-shaped crack. The intruders had stolen all the valuable items they could carry.

Antunez wanted to clean up the house, at least to sweep up the shattered glass, but Neruda's widow Matilde insisted they leave things as they found them. "It is a testimony of their brutality," she said. "We aren't going to hide this. Pablo is here with us, with the broken glass on the floor."

Neruda's funeral the next day turned into the first demonstration against the new military regime. At a time when so many Chileans with any left-wing connections had gone into hiding, thousands of people turned up at Santiago's general cemetery to bid farewell to the country's great poet. Antunez went by car with the Mexican ambassador, but when they were within six blocks of the cemetery the press of the crowd forced them to get out and walk. Someone in the crowd began humming a few bars of "Internationale," the socialist anthem. By the time they reached the entrance to the cemetery, Neruda's mourners were singing it loudly and shouting, "¡Pablo Neruda!"

"¡Presente!"

"¡Ahora y siempre!" (Now and forever!)

"¡Compañero Salvador Allende!"

"¡Presente!"

"¡Ahora y siempre!"

There were speeches at the gravesite and poems composed by Neruda's admirers, including some written the night before when the poets learned of his death. It was a cloudy, overcast day, but at one point the sun broke through. The man who was speaking at the time looked up at the sky and said, "The sun is a host; do you know what a host is? The host is communion, the common union, and we all have to unite in the face of this act of horror that is the coup and in wake of the death of our great poet."

About two thousand people turned out for Pablo Neruda's funeral, including members of the Chilean Communist Party. But when the speeches ended and the last poems were read, the crowd began to disperse, with the more politically vulnerable mourners exiting from the side entrance. Those departing through the cemetery's main gate found a line of soldiers with their guns pointing at them, like a firing squad, as they passed.

On Saturday, September 15, Dr. Patricio Guijón, the lone witness to Allende's death, and approximately thirty-five other deposed

Allende government officials were moved from the military academy in Santiago and flown to Punta Arenas, in Chile's extreme south. It was a slow flight in a military cargo plane that lasted about eight hours.[8] Forbidden to speak, the prisoners were positioned with empty seats between them. No one would say where they were going. At the Punta Arenas airport they were ordered to pull their shirts or jackets up over their heads to block their view and were taken in a boat to Dawson Island, another six hours away.

There was snow on the ground when they finally arrived at about four or five o'clock in the morning. The prisoners were taken to their quarters, flimsy wooden barracks, where they were met by the Dawson Island naval commander, who gave them breakfast and informed them they had come as prisoners of war. The naval base commander even read them their rights under the Geneva Convention, according to Guijón.

The prisoners' daily routine began with a dawn lineup before the commander, and the singing of the Chilean national anthem. Then they worked in Dawson Island's subfreezing temperatures: driving stakes into the ground, planting telephone poles, and picking up boulders for a fence the navy was constructing. They were never given any coats or clothing appropriate to the frigid climate, though after a few weeks packages began to arrive from their families. There were small humiliations, like having to ask permission to go to the toilet and taking care of one's necessities with a soldier standing guard, gun pointed at the prisoner. If they tried to escape, there was no place to run, nowhere to hide on the prison island.

Guijón and Allende's former health minister, Arturo Jirón, also acted as the prisoners' physicians. Some of the men could not work because of advanced age or medical problems: one had diabetes, another had a knee that would not bend. But the two doctors always tried to get everyone out of the barracks in the morning to keep them working and keep their minds occupied as much as possible.

"We realized that our welfare in that camp would depend on how well we acted," Guijón recalled. "So we kept our camp and ourselves as clean and orderly as possible, setting our dining-room table as correctly as possible, cleaning up thoroughly afterward." Cooperation among the prisoners was important; there could be no arguments. For that reason Guijón did not speak much about what he had seen the day of the coup; some of the former Popular Unity government officials believed, or wanted to believe, that Allende had died a martyr's death at the hands of the military.

After about a month on Dawson Island, representatives of the International Red Cross came to visit on a rare day when the prisoners were given a ball and told to play soccer. Although the Red Cross officials were not fooled by this hastily organized activity, they told the prisoners that some of the other detention camps they visited were even worse, like the one in Isla Mocha, in southern Chile, where the prisoners had no beds.

After the Red Cross officials left, there were more visitors, this time from one of the foreign television networks. The TV crew filmed the camp and its prisoners, who did not dare say anything negative before their guards. And they interviewed Guijón, who recounted his experience in the presidential palace the day of the coup.

The television crew did not believe that Guijón had witnessed Allende commit suicide, for if his story were true, why would the military hold him prisoner? But on the flight from Punta Arenas back to Santiago the crew met the Red Cross officials, who vouched for Guijón. A week later they were back on Dawson Island, requesting another interview with Guijón, claiming that the tape of the original interview had been accidentally erased. Guijón patiently told his story yet again.

"Marxist resistance is not finished," Pinochet told a press conference on September 21, 1973. "There are still extremists left. Chile continues in a state of internal war."[9]

First Corporal Nelson Morales Leal, a Chilean army reservist on patrol in central and western Santiago, was exhausted and somewhat demoralized by his duties. Orders always seemed to be changing: officers would come and go, shouting out different instructions of where to go, what to do.[10] Morales had first served in Temuco, an agricultural center in southern Chile, and received a citation when he left active duty. When he was called up for active duty a few days before the coup, he had been working as a civil servant in the Allende government's agrarian reform department. He reported to the Tacna regiment in Santiago, where the commander told the troops that the army was going to take power and liberate the country from Marxism.

The day of the coup Morales served in a backup unit in the downtown area, near La Moneda. He had watched the last Allende supporters leaving the presidential palace and witnessed several deaths that day. Some of the casualties were conscripts hit by left-wing snipers, including one youth holding a bazooka who died when a bullet hit the weapon and caused it to explode. But Morales saw far more civilians killed than soldiers.

Most of the conscripts had been brought from the provinces to the capital, where they tended not to know anyone. In this respect, the Chilean army had been very shrewd. These shaven-headed kids patrolled at night, shooting indiscriminately and spending bullets as if there were no limit. For the young recruits it was a joy to fire a weapon.

The patrol was supposed to intervene to stop fights, including disputes among families claiming that one of their members had been taken away because a neighbor had denounced him or her. But after a while the soldiers didn't bother; they were exhausted from their other duties, like checking the passengers at the railway station. And then there were the confusing cases when leftists denounced rightists as leftists, in a kind of revenge for the coup.

At one point, Morales's patrol went to a hospital where his brother, a Christian Democrat, was working. One of the young conscripts had been injured when he was kicked by another soldier and the blow caused his rifle to discharge. The bullet passed through his middle and index fingers, and the patrol took him to the nearest hospital. As they were waiting one of the hospital employees called Morales to the side and presented him with a list of five supposed communists working there. The second name on the list was his brother's.

Morales took a good look at the man who had given him the list, memorizing his mustache and his features, and then went to find his brother, who was on duty that night. The man with the mustache, his brother told him, was a member of the Movement of the Revolutionary Left, who had begun working there six months earlier. In the confusion and tension of the coup's aftermath, it was becoming harder and harder to tell who was who.

The military takeover that was supposed to be imposing order in Chile often produced the opposite effect: Santiago's criminal element was operating more freely as well. With so many people being killed, it was easier to commit a robbery and kill the victim or any other witnesses present, leaving behind corpses that were indistinguishable from Chileans killed by the military. Bodies were dumped along roadsides, in the Mapocho River, which winds through Santiago, and near the cemetery.

But criminals were not the only ones abusing private property. There were soldiers who would forcibly enter a suspect's home and proceed to break all the windows and all the dishes. In such cases there was no one to complain to other than the officer in charge, and even if the incident was reported there was no chance of compensation. Once Morales's patrol was ordered to raid a house where according to a neighbor communists were holding meetings every night. The troops raided the house, beating everyone inside. The more the people screamed, the more they were beaten in a clumsy attempt to shut them up. No one was given a chance to explain.

The atmosphere was different in the upper-income suburbs of eastern Santiago, where support for the coup was much stronger. Many residents there opened bottles of champagne and in some cases even partied in the streets. Sometimes the residents applauded the army patrols as they drove past. Meanwhile, however, middle-class Chilean leftists were negotiating for safe conduct out of the country via relatives and friends on this side of the political spectrum.

A right-wing member of Chile's newly closed congress explained in detail how he and his wife smuggled a leftist friend, one of the more than ten thousand Chileans to seek asylum after the coup, in the trunk of their car to a foreign embassy. In describing the incident, the former legislator said that he and his wife had taken a "great personal risk" in this action and asked that neither their names nor that of their friend, a well-known figure in Chilean political circles, be mentioned. At the same time, he emphasized how widespread was the support for Chile's new military regime.

"Everyone wanted the military to take over," he asserted. "Almost everyone." This peculiar juxtaposition of enthusiasm for the country's new order and the acknowledgment that the lives of many people, including relatives and longtime friends, were in danger was not unusual, although many Chileans supporting the new regime were either unaware of such abuses or else quickly learned to mentally block out any evidence to this effect. Food and other basic goods quickly reappeared on the store shelves, and there were no strikes or disruptive demonstrations in the new military-ruled Chile. Grateful that such aggravations had ceased, many Chileans found it easy to close their eyes. "There were a lot of things I objected to, but there was this mystique," said a Christian Democrat who briefly collaborated with the regime. "When you believe very fervently in something, disillusion doesn't set in right away. When you see mistakes, you think those mistakes can be corrected."

Some regime backers developed elaborate explanations or justifications for the authorities' more ham-fisted actions. Chilean novelist Jorge Edwards, a former career diplomat who was fired after the coup, recalled a dinner party he attended in Santiago at which one guest vehemently denied that the Chilean military had burned books in the wake of the coup. When asked about a well-known news photograph of soldiers burning books piled outside a Santiago apartment complex, the guest explained that the September nights in the capital are chilly, so the soldiers had furtively set a heap of confiscated Soviet propaganda on fire to warm themselves. Edwards and the other guests burst out laughing at this version of events.[11]

The National Stadium in Santiago was built in 1938, with a seating capacity of about fifty thousand. In the aftermath of World War II the sports complex served as a reception center for immigrants and refugees from Europe. But in the wake of the coup it became the most notorious site of detention and execution for prisoners, both Chilean and foreign. Detainees were brought to the stadium in police buses, army jeeps, ambulances, and trucks and hustled into the halls inside. According to eyewitness accounts compiled by Chilean human rights groups, arriving prisoners were formed into two lines of twenty people each and ordered to lean spread-eagled against the walls for several hours at a time. Soldiers or carabineros kicked the prisoners or hit them with their rifle butts before ordering them to a reception table.

The detainees were then booked and sent to different sections of the stadium according to the charges leveled against them, such as "dangerous extremist," or "Soviet spy." Sometimes the army and police officials referred to file folders to determine the prisoner's status, and in some cases they relied on the advice of a masked informant, usually a former leftist. These hooded informants, or *encapuchados*, would nod or silently extend a finger toward a former political associate. Individual interrogation sessions followed, almost always accompanied by more beatings and torture.[12]

María Cristina González, a former detainee held at the stadium in the aftermath of the coup, said she and about two hundred other women were kept for a time in the sports complex's emptied swimming pool. At one point they witnessed soldiers leading a group of fifteen other women back from interrogation, all bearing unmistakable signs of physical suffering. One woman, a left-wing physician, had been gang-raped and beaten. Her head was still dripping blood. When González's turn came, she was blindfolded and marched to an enclosed room. During hours of beatings, electric-shock torture, and threats to kill her, González was asked repeatedly about her husband, Francisco Aedo, a Socialist party member and architect who had worked in the Allende government's housing ministry. Who were their friends, who had visited their home, and what did she know about a supposed leftist plot to kill senior military officers and opponents of the Allende government?[13]

Hundreds of foreigners visiting or residing in Chile at the time were also arrested, and in some cases tortured and killed along with Chilean prisoners. Diplomats, business executives, and their families rarely faced such dangers, but students, budget travelers, and other less well-connected foreigners found themselves the object of a xenophobic campaign in the military-controlled media, which urged the Chilean public to denounce any "foreign subversives" in their midst.

Charles Horman, an American freelance writer and filmmaker who lived in a rented house in a lower-middle-class section of Santiago, was perhaps the best-known victim of this wave of repression. Horman, who was the subject of the Costa Gavras film *Missing,* and Frank Teruggi, another U.S. citizen, were arrested and held in the National Stadium. Their bodies, recovered weeks after their detentions, bore multiple bullet wounds that suggested they had been shot by firing squads. Chilean authorities later refused to acknowledge that Horman had been arrested, and claimed that Teruggi had been detained briefly for violating the curfew and then released.[14]

Another twenty-three Americans were picked up by Chilean authorities during this period. Adam and Patricia Garrett-Schesch were graduate students in history and sociology who had come to Chile to gather research material for their dissertations. The couple, arrested three days after the coup, was brought to the National Stadium where they were held for one week. On September 28 they testified before a U.S. Senate committee hearing on Chile chaired by Senator Edward Kennedy. Patricia told the hearing:

We saw the soldiers take people and select out from, let us say, a group of or a line of five or six people who were standing with hands over their heads like this, one person to beat up. They would take their automatic rifles and start on the backs, sides, and feet. We saw people lined up against the wall in the typical police position and see the soldiers take the rifle and just jam it right down on their feet, people standing doing absolutely nothing. . . . We saw other people when we went to the bathroom who were totally beaten up. Their faces were black and blue and a bloody mess. We saw people led down from the cells to the clinic area who could hardly walk. They were hobbling: young men, old men. We also heard women being beaten. We do not know whether the people who were beaten were Chilean or foreigners.[15]

Adam Garrett-Schesch was beaten during his interrogation, and both he and his wife were threatened with execution. Patricia testified that on Saturday, September 15, 1973, she witnessed groups of prisoners being led to a field just outside her view:

Within a couple of minutes the people outside began singing. At that point there was heavy automatic weapons fire. As the firing continued, fewer and fewer people were singing. Finally, the singing stopped and the continuous fire stopped also.

Shortly thereafter a soldier returned and spoke to a guard standing by the processing desk which was off to my right and said there were thirty-seven people in that group.[16]

Patricia Garrett-Schesch counted about four hundred prisoners who were eventually led out in this fashion. Nathaniel Davis, the U.S. ambassador to Chile at the time, was able to obtain the couple's release after signing a document vouching for their "good conduct," an implied promise that they would not publicize their experiences as prisoners. The Garrett-Scheschses naturally did not remain silent and their testimony, Davis noted, "created just the kind of furor in the world press I suppose the junta authorities were trying to forestall."[17]

Davis also said that Patricia Garrett-Schesch had not actually witnessed any executions, just prisoners being led away and subsequent
sounds of gunfire. But if what she saw and heard were not executions,
but rather a sadistic exercise designed to torment and further break
down the prisoners at the National Stadium, it seems likely that
Garrett-Schesch would have heard more singing or cries from the
prisoners once the shooting stopped. Simulated executions were one
of the many forms of abuse inflicted on political detainees during this
period, yet former prisoners at the National Stadium and other detention centers whom I interviewed, along with accounts compiled by
the Chilean human rights commission, indicate that this technique
was usually applied to individual prisoners rather than to large groups.

In such cases the guards and interrogators would stage an elaborate
show of preparing a firing squad, leading the blindfolded prisoners to
the execution area at dawn, and sometimes even introducing a
"priest" who offered to hear a last confession. The soldiers fired their
rifles either into the air or around the victim, while a guard standing silently to one side would knock the prisoner unconscious with a
blunt object.[18]

In *The Last Two Years of Salvador Allende,* Davis wrote that the
U.S. embassy's officers and Chilean staff "toured carabinero and military stations, the Santiago stadiums, the hospitals, the morgue, and
other points in the city to locate and obtain the release of any U.S. citizens who had been detained." But any efforts Davis and other U.S.
embassy personnel may have made in this regard compare poorly
with actions taken by other foreign embassies to protect their nationals during this period. A report by the U.S. General Accounting Office
(GAO) said that "prompt and effective protests by high-level U.S.
officials in behalf of arrested and detained Americans were not always made."[19]

The GAO report noted that although U.S. officials were holding
high-level discussions with the new military regime's top officials after
the coup, the plight of detained U.S. citizens was not discussed, nor
were any formal protests made. Even when Americans reported their
money or personal property had been stolen by Chilean soldiers, the
embassy made no formal protests.

The GAO report also studied the French, Swedish, Dutch, Bel-
gian, and Venezuelan embassies in Santiago, noting that all these em-

bassies offered shelter to their citizens and that one even arranged a special flight for those wishing to leave the country. In one particularly damning case cited by the GAO, two detained American missionaries held eleven days were visited twice in their cell by a Dutch embassy official—who was at the National Stadium seeking the release of Dutch nationals held there—before any U.S. consular officer visited them. It is difficult to imagine why a small embassy such as that of The Netherlands was able to pull more strings and locate and assist its citizens so much more effectively than the larger, more influential U.S. embassy, unless one considers the two embassies' different views of the coup. American officials tended to downplay the extent of the repression and bloodshed during this period. Military officials who arrested foreign nationals in the coup's aftermath habitually failed to notify the prisoners' embassies as required by the Vienna Convention, but the U.S. embassy rarely protested these violations. Indeed, those few protests to authorities concerning the treatment of U.S. citizens were made only belatedly, following inquiries by members of the U.S. Congress or reports in the American press.[20]

Many of the post-coup killings did not come to light until well over a decade later, when intimidated relatives finally began to gather enough courage to report what they had witnessed. As late as 1988 relatives of executed prisoners, under the auspices of the Chilean human rights commission, prepared a report on a massacre of most of the adult male population in a small farm community near Valdivia, in southern Chile.[21] The relatives' group compiled partial lists of executions in other regions of the country: 13 killed in Chillán; 21 in the Pisagua prison camp in northern Chile; 14 men—including a Bolivian university student on scholarship at the prestigious Facultad Latinoamericana de Ciencias Sociales (FLACSO) and Chilean folksinger Victor Jara—at the Chile Stadium; and 17 prisoners, including six detainees who died "while trying to escape" at the Tejas Verdes center in San Antonio, a port town west of Santiago.

In the southern forestry towns of Laja and Villarrica, Chilean carabineros executed at least seventeen men, mostly sawmill workers and other laborers who belonged to the Socialist party. Another five men were killed in Llanquihue, a lakeside town farther south. Most of the committee's listings of prisoner executions around the country end with the sad postscript "among others."

In succeeding years, the discovery of unmarked mass graves provided a grim reminder of the coup's bloody aftermath. In 1978 the
Catholic Church announced that the remains of fifteen people had
been found crammed into a lime kiln on a ranch in Lonquen, a few
miles north of Santiago. The victims included a father and his four
grown sons, another father and his two sons, and three brothers. All
had been arrested on October 6 and 7, 1973, by the carabineros, who
later told a judicial investigator that the men had died during a noc-
turnal shootout with the authorities. But autopsies of the remains told
a different story: because only one of the cadavers bore any bullet
wounds, it appeared that the victims might still have been alive when
they were brought to the kiln. Because members of the military were
involved, the civilian court that began investigating the Lonquen incident was forced to turn the case over to a military judge, who subsequently invoked a new amnesty law decreed by the regime that ab-
solved the carabineros of any wrongdoing.[22]

In Paine, a country town just outside the Chilean capital, two
dozen men were arrested on October 16, 1973, and were never seen
again. At least fifty-nine Paine inhabitants were either executed or
missing following their arrest during a three-month period after the
coup, giving the town the most political killings per capita in Chile.
Human rights activists speculated that the real figure is probably
much higher, with many families reluctant to report their relatives' arrests for fear of reprisals.[23]

Most of the dead from Paine were probably buried in unmarked
graves in section twenty-nine of Santiago's general cemetery. When
the Catholic Church denounced the existence of the graves in 1979,
authorities forbade photographs of the site. The cemetery's director,
when questioned about the prohibition, said that some of the graves
were in poor condition and that he and other officials wanted to show
"the positive side of Chile."[24] Photographs of section twenty-nine
were taken surreptitiously nevertheless, and showed individual graves
with crosses bearing the initials "N. N."—"no name"— along with
dates referring to either the burial or execution.

To the casual visitor, Paine is a pleasant, rather picturesque town,
with open-air restaurants serving grilled meat and other Chilean spe-
cialties that attract a sizable crowd from Santiago on weekends. But for
many the town bears a stigma. A retired general said that he and

another former officer were driving through Paine years later and were thinking of stopping for lunch when the general suddenly remembered what had happened there. "This is the *pueblo de las viudas* [town of widows]. We had better not linger here, it could be dangerous for us," he said.

Less than a week had passed since the coup, and Moy de Tohá and Isabel Morel de Letelier had decided to approach the defense ministry for information concerning their husbands, who had each served as defense minister during the Allende government. The two women were searched thoroughly at the entrance to the gray granite building, then allowed to wander through the halls, hoping to find some military friend to help in their husbands' cases.[25]

Tohá, Letelier, and most Allende civilian officials were being held on Dawson Island. Their wives wanted to know their legal situation—the exact charges against these men, who only days before had been government officials—and how they were being treated. No one seemed to know. The two women found one general who had once been a personal friend and who in fact had served for a few weeks as a minister in the last Allende cabinet. He was polite and called in another officer who had been recently appointed a military judge to explain everything. But this officer had just taken on the job and had very little idea of what was going to happen to Tohá, Letelier, and the other prisoners on Dawson Island.

Back in the halls of the defense ministry, the two women found themselves nearing the offices of the Chilean army commander, vacated less than a month earlier by General Carlos Prats. It was then that they saw Prats's successor approaching.

General Augusto Pinochet, in full dress uniform, was surrounded by reporters, with a press agent at his side who had once worked with a Chilean country musical group. There were foreign camera crews—the BBC, the American networks—and crews from the Chilean television stations as well. Pinochet talked into one microphone then turned to answer a different question into another. All the journalists scuffled around him, trying to catch his words.

Moy de Tohá froze in her tracks, dumbfounded, with Isabel de Letelier standing behind her. Pinochet, who was about forty feet away, spotted her and smiled as if nothing had happened, as if she had run into him during any of the thousand days of the Allende government when he was a loyal, apolitical general. "He's going to give you a hug," Isabel de Letelier whispered. Moy de Tohá stiffened, placing her hands behind her back, unsure of what to do. Pinochet must have noticed her expression, for he suddenly, violently threw his hands up at the gaggle of reporters around him. The questions stopped, the cameras and the microphones were turned off. How would it look if this woman rebuffed him, the commander of the Chilean army and member of the new ruling junta?

The TV cameras may have been turned off, but the reporters were still standing by. Pinochet came up to the frightened woman and gave her an *abrazo* anyway. Moy de Tohá threw her head backward and told Pinochet that she had to talk to him.

"Keep calm, nothing is happening," Pinochet said.

"What do you mean, nothing is happening?" she demanded. "José is in Dawson Island." How had she come by this information, Pinochet wanted to know. She knew, she knew. So Pinochet told her to speak to his aide, an officer who had also worked with Prats, and advise him that she was to have the very first audience the next day.

Moy de Tohá made a tactical error the following day, one she would recognize in hindsight. She arrived at the scheduled appointment not alone, but with Isabel Morel de Letelier, whom Pinochet had met only a few times, and with Irma Caceres de Almeyda, the wife of Allende's foreign minister, who was also on Dawson Island. Pinochet had never met this third woman, a lawyer and university professor, and she was just the sort of person who had always made him uneasy. But Moy de Tohá believed she should use whatever resources she could muster. Besides, the Almeydas and the Leteliers would have met Pinochet at the little farewell party she had wanted to give for Prats a few days before the coup.

The three women were shown into the army commander's office, and Pinochet entered, shouting at the top of his lungs about the Marxists, about how Allende's Popular Unity government had plans to cut the throats of the Chilean military's high command. Salvador Allende, already dead and buried, received special abuse. This screaming, raving Pinochet was not the warmhearted, if slow-witted, general who had dined with his wife at Moy de Tohá's house.

"Your husbands are well, they are well cared for and well fed, they receive medical attention and you have no reason to worry," Pinochet told them. "And the weather is mild where they are." This was difficult to believe, for at that time of year Dawson Island still had snow, and temperatures were made even colder from the strong winds.

Irma de Almeyda, the lawyer, began arguing that there was no reason for their husbands' detention, citing legal provisions. Pinochet did not take well to her exposition—he had never been comfortable around intellectual types, much less intellectual women, and the two ended up shouting. Had Moy de Tohá come alone, and played the role of the traditional wife and family friend, Pinochet's reaction might have been less violent, though perhaps no more helpful. The meeting lasted about twenty minutes, and as the women were leaving Pinochet approached Moy de Tohá and said, "You can send a suitcase of things for your husband to Dawson Island."

"And we can as well," Irma de Almeyda interjected.

"All right, go ahead," Pinochet said.

Lincoyán Zepeda was arrested eleven days after the coup in Copiapó at his job at ENAMI, the state enterprise for small and medium mining, where he was a technician. Copiapó, a mining town in Chile's northern Atacama desert, had a population of about thirty thousand, and if it had a disproportionate number of Allende government sympathizers, it was also the kind of provincial backwater where all the men (and few women) of any influence—Left, Right, and center—tended to be acquainted.

There had been very little resistance to the coup in Copiapó, save for a couple of student occupations of university and secondary school buildings, each lasting no more than a day. And in contrast to prisoners' treatment in Santiago, detainees were allowed brief visits by relatives. So when Zepeda, a Socialist party member, was brought before a military judge that day, he was not too surprised to be facing an army major whom he had met once before.[26] Two or three months prior to the coup he had gone to the army, which controlled the distribution of dynamite and other explosives in the area, to see if ENAMI could obtain some material for a copper mine the enterprise was operating. At the time, this army major had seemed a pleasant, agreeable sort. But now he and other officers appeared to be under heavy pressure from their superiors in Santiago to uncover leftist arms caches to demonstrate that they were doing their job.

The interrogation with the army major lasted about two hours, and its purpose was apparently to extract information about any armaments that Zepeda's Socialist party might be planning to use against the Chilean armed forces. There were psychological pressures, implied and explicit threats of torture and execution, and hints that Zepeda's brother, another Socialist party member arrested that day, might be killed. Despite the danger he was facing, the young mining technician had difficulty believing what he heard. At one point he asked the army major why he was making such accusations, since Zepeda had never even done his military service, much less had any outside experience with weapons. For a fleeting moment the officer seemed to believe him.

Zepeda spent that night in a tiny cell at the Copiapó army regiment, where every few hours soldiers would bang on his door, demanding that he identify himself. "Lincoyán Zepeda? Oh, we're going to execute you at 5 A.M." But another soldier, who seemed to be a noncommissioned officer, stopped by, offered him a cigarette, and inquired to which political party he had belonged.

"Socialist," the officer repeated. "This is a difficult time for you, isn't it?" It was the only humane gesture that night. Zepeda spent two more nights in that cell before he, his badly tortured brother, and a mutual friend named Jaime Sierra were moved into a warehouse-like building on the army base with thirty other prisoners.

Most of Zepeda's fellow prisoners belonged to one of the Popular Unity coalition parties, though many of them were not leaders or even well-known within their organizations. Some were very young, in their late teens. The treatment over the next few days was standard prison camp routine: up at 5:30 or 6 A.M., work detail, calisthenics. There were insults from the guards, occasional blows, and the psychological pressure of knowing that several of the men had been tortured and might be tortured again. Zepeda, who had only been beaten, considered himself lucky.

It was around 10 or 11 A.M. on October 16 when the prisoners were told that a general had arrived from Santiago. They were instructed to have everything looking orderly, for this army general—whose name they were not told—was going to review all their cases and there might be good news for some of the detainees. The Copiapó prisoners had all been held without any legal processes, not even a cursory trial by a military court. Zepeda, whose only charges were that he was a Socialist party member and belonged to some supposedly underground wing of the party, was hopeful he might be among those released.

General Sergio Arellano Stark, who had been one of the principal coup backers in the Chilean army, led a committee of officers on a helicopter tour of military bases, a tour that would earn him the nickname "the butcher of the north." The general and his committee first landed in La Serena, a pretty Spanish colonial town 480 kilometers north of Santiago. A group of sixteen political prisoners, including the director of a local children's orchestra, were moved from La Serena's jail to an army base and executed on October 16, 1973.[27]

That afternoon the atmosphere at the Copiapó regiment became more tense. The patrol in charge of Zepeda and other prisoners had consisted of a noncommissioned officer and a group of conscripts, and after a month of daily enforced contact they had grown used to each other. There was conversation and the occasional kindness. It was always the higher-ranking officers at the regiment, never their own patrol guards, who beat them or forced them to do backbreaking tasks. But now the prisoners were ordered back into their warehouse barracks, forbidden to speak, and made to stand at attention by their beds.

At around 9 P.M. a group of officers whom Zepeda had never seen entered the prisoners' quarters. They looked around at the detainees, and one of them commented ironically, "So here are the little doves." Another official said they would come back for "these bastards," and they left.

About two hours later the officers were back, this time with an army captain from the Copiapó regiment who read a list of names. One of the prisoners called was Zepeda's friend Jaime Sierra, arrested the same day Zepeda was detained. There did not seem to be any reason for the selection, and for a long time afterward Zepeda wondered why some of the prisoners were taken and others left in the warehouse.

The men whose names were called dressed silently, and no one ventured to ask the officers where they were being taken. But Sierra, who had occupied the top bunk of a bed next to Zepeda's, asked in a whisper if he knew what was happening. The thirteen men were led out in silence. At the time it looked as though they might be going to further interrogation sessions, or perhaps were going to be released.

That night Zepeda slept very soundly, exhausted by the day's tension. The prisoners got up the next day at their usual hour, and found the noncommissioned officer who had been on night guard duty waiting outside their quarters. Zepeda asked him how he had passed the night. "It was terrible," the officer said. Zepeda asked why. "Didn't you hear the screams?" the officer asked him. No, Zepeda had not heard anything. Where had they taken his friend Jaime Sierra and the others? The army official looked very upset, but said he did not know. The other prisoners began to talk among themselves, though no one dared speculate aloud about the worst possibility.

At around 7 A.M. another noncommissioned officer, a man with whom the prisoners had been able to talk at length, came to relieve the night duty guard. He seemed very happy to see Zepeda. "Lincoyán, it's good to find you here," he said. Zepeda asked if he knew what had happened to the other prisoners. "They killed them."

Zepeda broke down, and the noncommissioned officer asked him to calm down, for it would compromise him if the other officials heard. But Zepeda and the other prisoners could probably rest easy, he said, for it looked as though the worst was over. Zepeda, visibly upset, began to shout that it couldn't have happened, that it couldn't be true. His army friend persuaded him to lower his voice, to let the other prisoners know what had happened but also to reassure them that they were probably safe for the time being.

The killings haunted some of the army officials in the Copiapó regiment. Another young officer who had been on fairly cordial terms with the prisoners suffered nightmares and began drinking heavily. He had been in charge of burying the bodies, and oversaw a patrol of conscripts who were plied with pisco, a strong alcoholic spirit made from grapes, to get them through the grave digging. They began digging at midnight, but stopped at daybreak, fearing they could be seen from a hillside neighborhood across the valley. Since the grave was not very deep, the soldiers threw in some lime to help decompose the bodies.

Some of the bodies, when finally exhumed years later and delivered to the prisoners' families for burial, bore bullet wounds, but several of the victims had been stabbed and bludgeoned to death. The cadaver of Jaime Sierra, Zepeda's friend, bore a deep knife wound in his side that exposed part of his intestines.[28]

"These guys from Santiago were murderers," another Copiapó official later told Zepeda. This official had been with the regiment's commander when some of the thirteen prisoners were brought in. The first thing the officers from Santiago did was strike each man in the face with the butt of a machine gun. His commander, the officer recalled, blanched when he saw that.

Zepeda and the surviving prisoners at Copiapó noticed an improvement in their treatment in the wake of the killings, as if the massacre had shaken even the most hardline officers of the regiment.[29] But even if the Copiapó officers suffered pangs of conscience over what had occurred at their army base, none dared to challenge the official version of events as stated in an army communiqué the following day. The communiqué, dutifully published in full by the local newspaper, reported that the thirteen prisoners had been in the process of being transferred from the Copiapó jail to the facility in La Serena when the vehicle transporting them broke down and the prisoners attempted to escape. "Despite the fact that the sentries shouted 'Halt!' various times and even fired into the air to warn them, [the prisoners] did not stop," the communiqué said. "In view of this situation, [the sentries] proceeded to fire on the fugitives, wounding thirteen who died on the spot."[30]

General Arellano's helicopter tour flew further north into the Atacama desert, to Antofagasta, a port city 1,373 kilometers from Santiago, where another group of thirteen prisoners was summarily executed. The committee's last stop was Calama, a town adjacent to Chile's largest copper mine, Chuquicamata.

In *The Crucial Day*, Pinochet said that this northern mining area was one of his major concerns because the military had reports of well-armed leftist groups with combat training who might be able to isolate the local army unit.[31] If such reports did exist, and Pinochet was in fact concerned about such a security threat near the economically strategic Chuquicamata mine, his concerns did not lead him to notify either the commander of the Calama army regiment, Colonel Eugenio Rivera, or his immediate superior, General Joaquín Lagos of the Chilean army's first division in Antofagasta, about the military's plans for the coup on September 11, 1973. On that morning Colonel Rivera happened to be meeting in his office with a local Allende government official when the first reports of the military actions reached him. The Calama army commander immediately telephoned General Lagos, who indicated that he, too, was awaiting orders from Santiago.[32]

There was little resistance to the coup in this region: only one death—a man shot and killed while on the streets after curfew—and many of the political prisoners arrested had responded voluntarily to radio and television announcements ordering them to report to authorities.[33] A provincial military court in Calama had already tried and sentenced the twenty-six prisoners executed during General Arellano's visit, but the local authorities' handling of their cases was not severe enough to satisfy their military superiors in Santiago. Commander Fernando Reveco, who had served on the Calama military court, was ordered back to the Chilean capital where he was arrested and court-martialed for acting with "a lack of rigor" in carrying out military justice.[34]

"What we were most concerned about was whether there had been any arms in possession of civilians in the area," Reveco told a Chilean newsmagazine years later. "We never found anything, and it seems that none of the people we tried had anything to do with arms. In other areas there were people with arms, but not in Calama." His conscience, he said, did not permit him to judge individuals who had already been defeated and disarmed. These prisoners had already lost their government and their jobs, and on top of everything else were facing prison sentences. (One of the shortest sentences, sixty-one days, was that for the director of a local radio station, who had defied a military order to shut down the station the day of the coup. But his name was on the lists that General Arellano's committee brought from Santiago.) Commander Reveco was held in three different military installations where he was interrogated and tortured. While in detention Reveco learned to his horror that the same detainees serving prison sentences he had dictated, which ranged from fifteen days to twenty years, had been killed.

Colonel Eugenio Rivera, commander of the Calama army regiment at the time, had not been informed of the reason for General Arellano's visit, and had prepared an official program for the general: a troop review, a tour of the base, and a formal luncheon in his honor.[35] The band was ready to play and the Calama regiment's soldiers were standing at attention on October 19, 1973, when the Puma helicopter landed. A group of officers wearing combat uniforms and steel helmets and carrying automatic weapons climbed out, looking as if they expected to be met with enemy fire. Arellano rejected most of the proposed program and showed Rivera a document designating him General Augusto Pinochet's delegate. Arellano asked to see the prisoners' files, saying he had come to review the cases, and after looking through the papers he asked that the war tribunal be summoned after lunch. Shortly before the tribunal convened, Commander Sergio Arredondo, an officer from Arellano's group, approached and asked to interrogate the prisoners. Arellano gave him permission, and while the war tribunal met Rivera took Arellano on an informal tour of the Calama army base and the Chuquicamata copper mine, sixteen kilometers away.[36]

When the two men returned that evening, a guard told them the officers were in the dining room where the farewell dinner for General Arellano would be held. Rivera asked about the war tribunal. The guard said it had finished.

As Rivera and Arellano headed toward the officers' dining room, another official approached and told the general, "It is all liquidated," and handed Arellano some papers to sign.[37] After hurriedly signing the documents, the general entered the dining room with Rivera, who was still unaware that anything out of the ordinary had taken place at his army base. But after the dinner the colonel noticed that his second in command seemed agitated, and when Arellano's helicopter took off he asked his subordinate what was wrong.

The officer blurted out that the war tribunal had convened as Arellano ordered, but when they ordered the prisoners to appear they were told that the twenty-six men had already been executed on orders of Commander Sergio Arredondo. Rivera hurried back to the base and tried to convene a meeting of all the officers, several of whom seemed in a state of shock. One of the dead prisoners had been the brother of a noncommissioned officer there at the regiment. But the meeting could not take place until morning, for some of the officials were burying the bodies as Arredondo had ordered.

Rivera's deputy commander, believing that some record should be made of the prisoners' deaths, drew up execution orders following the killings and presented them to General Arellano to sign on their return to the base that evening. Rivera telephoned his immediate superior in Antofagasta, division general Joaquín Lagos Osorio, and learned that prisoners had been executed in that city as well. Arellano's helicopter had returned to Antofagasta for refueling, and Lagos ordered that the aircraft not be allowed to leave again without prior clearance from his office. In a notarized statement submitted to a civilian court thirteen years later, Lagos said Arellano telephoned him the morning after the Calama executions to thank him for his hospitality while in the region. Lagos angrily told him to come to his office and explain his committee's actions. "I expressed my indignation for the crimes committed behind my back, in my own area of jurisdiction," the statement said.[38]

Arellano arrived a short time later at Lagos's office, accompanied by the notorious Commander Arredondo. Lagos made Arredondo wait outside while he confronted Arellano, who in turn "apologized, saying that Commander Arredondo had acted on his own initiative and without his authorization." This rather vague explanation did not mollify Lagos. That afternoon Pinochet arrived in Antofagasta, where his wife was visiting relatives, and Lagos managed to report to him in private at the airport and ask to be relieved of his post. According to Lagos's statement, Pinochet indicated he had no idea Arellano would take such actions (though the general was ostensibly acting on Pinochet's orders as his "special delegate"). He ordered Arellano and his group, who were scheduled to continue their trip farther north (to the cities of Iquique and Arica), to return to Santiago. Whether Pinochet truly did not know that Arellano's tour of northern Chile would result in mass executions is open to question, but Lagos's outrage over what had happened almost certainly prevented more executions in the region. Within a year both he and Colonel Rivera had resigned from the

Chilean army, the institution that they had once been so proud to serve.

_____

"As for me, I saw so many things, well, I took to meditating on them at night. Why did I have to be witnessing such things?"[39]

Army first corporal Nelson Morales Leal did not dare express his discontent openly, for that could land him in front of a firing squad. But after taking part in a raid on the house where soldiers mercilessly beat the screaming inhabitants, he began thinking of ways to get out of the military.

The next time Morales had a one-day pass he walked down to Santiago's main avenue, with a plan he had not revealed to anyone. He found a fight in progress, four men slugging it out, the kind of post-coup scene he had seen so often while on duty. A military patrol had just arrived and was trying to break it up. Morales joined in and fought against the soldiers, who obligingly arrested him and turned him over to a police commissary on charges of disorderly conduct. Someone planted a pistol in his jacket, and a military court prosecuted him for disorderly conduct, illegal weapons possession, and being absent without leave. On October 29, 1973, the former army reserve officer was sent to Santiago's public jail, and found himself in the wing where political prisoners were held. Some of these men might even have been arrested by his own military patrol.

His fellow detainees found Morales's case funny—the soldier-turned-prisoner. *Indio*, or "Indian," they nicknamed him, for he was darker in coloring than most of the middle-class inmates in that wing. There were two journalists, one a socialist from the government newspaper *La Nación* and another from the communist newspaper *Puro Chile*, who frequently argued about ideology, about strategy, and about who was really responsible for mistakes made during the Allende government. More than once the other prisoners had to intervene. The prisoners' existence in the Santiago prison was not as harsh as that in other detention centers around the country: there were soccer games, the prisoners did some copper engraving, and on

Thursdays a priest came to lead Mass. But many of the prisoners were interrogated.

Morales's cellmate was a seventeen-year-old university student, Denrio Álvarez, who was taken for interrogation one day and never returned. A few days later it was Álvarez's birthday, and his mother arrived at the public jail with presents. Álvarez's father, a fishmonger, had sent seafood along with the birthday cake. At the time Morales and the other prisoners didn't know what had happened, only that the young prisoner had been taken to interrogation and had not returned; that was all he could tell his cellmate's frightened mother. She left, and later that morning a corporal arrived and beckoned to him.

"Indio, did you know your cellmate was found dead in La Pincoya [a low-income municipality of Santiago]?" The official turned over Álverez's identity card and other personal effects to Morales. At noon his cellmate's mother returned and Morales had to give her the news. "Look, ma'am, we've just received this information, and now you have to go to the coroner's office to see if it is true," he said.

It was true. And that day when Morales learned what had happened he began banging on a trash can to get the other prisoners' attention and announced the news. "A moment of silence for Denrio Álvarez! A moment of silence for Denrio Álvarez!"[40] The prisoners stopped what they were doing, rose to their feet, and stood quietly for a minute or so. The same fate could easily befall any of them.

Other Chilean military officers were held at the prison, including a handful of high-ranking officials who had opposed the coup. There was a group of air force officer candidates who had just finished their course and were sent on a trip to China and the former Soviet Union as their reward. When they returned to Santiago, they were arrested as they disembarked from the plane, thrown into a van, and brought directly to the jail.

Another air force officer held at the prison was General Alberto Bachelet, who had headed the Allende government's food-rationing program and who had been arrested the day of the coup at his office in the Chilean defense ministry but released that evening. Three days later soldiers raided his home and took him to the War Academy, where he was blindfolded, beaten, and tortured, sometimes by air force officials who had been his subordinates before the coup. Bachelet, who had heart trouble, was later transferred to the air force hospital, then sent back to his home where he was placed under house arrest. On December 18, 1973, he was arrested yet again and taken to the public jail, where he was subjected to periodic interrogations and torture.[41]

On March 12, 1974, as Morales and the other prisoners were being herded out of their cells for lunch, Bachelet collapsed on the floor, scraping the side of his face. Morales went to look for a stretcher and the other prisoners brought him back to his cell, where he died, the victim of a heart attack. Radio Balmaceda, one of the more independent radio stations still operating after the coup, reported Bachelet's death within two hours of the incident; the station had been alerted by a sympathetic prison guard. Consequently, the regime ordered Radio Balmaceda shut down.

Morales was eventually sentenced for assault, but his lawyer managed to get the military court to drop the illegal weapons possession charge, since the pistol had been planted on him. He spent just under a year in jail, but at least he would never have to go back to the army. His conscience was clear.[42]

Hortensia Bussi de Allende's revised version of her husband's death spread around the world, but the military regime would understand only belatedly that it was not in its own interest to hold Dr. Patricio Guijón indefinitely. After three months on Dawson Island, the surgeon was finally moved, first to the naval hospital in Punta Arenas and then back to Santiago. Afterward, he was turned over to Investigaciones, Chile's detective police, who promptly declared him incommunicado and proceeded to hold him in a cell for five or six days over Christmas. For three days he had almost nothing to eat: the guards, wanting to isolate him from the other prisoners, took him to the dining hall only after the others had eaten and there was no food left. On the last day, at about 11 A.M., he was taken from his cell and interrogated yet again about what he had seen that day at the La Moneda presidential palace. He repeated his story.[43]

"Very good," he was told. "Now you're going to have a television session, so go have a shower, shave, and change your clothes." No one ever offered any explanation as to why Guijón was being held, what his legal situation was, or what they were going to do with him. He was driven to Channel 7, Chile's government television station, and placed before a camera. There was not even a journalist there to interview him. "Just say again what you saw," he was instructed.

Chilean television viewers that evening saw a timid, soft-spoken man whose slight build had been further diminished by three months of prison-camp hardship. Those who believed Allende had been killed, and had not committed suicide, would hardly have been convinced by this forced television appearance.

The Investigaciones police then released Guijón but warned him not to leave his house for at least a week. Afterward he went back to Santiago's Salvador Hospital as a staff surgeon, only to be told two weeks later that he was to leave his job. He wasn't told who had given the order, or why.

"So I spent the next six weeks at home, being a house husband," he recalled. A colleague at a Santiago cancer facility contacted him, asking him to work there, and Guijón accepted the offer, working there from March to September of 1974. But the job did not use Guijón's skills as a surgeon.

His family was German on his mother's side, and through some contacts Guijón was offered a surgeon's post in West Germany, which he wanted to take. Many Chilean professionals were leaving the country, and Germany seemed to offer good prospects. But the Chilean interior ministry refused to grant him permission to leave the country, arguing that it was "not in the national interest." An official there, however, did ask him why he wanted to leave. Guijón told him.[44] "No problem. Just go back to the Salvador Hospital."

So Guijón was given his old job back, and the post in West Germany went to someone else. For economic rather than political reasons, he never tried to leave Chile after that. Physicians derive only a small portion of their income from their hospital work; they depend on their private practice fees. And surgeons, like most specialists, base their practice on referrals from internists.

Guijón, a marked man, did not get many referrals. Right-wing colleagues associated him with the Allende government, reasoning that if he had been a prisoner on Dawson Island he must have been guilty of some punishable offense. And some leftists who stayed in the country suspected him of being a regime stooge. But Guijón never changed his story; he would repeat it countless times to the journalists who asked.

Gradually, people in Chile began to forget, and Guijón's medical practice was slowly restored. Very rarely did a patient make the association between the doctor and the coup. The other Chilean doctors who were part of Allende's medical staff and who were with Guijón that day had all left the country.

Some of Guijón's fellow prisoners on Dawson Island did not survive their detention. José Tohá, Allende's former interior and defense minister, seemed consumed by a malady that had no medical explanation. He ate his meals; Drs. Guijón and Jirón examined him; but his weight seemed to drop no matter what they did.[45] He had always been thin—170 pounds and over six feet tall—and after only a month his weight dropped to less than 130 pounds. At Guijón's and Jirón's insistence, Tohá and some other sick prisoners were moved to a Chilean naval hospital in Punta Arenas. When the Red Cross informed Moy de Tohá that her husband had been hospitalized, she began making a series of desperate phone calls to the Chilean defense ministry trying to obtain authorization to travel to Punta Arenas to see him. An aide to the regime's defense minister, Admiral Patricio Carvajal, refused to pass on her message, saying that the official "had much more important things to do than concern himself with Mr. Tohá's health."[46] She called the defense ministry again and spoke to a sympathetic Chilean air force official who promised to see what he could do. He telephoned back and said her husband's case was not a matter for the defense ministry, but was appropriate for the Chilean interior ministry, which handles internal security matters, or perhaps for the junta directly. No one, it seemed, wanted to acknowledge responsibility.

She telephoned the regime's newly created prisoner department, and spoke to a colonel who flatly informed her she could not travel to Punta Arenas. "If anything can be done for your husband, the doctors will do it, and if they can do nothing I assure you we will deliver the cadaver to you," he said.[47]

Moy de Tohá then spoke to an aide to the Chilean air force commander, Gustavo Leigh, who suggested she draft a letter requesting authorization. She brought the letter to the officer's house that afternoon, and the following day he telephoned to say her trip to Punta Arenas to visit her husband had been approved.

At the naval hospital in Punta Arenas, Moy de Tohá was harassed by military guards, who searched her and inspected the gifts she was carrying. Her husband, walking slowly between two soldiers carrying machine guns, was finally brought in to see her. They could have fifteen minutes together, the guards said, and were allowed to talk only about family matters.

But Moy de Tohá defied them: She tried to lift her defeated husband's spirits by telling him about Chilean military officers who might help him and about the offers of political asylum the family had received from Mexico, Venezuela, and Spain. There were three more visits over the next few days, two an hour long and a final encounter cut short by a young official who told her he was about to leave for the cinema but that he would allow the Tohás an extra minute for a sexual encounter if they wished.

She returned to Santiago and again began contacting former military acquaintances and friends on behalf of her husband, who was sent back to Dawson Island and later moved to a military hospital in Santiago. José Tohá's condition was deteriorating rapidly, yet the authorities still subjected him to periodic interrogations. In desperation Moy de Tohá decided to request a formal interview with Pinochet. This time she would go alone.

Pinochet still retained his army commander's office in the defense ministry, but he and other members of the junta had moved the regime's headquarters to the Diego Portales building, a multi-story edifice originally built for a United Nations conference on trade and development during the Allende government. Arriving five minutes early, Moy de Tohá stopped by the office of an air force official who had once been a friend. He gave her a cup of coffee and they talked. José Tohá, the former defense minister, was being judged by a special war tribunal, whose magistrate's previous posting had been that of a police dog trainer.

"I want you to tell me if it is true that the military judge handling my husband's case is a police dog trainer," she said.[48] The officer looked uncomfortable.

"Well, anyone can be appointed military judge," he told her.

"I want you to tell me if this man is or is not a police dog trainer," Moy de Tohá insisted.

"Well, he has trained dogs," the official said, evasively. He called upstairs to Pinochet's office to announce Moy de Tohá's arrival. His office was on the next to last floor, and was accessible only by a narrow staircase. He was waiting for her at the top of the landing.

"Mrs. Tohá, up here." Pinochet did not call her by her first name, as he had done in the past. But she tried to move the encounter to a more familiar setting.

"Look, Augusto, I didn't come to see the head of the military junta, I came to see Augusto Pinochet, the person who was a guest in my house," she said, climbing the stairs.

"You ought to be grateful that I am receiving you at all at a time when there are long lines of people waiting months for an audience with me," Pinochet replied. "I am now head of the government junta."

"When you were a general and José was defense minister of this country you never needed an appointment to come to my house," she said. When she reached the top of the stairs, Moy de Tohá saw that Pinochet was smiling. He bent to embrace her, but even though she was trying to play the role of family friend, she couldn't bring herself to kiss him. She was too nervous, her husband had been held incommunicado for more than twenty days, and she knew how crucial this meeting could be.

Pinochet's new office was elaborately decorated, though not in the best of taste: velvet armchairs, a table with lots of little Chinese dragons and figurines. Their one-sided conversation began. "All over the world people are saying there are cadavers in the Mapocho River," he said. Moy de Tohá, along with most Santiago residents, had seen these bodies. "I don't know why you came to see me, I can't do anything. I have nothing against Tohá, nothing against him," Pinochet said. "I don't know if maybe the air force or the navy have something against him. We in the army don't have anything against Tohá."

But, he said, if we were to do something for José Tohá, it would be for his young son and daughter, "because whoever their father might be, children have a right to have a father." His words irritated Moy de Tohá.

"If you are going to do something, do it for José, because I can take charge of my children," she said. "And you'll do it because José is an upright man and you know that." Pinochet looked at her and smiled.

"You are a Marxist and I haven't taken you prisoner," he said. "I am not a Marxist," she replied, "though I married a Marxist and have friends who are Marxists. I consider myself too ignorant to be a Marxist."

The meeting lasted more than thirty minutes, and Moy de Tohá did not afterward remember all that was said. They spoke of her husband and his friendship with Pinochet, but Pinochet said much more than she did. He paced around the room and shouted, avoiding eye contact with her. The meeting was not accomplishing anything; Pinochet reacted badly when she tried to get a word in edgewise. In fact, it seemed to horrify him when she spoke.

He began to grumble about Hortensia Bussi de Allende and her campaign against the regime. It was as if he were throwing out every thought that entered into his head, whether or not it was pertinent to the matter at hand. The general who had eaten at the Tohás' house, who had brought little gifts to her children, had become a stranger.

After their meeting, Moy de Tohá kept telephoning and contacting other Chilean military officials, trying to enlist the help of any officer who had known her husband when he was defense minister. Some were courteous, but they did nothing practical to assist José Tohá, failing either to secure better treatment for him or to accelerate the war tribunal's prosecution against him.

Six months after the coup, Allende's former defense minister died in the military hospital. He weighed less than 110 pounds.[49] When Moy de Tohá retrieved his body she found a red ring around his neck, as if he had died by strangulation or hanging. But she would never learn the precise manner of his death.

Afterward several Chilean military officers who had known José Tohá telephoned to express their condolences. Maybe because the government was now in their hands, they could afford the luxury of offering superficial courtesies to Moy de Tohá, who would soon go into exile in Mexico. The Tohás' former friends had become powerful, and the dictatorship was in place.

Chapter Three

Military Government

I am Chilean, and I know our idiosyncrasies, which do not permit someone to perpetuate himself in power.
—General Augusto Pinochet, September 4, 1974

I will die, and he who succeeds me will die, but there will be no elections.
—General Augusto Pinochet, June 16, 1975

Chile's new military junta was officially sworn in the night of September 11, 1973, in a brief ceremony at the military academy where Dr. Patricio Guijón and other Allende government functionaries were being held prisoner. The four men who now led a new government had not even headed their respective services for long: Pinochet had taken command of the army barely three weeks earlier when his predecessor, General Carlos Prats, had been forced to resign. General Gustavo Leigh, the air force commander, had held his post since August 20—his predecessor was forced to leave the institution after he decided to resign from his cabinet post in the Allende government. The naval commander who occupied the position before Admiral José Merino had a similar experience; he reluctantly turned in his resignation on August 31. Although Allende had not accepted the decision, Merino, the navy's second-ranking admiral, had been acting commander by the time of the coup.

The last member of the junta, César Mendoza of the carabineros, had been the police force's sixth-ranking general at the time of the coup. Some of his superiors, in fact, had been with Allende at La Moneda early on the day of the coup, withdrawing when the carabinero palace guards left around 9 A.M. This defection was decisive, for the carabineros were a well-armed paramilitary force of 35,000 who might have posed a serious challenge to the coup's organizers had they sided with the Allende government.

These four men—Pinochet, Leigh, Merino, and Mendoza—were little known to the Chilean public, and to the foreign governments whose embassies in Santiago were frantically trying to ascertain what was happening based on the scarce information available. The brief statements each of the new junta members made following the televised swearing-in ceremony were markedly different in tone and content and hardly helped to clarify the picture.[1] Pinochet, the first to speak, indicated that military officials would be appointed as governors and cabinet ministers, and civilian advisers would be assigned to the latter. The Chilean congress, he said, was "in recess" until further notice, but the judiciary and the comptroller general's office would be maintained. Chile would keep diplomatic relations with all countries except Cuba, he said.[2]

Naval commander José Merino then spoke, acknowledging Chile's democratic tradition but saying that the executive branch (read Allende) had forgotten its duties and the armed forces were obliged to take over. As if to deflect attention from the navy's leading role in plotting the coup, Merino's words took a nearly eloquent turn when he said Chileans "must realize that for sailors it is much pleasanter to be by the sea, near our ships. But when the task is so vast, all thoughts of pleasure are forgotten, hearts unite, services unite, for our native land is above individual desires and to her we devote our efforts."

Air force commander Gustavo Leigh, who five years later would be ousted from his junta post over disagreements with Pinochet concerning the timing of a return to civilian government, took the most hardline approach, with three references to Marxism or the "Marxist cancer" and the need to extirpate it. Yet he described the military takeover as a "sad and sorrowful mission." Carabinero general César Mendoza said the junta's goal was to restore law and order and compliance with the Chilean constitution. It was not, he said, a question of ideology or personal vengeance.

The Chilean military's role was enlarged from national defense to enforcement of government policy. But aside from crushing the Allende government and its supporters, the junta appeared to have little or no plan for what to do with the governmental apparatus it now controlled.

The four junta members met again the following morning at the defense ministry, across the street from the still-smoking La Moneda presidential palace. The center of the Chilean capital was relatively calm, although navy commander José Merino took the precaution of arriving in a Swiss-built Mowag armored vehicle, startling the soldiers guarding the building.[3] Inside, the junta began to put together a government, a process that seemed improvised at best.

The first order of business was to draw up an official document constituting the junta as Chile's "supreme power." The first draft of the document designated Pinochet as junta president, an office that would be rotated among the four military commanders. Pinochet requested that this provision for rotating the junta presidency not be set down in writing, but be understood as a gentlemen's agreement.[4] His request was granted. Other decrees were added imposing a state of siege throughout the country and appointing twenty-eight military officers, mostly army colonels, to administer martial law throughout the country's provinces.

The regime's first cabinet appointments were made over a three-week period from September 12 to October 11, 1973. The ministries were divided among the four branches of the military and two civilians were chosen to lead the departments of education and justice. These first appointments, judging from accounts by former regime officials, were often hurried decisions as the junta tried to put together a functioning government as quickly as possible. The important post of interior minister, the leadership position within the cabinet, was initially considered an appropriate job for a carabinero officer, since the police institution at the time came under the jurisdiction of the interior ministry (later it would be transferred to the defense ministry). But General César Mendoza, the carabinero commander who suddenly found himself head of the institution the day of the coup, was so unprepared for his new role that he had no candidates, though three other carabinero officers were placed in less-strategic cabinet posts. The interior minister's job went to General Oscar Bonilla, who had been one of the chief coup plotters within the army.

The junta named two civilians as ministers of education and justice. The former official in charge of education, José Navarro, who had once been Pinochet's professor at the military academy and who was hurriedly invited to join the government the day after the coup, lasted barely two weeks before he was replaced by a navy admiral. An army general who was appointed economy minister also had a brief term in office as justice minister; he was replaced at the end of the month by a civilian businessman.[5]

In many cases military officers were unenthusiastic about their new jobs in the government ministries, where a number of left-leaning and Christian Democratic employees still worked. Though the imposition of a state of siege and the accompanying climate of intimidation made open defiance unlikely, the new military cabinet officials sometimes encountered a passively uncooperative staff as they struggled to master the finer points of agriculture or urban development. In addition, many Chilean officers remembered only too well the negative experiences of some of their colleagues who had served briefly in the Allende cabinet.

The experience of Nicanor Díaz Estrada, an air force general who served as labor minister for eighteen months beginning in mid-1974, illustrates the haphazard way officials were moved in and out of the regime's cabinet and the often comic disorganization of the ministries under military administration.[6] "One day I got a call from the air force chief of staff who told me, 'General Pinochet is going to appoint you labor minister.' " When Díaz said he did not want the job, his superior officer said the appointment was an order like any other. Called the next day to a government assembly, Díaz, who had expected at least a preliminary meeting with Pinochet, found himself being sworn in as the new minister. Confronted with reporters asking about his plans for the labor ministry, the startled air force general managed to say that it was not the time to make public statements, but to work.

Díaz's predecessor had been Mario Mackay, a carabinero general who had caused a minor uproar when he and the regime's minister of mines, another carabinero general, had traveled to the El Teniente copper mine south of the capital and been photographed giving *abrazos* to two leaders of the copper mine workers' union. That in itself was no crime, but those particular leaders happened to be the last two remaining leftists on El Teniente's labor board. Díaz said he asked Mackay to leave four other carabinero officers who had been working under him at the labor ministry on the job for a few days while Díaz settled into his new post. Mackay agreed, but when Díaz arrived at the ministry the following day he discovered that three of the four carabineros had already left. Furious, he ordered the remaining carabinero ministry functionary to leave. When Díaz examined a stack of file folders on different ministerial commissions studying such topics as labor-code modifications and social security reforms, he found nothing but blank pages.

Díaz asked air force leaders to assign some of their officers to fill the vacancies at his ministry, but they proved extremely reluctant to do so. At a meeting of air force generals, Díaz, frustrated by the lack of cooperation, stormed out of the room without even asking leave of the commander, General Gustavo Leigh. He eventually managed to secure two junior officers by pulling rank and simply ordering them to report to him at the labor ministry.

But news of intraservice feuds and other cases of government disorganization rarely escaped the thick wall of censorship in place since the coup. The junta's civilian press secretary, Frederico Willoughby, was a civilian rightist who had joined the regime the day of the coup, arriving at the defense ministry to help draft the first public statements. "The junta was composed of people who had not even known each other very well before," Willoughby recalled. "While they were sorting out their differences I . . . channeled information to the press, so there wouldn't be contradictory opinions on the same issue. One junta member might express one view and another something different. Whenever this threatened to occur, it was my job to put out the fire, so to speak."[7]

Like press secretaries in most governments, Willoughby arranged interviews with junta members, meeting with them beforehand to review questions likely to be raised and to suggest the wording of appropriate statements to be made in response. Instilling a sense of public relations in the four commanders was no easy task, although General Gustavo Leigh of the air force seemed the most adept with the press. Pinochet, on the other hand, had to be persuaded not to wear dark glasses when photographers were present in order to avoid enduring images such as the photo of him sitting with his arms crossed, glaring into the camera from behind thick sunglasses. Years later Pinochet recalled that photo, claiming that it had been taken when he had not slept in days, and had been deliberately used against him.[8]

During the regime's first few days in power, the defense ministry received an avalanche of letters, telegrams, flowers, and other congratulations from Chileans backing the coup. There were donations of jewelry delivered to the central bank to help "rebuild" the country; some couples even gave their wedding rings, receiving copper bands in return to be worn as a symbol of support for the new regime. Photographs of these piles of jewelry and reprints of the messages of support from prominent Chileans filled the pages of the newspapers, helping the regime to create an impression of broad public support.

One cabinet-level post, the government secretariat general, would take charge of propaganda and ideology. One of the department's first efforts, led by army colonel Pedro Ewing, was the *Libro Blanco* (White Book), a clumsily written official justification for the coup whose publication was financed by the CIA. The book alludes to "Plan Z," an alleged left-wing plot to murder senior military officials and opponents of the Allende government. Plan Z gave a tentative date for the leftist uprising of September 19, when the Chilean military held their traditional parade, though it was unclear from the content of *Libro Blanco* whether Allende was supposed to have approved the plan or whether the Chilean military commanders were supposed to have known of the plan prior to the coup. The obvious intention of the writers of the book was to cast the Chilean left in the role of the military's armed opponent, obscuring the Right's involvement in terrorist activity and the murder of military officers such as former army commander René Schneider and Allende's naval attaché, Arturo Araya.

To this end, *Libro Blanco* included another "secret document": a forged Socialist party document indicating that party members had taken part in the Araya assassination, which in fact had been committed by a breakaway faction of the right-wing extremist group Patria y Libertad. Araya's name was included in the book's list of ninety-six people killed in "violent incidents attributed to social or political motives" during the three years of the Allende government, including leftists, Christian Democrats, and workers. This list looks insignificant now beside the numbers of people killed during the coup and the regime's first few weeks in power, but at that time the coup's bloody aftermath was not being reported inside Chile.

Plan Z allegedly mentioned the "fundamental importance of eliminating the high command and the officials heading the regional units of the enemy forces" during the September 18 military parade and at an officers' luncheon held at La Moneda, which presumably Allende would attend, but there were no details as to just how this was to be accomplished.[9]

One general holding a high ranking defense ministry post before the coup told me that no such plan was even discussed during the coup-plotting meetings he attended. If there had been any Plan Z, he said, his people would surely have known of it. Belief in such a leftist plot, however, quickly spread through the regime's lower ranks to those interrogating and torturing political prisoners, who demanded to know what their captives knew about Plan Z.

Every Chilean newspaper, magazine, television station, and radio station had a regime-appointed censor whose job was to scrutinize press reports before they were aired or published. Approval from an in-house censor, however, did not necessarily protect the press from official wrath at a higher level. One Christian Democratic newsmagazine was reprimanded for printing a photograph of Interior Minister Oscar Bonilla with a button of his uniform unfastened, and for a seemingly inoffensive human-interest story about a man from a low-income district of Santiago who had managed to obtain a university degree in engineering while working full time. The story, which noted that this graduate had received better grades than many of his nonworking classmates, was criticized by the regime's propaganda division for "stimulating class struggle." Even staunchly proregime publications were sometimes sanctioned: the tabloid *La Segunda*, part of the *El Mercurio* newspaper chain, was shut down four months after the coup for publishing a front-page story about the shortage of cigarettes. The official resolution closing the paper for one day claimed the report had "altered the citizens' tranquility."[10]

The University of Chile, which had been closed for the first few days following the coup, was still under civilian control as its rector, Edgardo Boeninger, tried to put the institution in working order. Many of the left-wing professors and students at the university, who accounted for roughly half the twenty thousand students in Chile's higher-education system, had either been arrested or taken refuge. And right-wing academics were urging that remaining leftists on the faculty be fired, or, more ominously, that the military intervene and put the University of Chile under its administration. A group of professors at the university's Valparaiso campus had voted to ask the navy to take control, and Boeninger, a Christian Democrat, whom I interviewed in Santiago, hastened to try to avert such a disaster.

The right-wing faculty members were adamant. "The campus is full of Marxists, who have done the most horrible things to us in the past," they told Boeninger. "Someone has to do the dirty work, and this dirty work should be done by the military. But don't worry, rector, we support you." Boeninger then paid a visit to Admiral Hugo Castro, who was about to become the regime's education minister, and the two men began a friendly conversation over drinks.

Military intervention would be a very bad mistake, Boeninger told the admiral, for any changes in faculty or administration should be done by the university itself. Academic standards must be maintained. "Look, rector, I don't understand," Admiral Castro responded. "We have decided to take over the port authority, and how can you ask us not to do the same with the universities, considering that there are more Marxists there than in the port authority?"

"Admiral, these are two very different entities," Boeninger started to say, but realized then that further discussion would be useless. He returned to Santiago and called a meeting of faculty, students, and administrative personnel to announce his resignation.

Barely two hours later Boeninger received a telephone call from one of the academics at the meeting, a law professor with good contacts with the armed forces. The junta was very surprised by his resignation, Boeninger was told. Would he be willing to discuss this? Boeninger, accompanied by the rectors of two other Chilean universities, went to a meeting at the defense ministry. Pinochet sat at the head of the table, and Boeninger was seated next to Merino, the navy commander, who removed a pistol from his pocket and placed it on the table. Pinochet gruffly asked the rector to state his position. Boeninger, though uncomfortable with Merino's gun and Pinochet's tone of voice, spoke of the need to preserve academic freedom and how military intervention would be wrong, trying to phrase his comments as diplomatically as possible. Leigh, the Chilean air force commander, told him he had made a very convincing presentation and asked if he would be willing to put it in writing.

Boeninger composed a memorandum using the most conciliatory
language possible to describe what he felt were the basic elements of
a university. One heading cited the shared goals of peace and reconciliation. He sent the memo to the junta and waited for their response, receiving telephone calls from right-wing friends who assured
him that the junta was reacting favorably to his recommendations.
Three days later he went to the defense ministry for another meeting
with the junta, this time with the rectors of Chile's other universities.

Once again, Pinochet sat at the head of the table, and once again
Admiral Merino removed a pistol from his pocket and placed it on the
table. A few seconds later, a television crew burst in to film the beginning of the meeting, and Merino grabbed his gun and hid it until
the cameras had left the room.

The meeting began with Pinochet saying that the junta would state
its position on the subject of military intervention. He then asked
whether anyone had something to say beforehand. Boeninger indicated he had already presented his views. "Then you are all in agreement?" he asked the other rectors, who nodded.

"The junta is in total disagreement, but I would like Admiral Castro
[the education minister] to state the government's views," Pinochet
said. Boeninger, who was sitting next to Castro, saw that he held a
copy of the memo and had scribbled several comments across the
pages. He pointed to the heading "shared goals."

"I want you to know there is no such thing as 'shared goals,' " he
said. "There are only the government's objectives, and the citizens
must comply with them." Castro continued to speak for ten to fifteen
minutes about the Marxists and how eliminating their presence in the
universities could not be done by civilians. Although they would have
liked to have Boeninger, a Christian Democrat, and some of the other
rectors remain in their jobs, Castro said, the junta had decided to appoint "military delegate rectors" in their place. Boeninger sat stone-
faced through the meeting.

A few weeks later Boeninger was shocked to learn that the director
of the children's orchestra had been summarily executed in La Serena
during General Sergio Arellano's tour of northern Chile. The children's orchestra had been part of a University of Chile extension program, and Boeninger had been good friends with its director, a socialist, visiting him in his home whenever he traveled to La Serena. Four

or five days after hearing this news he received another telephone call from the regime, this time from a civilian working as an adviser to the economy ministry.

The adviser told him that the country needed to buy some wheat from Australia, for it was facing a huge grain shortage, and there were difficulties involved in securing this purchase. Boeninger had been a guest of the Australian government only four months before the coup, and had signed some academic agreements with Australian universities. In addition, he was friendly with the Australian embassy in Santiago. Would he be willing to go to Australia and negotiate a wheat shipment in behalf of the Chilean government?

Boeninger told him he could go to Australia. "The only problem is that people will ask me about events in Chile and I will tell the truth as I see it," he said. "I will say that I thought the coup was inevitable but I will also be very frank about the repression, that people have been murdered, including friends of mine. All this I will state very frankly." The adviser to the economy ministry hung up, and Boeninger received no more requests for assistance from the regime.[11]

But the regime did not lack civilian collaborators to assist the military in running the government, and it was able to call on Chile's center-right political and business groups for additional help. The Christian Democrats, who were the country's largest political party and who had led the opposition to the Allende government in congress, were divided over the coup. A statement issued by the party indicated the Christian Democrats viewed the coup as the inevitable result of "economic disaster, institutional chaos, armed violence, and moral crisis," but said they expected the armed forces to return the government to civilian rule once these difficulties were overcome. The statement authorized party members to hold government jobs; but even though Christian Democrats continued to fill much of the government bureaucracy, the party itself soon became a target of official persecution.

The rightist National party not only applauded the coup but said the junta was opening up a new stage in Chilean history. Although many party members were uncomfortable with the move to close congress and the decision by Sergio Jarpa, then party president, to dissolve the party organization, the reference to a "new stage" was revealing. It showed that much of the Chilean right viewed the coup as not only a means to oust a socialist government but an opportunity to impose a project of its own without the bother of negotiating with political opponents. Yet many Chilean rightists found the term *golpe de estado* distasteful, and "military pronouncement" became the preferred expression, masking the violence and bloodshed involved.

On Saturday, September 15, 1973, Chilean army patrols escorted six of Chile's most prominent businessmen to a ceremony at the defense ministry, where the four junta members offered them a tribute for their role in bringing down the Allende government. One of those invited was Orlando Saenz, president of the Chilean industrial society, who had helped to draw up an alternative economic plan for a post-Allende government. The regime's foreign minister, Admiral Ismael Huerta, asked Saenz to work in his economics advisory department to reestablish new lines of overseas credit, which had virtually dried up during the previous three years. Bilateral assistance from the United States, which had been Chile's biggest source of loans and aid, shrank to $24.5 million during the Allende government, less than the country had received during any single year while Allende's predecessor, Christian Democrat Eduardo Frei, was in office.[12] The United States also used its influence to block loans to Chile from multilateral lending institutions such as the World Bank and the Inter-American Development Bank (IADB). By 1973, according to central bank figures, Chile's foreign reserves had shrunk from $393.8 million in 1970 to $12.9 million. But Allende's overthrow did not mean that the international credit spigot would open again automatically, and most worrisome to regime officials was the fact that opposition to renewed aid to Chile was already mounting.

A U.S. Senate subcommittee on refugee affairs headed by Edward Kennedy had held hearings on Chile, listening to testimony from Americans such as Adam and Patricia Garrett-Schesch, who had been detained for a week in Santiago's National Stadium. The United States, Kennedy said, should be in no hurry to lend economic assistance to Chile. The State Department's assistant secretary for inter-

American affairs, Jack Kubisch, told the subcommittee that Washington would give economic and military aid to Chile if it was sought, and that the Nixon administration, while "considerably concerned" about the violence, regarded it as a Chilean affair.[13] Though Kubisch's statement hardly satisfied Kennedy or anyone else concerned with human rights in Chile, the regime's dirty work had become a subject of debate in Washington and other capitals. It was clear that strict censorship within Chile could not prevent reports of post-coup atrocities from reaching the outside world. The regime was going to have to move fast if it wanted to claim legitimacy, not to mention economic assistance, from other countries.

There had already been street demonstrations in New York against the new military regime when Orlando Saenz accompanied Admiral Huerta and the foreign ministry's political counselor to the United Nations during the first few days of October 1973. The security measures were so tight that the three Chileans were obliged to disembark from their plane on the landing strip, climb into waiting automobiles that brought them straight to the Plaza Hotel, and take an elevator directly to their rooms on a floor occupied only by the Chilean delegation and their guards. Huerta was due to address the United Nations General Assembly that weekend, delivering the regime's justification for the coup to a skeptical international community. But the day after their arrival something happened that pushed Chile back to a secondary level of interest, and forced Huerta to postpone his speech: Egypt attacked Israel on the Jewish Day of Atonement, Yom Kippur. Much to the Chilean delegation's relief, war in the Middle East distracted the international community from events in Chile.

That weekend the Chilean delegation was startled to receive a message from Israel's foreign minister, Abba Eban, requesting a meeting. Having no idea what the purpose might be, the panicked officials spent the day conferring by telephone with Santiago. But Eban, who spoke Spanish, said he had only wanted to welcome the Chilean delegation to the United Nations. Israel understood that they were under extreme pressure, he said, and he simply wanted to let them know that his country was on their side.[14] The three Chilean officials were elated.

From New York the delegation flew to Washington, where they had a brief protocol meeting with Secretary of State Henry Kissinger, who arrived a few minutes late. Kissinger apologized for the delay, suggesting to the Chileans that if their superiors in Santiago required an explanation they should say that it was due to "a little matter several thousand kilometers away," that is, the Yom Kippur war. The officials laughed, and Admiral Huerta, who had learned German years earlier while negotiating for a German-made ship for the Chilean navy, spoke to Kissinger in his native language.

The visit to New York and Washington left the Chilean officials with the impression that the United States was willing to help the new regime, and Orlando Saenz spent most of the next six months meeting with foreign bankers to seek economic assistance. Manufacturers Hanover Trust Company and ten other U.S. and Canadian banks offered Chile commercial loans totalling about $150 million in early November, and the U.S. agriculture department gave the regime $52 million in emergency credits to buy grain.[15] By spring the IADB, which had not approved a single loan requested by the Allende government, approved two loans of $22 million and $75.3 million. The latter, the largest IADB loan ever granted to Chile, was for the construction of a hydroelectric plant south of Santiago whose financing the Allende government had requested from the bank some seventeen months earlier.[16]

But the willingness of international banks to resume lending to Chile did not mean that the regime was on secure financial footing, for the country needed at least $600 million in external credits. In addition, the regime was facing an additional outflow of funds as it negotiated compensation packages with ITT, Anaconda Company, Cerro Corporation, and Kennecott Copper Corporation for holdings nationalized during the Allende administration. According to the settlements reached, ITT was to receive $100 million, Anaconda $253 million, Cerro $41.8 million, and Kennecott $54 million.[17] (The Allende government's move to nationalize the copper industry had been backed by its political opponents and supporters alike, although Allende's refusal to compensate the U.S. firms was a separate issue of contention.) Under these circumstances, many regime officials felt that Chile was giving at least as much as, if not more than, it was receiving from the international banking and business community. In addition,

more than one Chilean official had expected a more generous outpour-
ing of economic aid from the United States once the military had
ousted Allende.

"We thought the Americans were going to put together a Marshall
Plan for us," said General Horacio Toro, a retired army officer who
had served on the junta's advisory committee.[18] Not only was such aid
not forthcoming, but the signals coming from Washington seemed
mixed to the Chileans, despite the Nixon administration's apparent
support. In addition to the Kennedy subcommittee hearings on Chile
and public criticism of the regime's human rights abuses, the State
Department was pressing for a return of the remains of Charles Horman, one of two Americans killed in the coup's aftermath. According
to a former regime official who attended a government meeting in
which the Horman case was discussed, Pinochet was angered by the
State Department's interest in the matter (an interest prompted by
pressure from the Horman family). Interior Minister Oscar Bonilla
told the U.S. ambassador, David Popper, that the regime had delayed
releasing Horman's body "out of concern that the release be so timed
as to minimize use of the event to the detriment of Chile in the U.S.
media and public opinion." Some members of Congress contacted by
the Horman family had urged that military aid to Chile be cut off if the
remains were not returned. Even Henry Kissinger warned in a cable
that "continued Chilean failure to authorize shipment will keep the incident alive and fan the family's resentment."[19] The body was finally
returned to Horman's family more than six months after his murder,
but to the regime's frustration the affair was far from finished; it cul-
minated in a bestselling book and a film.

Other incidents involving the United States also annoyed the junta.
The chief of the U.S. military mission in Santiago, navy captain Ray
Davis, told the Pentagon that the Chilean government would not accept the appointment of a black U.S. army attaché to the country.
Davis had in fact rejected the black officer's nomination without consulting either Chilean authorities or the U.S. embassy in Santiago.
His decision set off a fracas involving the regime, the State Department, and the Pentagon. The Chilean embassy in Washington issued
a statement saying that any insinuation that the regime had rejected a
black officer was "a slander against both the Chilean government and
the people of Chile." The regime's new ambassador to Washington,

General Walter Heitmann, called a press conference to say that his government was never even consulted about the appointment; the State Department said it was unaware of "any special racial policy" of the regime.[20]

In an effort to counteract what it perceived as an orchestrated campaign against Chile, the regime sought the help of public-relations experts and conservative lobbyists in Washington—with often negative results. Shortly after the coup, the regime signed an agreement with Worden and Company, a Washington-based public relations firm, to advise the Chilean embassy on such issues as how to respond to negative articles in the U.S. press. The following year the regime signed another contract with a subsidiary of J. Walter Thompson, which withdrew from the agreement after the *Washington Post* published a story on the contract (September 13, 1974); the firm had, according to its executives, received at least one bomb threat.[21]

The regime also placed several heavy-handed advertisements in the *New York Times* and the *Washington Post*, often featuring personal attacks on Chilean leftists or Allende government sympathizers. One such advertisement described the late Victor Jara, a Chilean folksinger killed after his arrest, as "a second-rate musician" who had once been detained by police in "the company of homosexuals" (*Washington Post*, November 10, 1974). The most ambitious public-relations effort came in 1975, when the Consejo Chileno-Norteamericano, a Santiago-based organization supposedly made up of prominent pro-regime Chileans, hired the New York public-relations firm of Marvin Liebman to lobby on behalf of Chile under the guise of a U.S.-based American-Chilean council, which the firm was to organize. Liebman and the council contacted conservative members of Congress to lobby on behalf of continued military aid and arms sales to Chile, and published a series of pamphlets depicting the now sizable anti-regime lobby as having links to the Soviet Union. This public-relations effort backfired when the U.S. Justice Department filed suit against Liebman for violating the Foreign Agents Registration Act, which requires disclosure of any activities undertaken on behalf of foreign governments or political parties. The suit charged that the American-Chilean council was operated by the military regime and that a member of Chile's United Nations mission had given Liebman a check for $26,850 for the group's initial funding.[22]

If the junta was serious about improving its image abroad, it would need a corps of experienced foreign-service officers, which Chile had had prior to the coup. But the foreign ministry was purged of roughly 40 percent of its career diplomats within two months of the coup as part of the military's effort to rid the department of suspected leftists and Allende sympathizers. The intimidated and demoralized officials who remained were faced with the daunting task of explaining to the rest of the world why Chile, which had enjoyed four decades of orderly successions of elected presidents, had undergone a military coup and why so many of its citizens were being rounded up, tortured, and killed. The Chilean foreign ministry received countless inquiries and expressions of concern from governments and international organizations regarding the fate of political detainees, as well as demands for explanations as to why heavy-handed military authorities had failed to respect international agreements on such matters as diplomatic immunity or the treatment of foreign nationals under arrest. The ministry officials had to seek official explanations from Chilean military authorities—who were not accustomed to having to answer to anyone other than their commanding officers—and then, poker-faced, pass on their often ludicrous responses to governments abroad.

The Organization of American States requested information on the death of Chilean folksinger Victor Jara, who was arrested the day after the coup. Jara's body, bearing multiple bullet wounds, had been discovered four days after his arrest near Santiago's cemetery along with five other corpses, and the regime's official explanation of his death seemed to only further mar Chile's image. The Chilean foreign ministry, in a communiqué dated March 27, 1974 (over six months after Jara died), said that the folksinger "died at the hands of snipers who . . . fired repeatedly at the armed forces as well as the civilian population."[23] Foreign governments' interest in such matters provoked a furious reaction in the defensive and parochial Pinochet, causing him to lash out at the foreign-ministry officials acting as messengers of bad news. "Pinochet was always very concerned that we sweat our shirts for the government, showing absolute and unconditional loyalty to the government," Alvaro Zuñiga, a career foreign-service officer said. "That obviously is not the style of professional diplomats."[24]

Pinochet, the military man, had little respect for the art of diplomacy, and as the years passed he met only rarely with foreign ambassadors in Santiago. Several embassies in Santiago had sheltered political refugees, a situation that in the minds of military hardliners cast the foreign missions in the role of enemy collaborators. Swedish ambassador Harald Edelstam, a latter-day Raoul Wallenberg, protected dozens of Chileans and foreigners sought by the military and police; he was declared persona non grata and forced to leave the country a few months after the coup. Other governments, frustrated by Chilean authorities' reluctance to grant exit visas to the hundreds of refugees crowding their embassies in Santiago, withdrew their ambassadors temporarily in protest. When Colombia called its envoy back to Bogotá for consultations, Admiral Huerta publicly accused the ambassador of "having contacts with extremists and communists" and said he hoped the diplomat would not return to Chile.[25]

The vacancies left by the purge in the Chilean foreign ministry were filled by right-wing civilians and retired military officials, including several generals who were sent overseas as ambassadors—with mixed results. While these retired generals were not Chile's first politically appointed ambassadors, their backgrounds made them unlikely to work well with the experienced diplomats under their authority. Back in Santiago, military officers were appointed to the second- and third-ranking posts within the foreign ministry, often acting as Pinochet's eyes and ears in a government department he would never fully trust.

After a few repressive months in power, the junta could no longer claim a subversive threat as its raison d'être without calling into question its own soldierly competence. What was needed was a new sense of purpose, along with a governmental organization structured along rightist ideological lines. While retaining their military command offices in the Chilean defense ministry, the junta appropriated a multistory edifice built for the 1972 United Nations Conference on Trade and Development (UNCTAD), renaming it the Diego Portales building after an authoritarian nineteenth-century Chilean statesman. Each junta member had his own informal group of advisers, including prominent figures from Chile's extreme Right. Pablo Rodríguez Grez, leader of the fascistic Patria y Libertad organization, was a frequent visitor, as was Jaime Guzmán, an eccentric young lawyer who led a movement of Catholic traditionalists known as the gremialistas. *Gremio* means corporation or society, and the Chilean gremialistas envisioned an authoritarian society in which trade unions and other special interest groups were depoliticized but not completely independent of state control. Such a view, not surprisingly, was welcome in the upper ranks of the Chilean military, which had banned or else declared "in recess" the country's political parties but whose own structure made them view independent associations with suspicion.

While the gremialistas did not advocate armed actions to further their aims as did Patria y Libertad, they were inspired by European fascist movements of the thirties. Guzmán joined the government's secretariat general, remaining on its payroll until the regime's later years, and the department formed its own dependencies: the secretariats of youth, women, and labor, along with separate offices for civic and cultural organizations.

Of the four military commanders who formed the original junta, only two—Pinochet and navy commander José Merino—were still in office when the regime ended. But a psychologist studying the four men might not have predicted that Pinochet would be the one to become Chile's dictator for sixteen years. Both Merino and General Gustavo Leigh had more impressive military records than did Pinochet: Merino, who had spent part of his boyhood in England, had served in the Pacific during Chile's brief participation with the Allied forces during World War II and later went back to London with the Chilean naval mission for three years. Leigh had taken three training courses in the United States and another at the U.S. Escuela de las Américas in Panama, and had been Chile's air force attaché in Washington.

The fourth member of the junta, carabinero director General César Mendoza, was a career police officer whose greatest distinction was his horsemanship; he was a member of the Chilean equestrian team at the 1951 and 1960 Olympic games. Mendoza became the butt of many jokes in which he was cast as the least intelligent member of the junta; his brutish public statements added to his comical image. He left his directorship of the carabineros and the junta under a cloud of scandal in 1985 when a brave civilian judge implicated his officers in the murder of three Chilean leftists.

The Chilean navy, which had done most of the coup plotting and whose officers tended to come from slightly higher socioeconomic levels than did officers in the other services, had perhaps the closest ties with the country's right-wing groups. But Merino, whose heavy drinking became more evident as the years went by, was not as determined or ambitious as Pinochet proved to be. That left Leigh, the air force commander, as Pinochet's sole potential rival for control of the regime, and he led a force of eleven thousand men (compared to the Chilean army's fifty-three thousand troops). This meant that there were far more army officers to be placed within the government.

A formal advisory committee to the junta had been formed at the end of 1973, headed by a colonel who also directed the army's school for noncommissioned officers and staffed largely by other army officers. Leigh, uncomfortable with this army-dominated entity, sought to place three of his closest collaborators on the board, a move Pinochet reportedly agreed to but never implemented.[26]

One of the committee's first recommendations was that the junta discard the idea of a rotating presidency among the four military commanders, citing the administrative problems this would entail for both the government and the four services as well as the need to give the regime greater institutional coherence. The decision-making process would be more cumbersome if four military commanders had to reach agreement.

On March 11, 1974, the regime's six-month anniversary, the junta held a solemn ceremony at the Diego Portales building to read a statement of principles drawn up by the advisory board. The statement said the government respected human rights but that it could not permit a "naive democracy" to allow guerrilla groups espousing a totalitarian doctrine to operate in the country. For this reason, the statement said, Marxist movements would never again be allowed, and at an "opportune time" power would be handed over to a popularly elected president. The junta's declaration of principles, reflecting the semifascist leanings of Jaime Guzmán, an advisory board member, also spoke of a broad civilian-military movement with regional and local "vehicles of participation."[27]

Pinochet used the occasion to attack, though not by name, the Christian Democratic party, whose leaders had begun to press for a timetable for a return to civilian rule. Some politicians adopted a favorable attitude toward the government, he said, viewing the military's "liberation of Chile" as an opportunity to retake control of the government within a short period of time. "Today they have reacted contrarily when they realized how mistaken they were, and I ask myself, 'Are they patriots or are they traitors?' "[28] he said.

Pinochet's old lack of understanding of politics, which during previous governments had cast him in the role of a loyal, "constitutionalist" officer, had hardened and narrowed his view. The army general who had rejected overtures from procoup civilians during the Allende years was not going to listen to the same politicians whom he suspected of cynically seeking a piece of the government pie now that the military was in power. Only the most trustworthy civilians, such as the neofascist Jaime Guzmán and Pablo Rodríguez, would be allowed to participate, and then as advisers. A program of government, albeit a nebulous one, was now in place; the next step would be to position a president to lead it.

On one of his very few trips outside the country, Pinochet had traveled to Brasília earlier that year to attend the inauguration of Brazilian president Ernesto Geisel and had conferred with Bolivian dictator General Hugo Banzer, who was also attending the ceremony. Merino had taken over the junta leadership for the five days he was gone, but the episode was another reminder that Chile still had no clearly identifiable leader. The army-dominated junta advisory board began to rally around Pinochet as the logical choice for president.

The committee drew up a proposed decree, number 527, making Pinochet the regime's chief executive and Leigh, Merino, and Mendoza a legislative body. The other three commanders could veto in some cases, but the decree also established procedures for replacing junta members. The proposed measure did not sit well with senior officers in the Chilean navy and air force.

One admiral serving as cabinet minister caused an awkward silence when he asked if he was to report to Merino or Pinochet. The answer, of course, was to Pinochet, who as chief of state would reshuffle his cabinet more than a dozen times, usually ordering his ministers to resign en masse and then in a televised ceremony announcing which officials were to remain in their posts. Cabinet ministers would not always know beforehand whether they were about to be removed from office. Shortly before one cabinet swearing-in ceremony in late 1980, the agriculture minister, Alfonso Márquez de la Plata, was overheard happily remarking to his colleagues that surely the president was going to confirm him in his post.[29] Pinochet did not, nor did the agriculture minister's successor last much more than a year in the job.

Decree 527, making Pinochet supreme chief of the nation, was not simply issued in the regime's official government bulletin, as were most decree laws. Instead, Pinochet's closest collaborators quietly planned a solemn inauguration ceremony to be held at the Diego Portales government building, at which the president of Chile's supreme court—who was notified a few hours beforehand—would place a new presidential sash (the original had been lost when La Moneda burned the day of the coup) over Pinochet's shoulder. The other three junta members, whose institutions had given reluctant approval to the decree, were also not advised of the ceremony in advance.

Air force commander Leigh, in particular, was outraged when he learned of what was about to take place, and confronted Pinochet, accusing him of playing God. While regime officials, selected civilian supporters, and reporters from Chile's restricted news media assembled downstairs to wait for the ceremony to begin, the two men—who had commanded their respective institutions less than a year—screamed at each other. Pinochet responded by threatening to call off the ceremony, warning that any subsequent damage to the regime would be Leigh's fault, and brought his fist down so hard on the air force commander's desk that it cracked the sheet of glass covering the top.[30]

The four junta members, grim-faced, walked into the salon for the brief inauguration ceremony. After receiving the new presidential sash, Pinochet said that he "had never dreamed of, nor much less sought" the Chilean presidency. And so on June 27, 1974, Pinochet became the "supreme leader of the nation." He had commanded the Chilean army for just ten months.[31]

Although his participation in the events leading up to the coup had been almost nil, Pinochet threw himself wholeheartedly into the task before him, rising at dawn and working long hours. His most obsequious admirers depicted him as a self-taught intellectual, citing his two published books and his expanding library on military history. But the demanding schedule he imposed upon himself left little time for serious reading, as he himself admitted. "At ten o'clock I am already in bed, reading historical, philosophical, political materials," he told the center-right Chilean weekly *Qué Pasa* in 1981. "I read for a quarter of an hour."[32] And unlike many openly corrupt heads of state in developing nations, Pinochet was noticeably abstemious in his consumption and discreet in his personal habits.

"He was not a teetotaler, but he drank very little," one former regime official told me. "At formal dinners, when everybody else was having cocktails, Pinochet would be served some funny-colored vegetarian concoction." Indeed, it appeared that he had tied his own longevity to the regime's. In an interview two months later, Pinochet, asked how the Chilean public was able to influence government decision-making in the regime's brave new order, said, "There is much more direct contact with the people than before, inasmuch as intermediate mechanisms of a political character no longer exist, which used to obstruct the relation and interpretation of the aspirations and needs of the country's different sectors."

Asked about the "opportune time" for returning power to a popularly elected government, as cited in the junta's first declaration of principles, Pinochet became irritated. "Excuse me! I never said how long. No one ever said two or three years. The ones who set time periods were the politicians who always spoke of four, six, seven, or ten years. Because what did they want? [They wanted] us to clean house, leave it freshly painted, for which we dupes would be useful, and then they would come and occupy it again. And we would be back where we started!"[33]

If Chilean politicians were allowed to act in public life, he told his interviewer, the country would inevitably return to its precoup conditions. The regime, according to Pinochet, was attempting to unite Chileans, and political leaders would only hinder this process.

The battered Chilean economy did not recover significantly during the regime's first year in power, and if some of the central bank statistics showed modest progress in some areas, the scale of the crisis was no less evident. At the end of 1973 consumer price inflation was 508.1 percent annually; twelve months later the figure stood at 375.9 percent, according to Chile's National Statistical Institute. The balance-of-payments deficit was $111.9 million in 1973, shrinking to $45.1 million the next year and ballooning back up to a deficit of $275 million in 1975. The price of copper, Chile's chief export, had plummeted, cutting the country's earnings from this product from $1,623 million in 1974 to $868.2 million in 1975. If the regime wanted to survive, decisive action in the form of a coherent economic policy would have to be taken. The trouble was that Pinochet and the other junta members had almost no understanding of economics or finance, and military regimes have no natural inclination toward releasing state-controlled resources, even economic ones, to civilians.

Under the Allende government, the state had dramatically increased its economic holdings in an attempt to redistribute resources to the poorer sectors of Chilean society. In addition to nationalizing the copper industry, the government bought up shares of banks and other financial institutions until it controlled 85 percent of the Chilean financial sector. The Popular Unity government also either nationalized or took administrative control of hundreds of industrial firms whose profits were to be used for government social programs. Not surprisingly, Allende government authorities soon discovered that rather than provide the state with new sources of revenue, the government-controlled companies drained fiscal resources.[34]

A group of Chilean business leaders and right-wing civilian economists had been waiting in the wings for the chance to impose a free-market economic model. And with Pinochet sworn in as Chile's president, there was only one general to convince, rather than four. The regime returned some of the companies and farms taken over during the Allende government to their former owners, whose financial losses often made it impossible for them to reinvest enough capital to resuscitate these businesses. As a result, the regime ended up selling many state-controlled firms at fire-sale prices, but still faced a sizable budget deficit.

Chile sought the assistance of the International Monetary Fund, which agreed to help the country resolve its balance-of-payments crisis. The agreement with the IMF, however, required that Chile apply a series of austerity measures designed to further reduce its budget deficit, which the regime had already managed to cut from 24.6 percent of the country's gross domestic product in 1973 to 10.5 percent the following year. The decline in copper prices and the rapidly rising cost of imported oil, however, cut deeply into Chile's revenues. Jorge Cauas, a former World Bank official and Fulbright scholar who had become the regime's finance minister in mid-1974, decided to take drastic action. On April 24, 1975, Cauas appeared on Chilean television to announce a plan of shock treatment for the economy. Public spending would be reduced between 15 and 25 percent, he said, and these reductions would be implemented "at any cost, including the dismissal of functionaries unable to understand that the reduction of inflation receives top priority." He acknowledged that the measures would require sacrifices, but optimistically predicted that in the near future "poverty will be stamped out, and all Chileans will be able to benefit from the advantages of the modern world."[35]

The macroeconomic data for this period give a good idea of just how much sacrifice was required. In 1975 the Chilean economy shrank by a record 16.6 percent, while unemployment rose from 9 to 18 percent (and to 22 percent in 1976). For those who had jobs, real wages were 64 percent of what they were in 1970, the year Allende was elected. A survey sponsored by the Catholic Church indicated that in 1969 a Chilean earning the minimum wage could buy the items on a list of basic foodstuffs with slightly less than half his income and use the rest to cover other basic needs. Under the regime's austerity program, the same worker could spend his entire earnings and still only purchase 80 percent of essential food items. In the low-income neighborhoods ringing the capital, the Catholic Church set up soup kitchens (which regime officials decried as communist cells) to feed the hungry, but even with humanitarian assistance from abroad it could not meet the demand. Nevertheless, Cauas's plan succeeded in trimming the budget deficit down to 2.6 percent of GDP and cutting inflation from 369 percent to 343 percent, with further reductions to come over the next six years.[36]

It was the beginning of a harsh and radical economic experiment, one that attracted the attention of economists around the world. Cauas's austerity plan played a crucial role in restoring Chile's standing with the international banking community, though executing such a plan was considerably easier under military rule than it would have been under a civilian government, against which trade unions would have almost certainly organized strikes and protests. Many senior military officers would have also preferred a more populist economic program. Yet Cauas had sufficient diplomatic skills to press his policies without alienating the military.

The Chicago Boys were a different story. A group of younger, U.S.-trained economists who had become rising stars within the regime, the Chicago Boys often irritated military officers with their brashness and dogmatism. Since the coup the Chilean ministry responsible for government planning, ODEPLAN, had been under the control of Roberto Kelly, a former navy officer with close ties to the *El Mercurio* business group. He had hired several graduates of the University of Chicago's master's degree program in economics. Some of the Chicago Boys eventually assumed cabinet posts; Sergio de Castro, for example, succeeded Cauas as finance minister when Cauas was appointed ambassador to Washington in late 1976.

The University of Chicago, where the views of Milton Friedman and other free-market theorists reigned, had an academic agreement with Chile's Universidad Católica, and the Ford Foundation had provided several scholarships for the Chilean students' tuition and expenses. Yet the Chileans' experiences there as graduate students in the sixties and early seventies were not always broadening or gratifying. For the upper-middle-class young men who had lived at home with their parents during their undergraduate studies, life in the small student apartments near the university was often harsh and stressful. The neighborhood had a high crime rate, and students were advised to walk to and from campus in groups for their own protection. The snow and subfreezing temperatures of the Chicago winter were a rude contrast to the relatively mild winters in Santiago. Some of the Chileans had married shortly before beginning the program; for their wives, many of whom bore children during the two-and-a-half-year stay and who had been used to having extended family networks (and domestic servants) for support, the adjustment was even more difficult. The university's master's program in economics was competitive and demanding, with a high rate of failure for first-year students. The Chileans, who did not always speak English fluently upon arrival, usually spent even longer hours studying than their American counterparts did.

Miguel Kast, who later became one of the regime's economic planners, arrived at the University of Chicago in the fall of 1971, accompanied by his young wife. Kast had been born in Germany. His father, a veteran of Hitler's army, had moved the family to southern Chile shortly after World War II. Like most economics students from Chile studying at the University of Chicago, Kast was adamantly opposed to the Allende government. In March of 1973, when he was about to complete his degree, the Popular Unity coalition won 43 percent of the vote in the Chilean municipal elections. Kast decided to take a job in Mexico rather than return to Chile, and he urged three Chilean classmates—Ernesto Silva, Martin Costabal, and Juan Carlos Mendez—not to go back either, arguing that there was no future for them under the Popular Unity government.

"Miguel Kast knew that his stay in the United States was temporary, and he had never adapted to American habits," wrote his biographer, Joaquín Lavin, a fellow economics graduate of the University of Chicago.[37] Kast had already accepted the job in Mexico when the coup took place, while his Chilean classmates, back in Santiago, quickly found jobs in the new regime. Offered a job in the research department of the Chilean planning ministry, Kast, who had until then held German citizenship, hastily became a naturalized Chilean citizen. He became the planning ministry's deputy director in 1975 and its director three years later. Among his duties were to survey Chile's poor and develop plans for a scaled-down social welfare program limiting assistance to the most extreme cases of need.

Kast's admirers credit him with a sensitive concern for the country's poor; his biographer wrote that "the difficult years his family spent upon arriving in Chile left him especially sensitized to the problem."[38] Others found him pompous and out of touch with social realities. Former labor minister General Nicanor Díaz recalled in an interview that at one cabinet meeting he asked Kast if he had ever actually conversed with a Chilean worker. The young economist turned red, then said that his father had a farming business and that during school vacations he worked alongside him.

During government meetings to discuss economic policy, Kast often argued a more extreme position than he actually held, figuring that whatever compromise was eventually reached would be that much closer to his own stance. Whatever the efficacy of this tactic in achieving Kast's goals, it earned him the animosity of many military officials. These tensions worsened when the planning ministry, as part of Finance Minister Cauas's austerity program, wanted to assign a budgetary overseer to each government ministry in order to control expenditures. The defense ministry rejected the idea, as did Díaz's labor ministry. "With the finance minister and the guys from the planning ministry we would start arguing and within five minutes we would be cursing," Díaz said. "We couldn't reach any understanding with the economic team. I didn't call them the Chicago Boys but the Chicago Gang."[39]

Nevertheless, Kast and the other civilian economists remained in the regime, while military officers like Díaz—who had never really wanted cabinet posts in the first place—began leaving. This suited Pinochet, for generals in the cabinet tended to challenge his position more than civilians. "I am going to accept your resignation," Pinochet told Díaz. "I want a civilian minister there, because every now and then I feel like hurling a curse at a minister, and I can't do that to another general."

In late 1975 the U.S. Senate conducted hearings on attempts by the Central Intelligence Agency and the American embassy in Santiago to prevent Salvador Allende's election in 1970, undercut his government, and provoke a military coup. The Senate's hearings and subsequent report, which said that the United States had channeled $3.4 million into former president Eduardo Frei's 1964 campaign and another $7 million to anti-Allende groups during the Popular Unity government, proved extremely embarrassing to many Chilean Christian Democrats, who by then had become openly opposed to the regime. Another recipient of U.S. funds during the Allende years, according to the U.S. Senate Committee report, was the *El Mercurio* newspaper chain, said to have received $1.6 million to keep it afloat.[40] *El Mercurio* issued a furious front-page denial.

"To understand the infamy of the description of so-called economic aid that *El Mercurio* might have received it is sufficient to state that the monthly gross income of this newspaper is almost $1.5 million," the paper wrote December 6, 1975. The U.S. Senate also reported that the CIA had "remained close to the Chilean military officers in order to monitor developments within the armed forces." This of course might have embarrassed some of the officials who had plotted the coup, such as army generals Oscar Bonilla, Sergio Arellano Stark, and many Chilean naval and air force officers—but not, obviously, Pinochet, who had virtually nothing to do with the coup's planning and was among its most reluctant participants. The Senate hearings into U.S. covert action in Chile may have sparked some rethinking of the Central Intelligence Agency's role and of American foreign policy, but in Santiago the revelations produced an angry, defensive reaction on the part of regime officials and undoubtedly confirmed Pinochet's suspicion that the Americans were not to be trusted.

On January 25, 1976, the Chilean central bank, attempting to counteract what it called "a torrent of misinformation (premeditated or purposely fanciful) that warps all reality" about the country under the military regime, published a full-page paid insert in the *New York Times*. The advertisement, written in correct but awkward English, included statements by Finance Minister Cauas, the regime's tourism director, the president of the U.S. Chamber of Commerce in Chile, and other regime supporters who extolled the country's economic progress over the previous two years. The insert's authors made a point of not alluding to the coup, and mentioned the military junta only once in the entire four-thousand-word advertisement.

On February 18 of that year, the U.S. Senate passed an amendment sponsored by Edward Kennedy that prohibited military sales and deliveries to Chile. The amendment, approved by a vote of forty-eight to thirty-nine, was accompanied by sharp attacks on the regime by senators backing the measure.

"Why should we squander money on tyrants, giving them the weapons to hold down their own people?" Senator Alan Cranston asked. Hubert Humphrey said the United States should not be "aiding and abetting the most totalitarian government in South America."[41] In Santiago, there were equally harsh verbal attacks on Senator Kennedy, whom the regime had viewed as a bitter enemy and an instrument of communism ever since he led hearings on Chile shortly after the coup.

"Kennedy is a traitor," the regime-owned newspaper, *Cronista,* headlined on its front page. A few days later a group of about one hundred youths, mostly from the regime's secretariat of youth, marched past the U.S. embassy carrying placards denouncing Kennedy's "hypocritical" attitude. The embassy received telephone calls both for and against the arms cutoff, although embassy staffers' official Chilean contacts reacted negatively.

"Overall, we would characterize Chilean reaction as a blend of resentment and anxiety," the U.S. embassy reported in a cable to Washington a few days after the vote. The cable noted that the Chilean air force was the most concerned about the Kennedy amendment, for deliveries were about to begin on a purchase of eighteen Northrop F-5 planes.[42] Because the air force's payments on the planes were up-to-date, canceling the contract would involve "a number of legal and operational problems." The Chilean air force, which used more American equipment than the army or navy, was the military branch most affected by the measure.

The Kennedy amendment infuriated Pinochet, who attacked the U.S. senator publicly "as a puppet of Soviet imperialism" who had "put personal ambitions ahead of sacred interests of our country." Nevertheless, the Chilean military was able to receive the aircraft already paid for, as well as some additional supplies, before the measure actually went into effect. Senators Kennedy and Humphrey charged that the State Department was rushing a new $9.2 million commitment for the Chilean air force before the ban took effect and that it was seeking to supply Chile with spare airplane parts beyond the deadline.[43] But in later years the Chilean air force found it increasingly difficult to obtain replacement parts for its U.S.-built aircraft, and within a few years of the ban was unable even to buy safety equipment such as ejection seats. Other countries that had been the Chilean military's principal suppliers also halted arms sales, although these bans were in effect at different times: Great Britain, which had supplied the Chilean navy with much of its fleet, cut off sales until 1980, while France, which had been a steady arms supplier to the regime (selling Chile Mirage jets and Puma and Alouette helicopters), halted arms sales in 1981, when François Mitterrand took office. France also stopped deliveries on a previously ordered fleet of fifty AMX tanks on the grounds that they could be used for political repression.

Memories of the British-built Hawker Hunters strafing the La Moneda presidential palace during the coup fueled such debates, yet Chile had far less trouble procuring the sort of equipment used by the police and security forces. The regime bought some small weapons and anti-riot gear from South Africa, along with tanks, ammunition, and some small arms from Israel (including the Uzi submachine guns carried by the Chilean carabineros). The foreign arms embargoes did encourage the growth of a domestic arms industry within Chile, and by the early 1980s a company operated by the army was manufacturing small arms, grenades, ammunition, and mortars. The Chilean air force eventually developed a small training aircraft. In addition, a private Chilean company, Cardoen Industries (which in 1991 U.S. authorities would accuse of violating the U.N. embargo against sales to Iraq), began building armored personnel carriers under license from a Swiss firm.[44]

The arms embargoes by the United States and other countries may not have dented the regime's security apparatus, but they unquestionably hurt Chile's external defense capabilities. The country had a long-standing territorial dispute with Argentina over control of three tiny islets in the Beagle Channel, and the two countries nearly went to war over the issue in 1978 (the United States advised Chile that Argentina was preparing an attack). Peru and Bolivia, which had lost extensive territory to Chile during the 1879 War of the Pacific, were possible allies of Argentina in the event of such a war, and Peru had steadily increased its military purchases to the point where its navy was said to be better equipped than Chile's and its army and air force had Soviet tanks and fighter jets. Chile lacked important defense equipment such as antitank and antiaircraft weapons, and its few advantages lay in its defensive position and the superior organization and training of its military. Chile, under a military regime, was ironically weaker militarily than it had been under a civilian government, and was dependent more on diplomacy (and its weakened foreign service) to safeguard its borders.

Chapter Four

Dirty Warriors

I do not tolerate arbitrariness, or injustices, or abuses of power. Each time I have had knowledge of some action in this sense, I have ordered measures to be taken.
—General Augusto Pinochet, December 1985

Calle Londres is a narrow street behind an old colonial church in downtown Santiago, where a handful of period buildings have escaped demolition. One address, Londres No. 36, was once a ward office of the Chilean Socialist party, and was impounded by the military after the coup. The building became one of the first detention centers used by the Dirección de Inteligencia Nacional (DINA), the regime's security police. Guillermo Norambuena, a leader of the Socialist party's youth wing, was arrested in July 1974 and spent three weeks at this ward office–turned-prison, one of five different sites of detention he saw during a hellish two-year sojourn at the hands of the DINA.

Norambuena was first detained in the subterranean offices of the carabinero intelligence service, Servicios de Inteligencia de Carabineros (SICAR), located beneath the plaza facing the La Moneda presidential palace. He spent eight days there undergoing interrogations and torture. Then he was moved a few blocks to Londres No. 36, newly remodeled for use by the DINA. More beatings. More torture. Then on to Cuatro Alamos, another DINA installation, where he was held incommunicado for three months, and then out of Santiago to Ritoque, a one-time beach resort converted into a prison camp. Afterward he was returned to Santiago to a penitentiary where he spent Christmas and New Year. In March 1975 Norambuena was sent back to Ritoque, then again to Cuatro Alamos, before finally being released four months later. No formal criminal charges were ever made against him by regime authorities.[1]

Today the street numbers on Calle Londres have been rearranged so that Londres No. 36 no longer exists; in its place is Londres No. 40, which houses an institute named after the Chilean independence hero Bernardo O'Higgins. A short distance away, across the capital's main avenue and toward the northeast, is a nondescript office building in which the former DINA chief set up a private security agency. Retired army general Juan Manuel Contreras, founder and 98 percent owner of the Alfa-Omega Security Company, continued to be one of the most feared men in Chile more than a decade after leaving the regime and the Chilean army. Contreras, more than any other military official, helped Pinochet secure his grip on power during the first few years of the regime.

A former student of Pinochet's at the Chilean war academy, Contreras held the rank of lieutenant colonel at the time of the coup, commanding the Tejas Verdes army regiment in San Antonio, a port sixty-five miles west of Santiago that had been a center of leftist sympathies and militant trade-union activity. Contreras had proved himself to be ruthlessly efficient at crushing real and potential sources of unrest there. When San Antonio dockworkers called a strike after the coup to protest the military's suspension of labor union activity, Contreras called four union leaders to his office for a meeting. The trade unionists' bodies were delivered to their families in coffins the following day. Contreras often supervised the interrogation of prisoners himself at the army base he commanded, and by the time he was transferred to Santiago his reputation had preceded him. In time even other regime officials, both civilian and military, would come to fear him as the DINA extended its network of agents and informants to government offices and the armed forces as well as to the Chilean society at large.

The directors of intelligence services for the four military branches began holding weekly meetings at the Chilean defense ministry after the coup under the command of the ministry's chief of staff, air force general Nicanor Díaz. After receiving the reports from the different branches, Díaz handed out new assignments to each service's intelligence department, in order to prevent any duplication of effort. These interservice intelligence briefings had been taking place for several weeks when Contreras appeared at one of the meetings.

Like his former instructor, Contreras was a rough-edged but shrewd man who had trouble with social conversation and lost his temper easily. Unlike Pinochet, Contreras was considered by his fellow officers to be highly intelligent, "perhaps the most intelligent of the army officers at the time," one retired general told me. He had spent two years at the Army Career Officers School in Fort Belvoir, Virginia, but had no real background in police or intelligence work, a shortcoming that did not endear him to the more experienced officers in the field.

At the defense ministry Contreras officially presented his project for a new intelligence service, the Dirección de Inteligencia Nacional, or DINA. The DINA would incorporate the work of the Chilean army, navy, air force, and carabinero intelligence operations, he explained to the other officers. After giving each officer a protocol salute, he asked them their opinions of the project.

Commander Germán Campos, who headed the carabineros intelligence services, was the first to speak and immediately blasted out his criticisms of the DINA project. What were the DINA's internal regulations to be, and how would it be financed? The Chilean military had the country well under control, so what was the point of organizing a new security agency?

"There hadn't been any terrorist attacks, we were under an extremely strict state of siege, with curfews and people being arrested at all hours," Campos recalled. "People were being executed right and left in the army regiments, in the detention centers. There was a climate of terror. Nobody would dare lift a finger against the regime."[2] Campos and some of the other officers at the defense ministry meeting suspected that the DINA would be used to enhance Pinochet's personal power rather than serve any legitimate intelligence function.

Campos bluntly told Contreras that he and other intelligence officers were not going to leave their work "to a bunch of vulgar bodyguards." Contreras, unfazed, asked for the opinions of the other intelligence directors, who were vague or noncommittal in their responses. Afterward Campos, the most junior officer present, was approached by General Díaz, who warned him against further confrontations with Contreras. "I share your misgivings," he told him, "but you cannot go around talking like that because this project has already been approved by the junta." Campos lasted only four more months in his post as the carabineros' intelligence chief before being transferred to a police prefect's job in a provincial town in southern Chile.

The arrest and interrogation of prisoners after the coup was such a massive task that it was spawning its own bureaucracy, the Secretaría Ejecutiva Nacional de Detenidos (SENDET), a national prisoners' service. The ostensible aim of SENDET, located in the Chilean congress building, was to "fix the norms in which prisoners would be interrogated, to determine their degree of danger, and to maintain a permanent coordination among the intelligence services of the armed forces, of carabineros, and of Investigaciones [Chile's civilian detective police]." The junta had approved a decree law establishing SENDET at the end of 1973;[3] one article of this decree made DINA a SENDET department.

DINA's function within SENDET was to "determine the level of dangerousness" of each prisoner. It was a task that offered almost unlimited possibilities for expansion, with tens of thousands of detainees to be investigated, as well as their families, acquaintances, and contacts, in an ever-expanding web of suspicion. For Contreras, the DINA offered a fast track to advancement. For the regime, the suspects and plots uncovered by the security forces provided a continuing justification for military rule. Six months later the junta approved a new decree, number 521, officially constituting the DINA as a centralized intelligence organization. Chilean human rights groups had already detected a change in the way suspects were being arrested.

"By the end of 1973 the characteristic military action gave way notoriously to that of the intelligence services," said an internal report by the Catholic Church's human rights department, the Vicaría de la Solidaridad. Since January 1974, according to the report, the methods of arrest showed an unmistakable trend toward cracking down on members of banned political parties.

Many of the prisoners arrested by DINA had earlier, in the wake of the coup, been detained and released. One of these was Francisco Aedo, the socialist architect who had worked in the Allende government's housing ministry. Aedo had been arrested by carabineros after the coup and was released from the Chacabuco prison camp in northern Chile ten months later. But on September 7, 1974, four men in civilian dress pulled up outside his home in a light-blue Chevrolet pickup truck without license plates.[4]

Aedo's wife testified that the agents, who showed no arrest or search warrant, ransacked the house while supposedly looking for weapons. They confiscated a floor plan of the Chilean military hospital—an architectural expansion project on which Aedo had worked—and several classical music albums by Russian composers. When they led Aedo away, the DINA agents assured his horrified wife that he was only wanted for routine questioning, and that he would be back in a couple of hours.

One month later she received a phone call from a man who said he had seen her husband at the DINA's Cuatro Alamos detention center a few weeks earlier. Aedo was then being moved to another place of confinement. Over the next few years Aedo's wife received other, indirect reports from former prisoners and one ex–security agent who had seen him alive as late as 1975, but after that the scattered clues to the architect's fate ended.[5]

If the line between armed resistance and dissent had already blurred in the minds of many Chilean officers at the time of the coup, for Contreras and his DINA agents it could be said to never have existed at all, with each left-leaning Chilean a potential terrorist. Whatever Contreras lacked in intelligence training and finesse he made up for in zeal. He was forty-one at the time of the coup, five years younger than Pinochet had been when he became lieutenant colonel, and the bright and brutal Contreras had come to be the second most powerful man in Chile.

Theoretically the DINA was supposed to come under the junta's control, but in practice Contreras appears to have reported to no one but Pinochet, a fact that irked more senior officers. Contreras habitually arrived at Pinochet's official residence in eastern Santiago at 7:30 A.M. for breakfast and a briefing, and afterward the two men rode in the same chauffeured automobile to the Diego Portales government building. If Contreras had not finished his report by the time they arrived, he would accompany Pinochet to his office to continue the briefing and to receive any new instructions. His own office at the DINA headquarters, located about half a mile from the Diego Portales building, contained a two-way television hookup with Pinochet's office, allowing the two men to communicate easily during working hours.[6]

The DINA's upper echelons were filled mostly by Chilean army officers. Some of them formed a tight nucleus around Contreras, who in turn inspired a fierce and unquestioning loyalty. Service in his elite security squad held a kind of mystique for many young military officials. Retired general Horacio Toro, who had also taught for a time at Chile's war academy and at the military academy, observed marked changes among his former students who entered the DINA at that time.

"Many of these men had been excellent students, young men of high moral character," he said. "I saw them afterward profoundly, utterly changed. Their new environment was one without any scruples toward their fellow citizens who happened to belong to banned political parties." Junior officers who had excelled in combat training took to the DINA with special gusto. The Chilean army may not have fought a war since the 1879 War of the Pacific, but in Contreras's mind the regime was at full-scale war with Marxists (both Chilean and foreign) and any others who might dare to criticize the regime, and the situation required total and unquestioning commitment from its officials. General Toro said he had known of only one instance of an army officer requesting a transfer from the DINA to a more conventional assignment. The officer, a lieutenant colonel, left the army a short time later.

"The ideal DINA recruit was a young officer who had excelled in such areas as skydiving or special commando units—someone with an adventurous spirit," he said. "Then there were those who had training in some specialty the DINA needed—languages, for example—and those who were good at blending in with different surroundings. You know how some officers look dressed in civilian clothes, you can tell immediately by their bearing that they are military men? Well, the DINA needed men who could easily disguise themselves."[7]

The DINA also needed civilian collaborators, and the old Patria y Libertad network provided many of them. The right-wing extremist group had proffered its services since the day of the coup, and in some instances even acted as DINA's forerunner by approaching the military with lists of suspected leftists and urging that they be arrested. In Paine, the country town southwest of Santiago that had the highest per capita number of *desaparecidos* in Chile, witnesses reported that right-wing activists invariably accompanied the soldiers and police when making arrests.

"From the beginning, families of the victims told me two things: that their relatives were detained by military patrols accompanied by other persons in uniform, or partial uniform, and that those persons would unerringly identify the campesino leaders," said Andrés Aylwin, a human rights lawyer who represented relatives of the missing. "Repeatedly [the victims' families] would name certain civilians, linked to local landowners or far Right groups."[8]

The DINA also had as informers a smaller number of former left-wing activists who had either been blackmailed into collaborating with the security forces during their own arrest and torture or had broken with their political organizations prior to the coup. One such agent was Juan René Muñoz Alarcón, the ex–Socialist party member whom the military used to identify party members among the prisoners at the National Stadium. After working with the DINA for a few years, the guilt-stricken Muñoz approached the Catholic Church's human rights department to tell what he knew and to seek protection.

"I am the hooded man from the National Stadium," Muñoz said in a sworn statement dated October 7, 1977. In the statement, filed in the Vicaría de la Solidaridad archives, Muñoz described his recruitment and training in the DINA. He was first sent to Colonia Dignidad, an agricultural community in southern Chile that had lent its facilities to the DINA. The colony had been founded in the sixties by Paul Schaeffer, who fled West Germany after being charged with sexually abusing boys at the orphanage where he worked. About three hundred people of German origin lived and worked in Colonia Dignidad, located outside the town of Parral, 250 miles south of Santiago. Despite its small size, Colonia Dignidad had a school, hospital, mining and commercial activities, and its own airstrip. A handful of former residents who managed to flee the community described an authoritarian state-within-a-state where residents were forced to work long hours and forbidden to have contact with outsiders, and where rebelliousness was treated with beatings and drugs.[9] He described how prisoners were moved from Santiago to the colony, which had an extensive network of underground prison cells holding over one hundred prisoners at a time. Two weeks after he made his statement to the Vicaría de la Solidaridad, Muñoz's body, bearing multiple stab wounds, was found in an abandoned lot in north Santiago.

Air force commander General Gustavo Leigh was suspicious of the DINA and the cozy relationship between Pinochet and Contreras, and he did not want the anti-Marxist crusade to become the exclusive domain of the Chilean army. The Comando Conjunto, a new security group led by air force intelligence officials, was formed in 1974 to join in the campaign.

The group's target was the Chilean Communist Party, while the DINA tended to concentrate on socialists and the MIR guerrilla group. Until then the country's communists had not espoused armed resistance or guerrilla tactics, and in some ways the organization was considered more conservative than the Socialist party. Andrés Valenzuela Morales, a one-time Chilean air force intelligence agent who after seven troubled years decided to make his story public, described an organization whose methods were at least as vicious as the DINA's:

A Chilean air force helicopter arrived and they took out about ten or fifteen people. I remember clearly that there was an ex-councilman from Renca who limped, he was an old man, he must have been one of the ones caught in the dragnet. They drugged them, they gave them some pills, but they must not have been very effective because [the prisoners] seemed aware of what was happening.

One of the military men taking part, "Fifo," told me later that one of them woke up during the flight and was hit with an iron rod. Then they began to throw them out of the helicopter into the sea, near San Antonio, I believe. There were some army security commandos along, and they opened up the stomachs with a curved knife so the bodies would not float. Before throwing them out into the sea they opened them up. I remember another prisoner they took up in the helicopter, a guy of forty-five or fifty, a communist, bald, more or less dark-skinned. He had tried to commit suicide and had broken his arm. They took him to a doctor and he had a cast for a long time. He also went in the helicopter. There was another prisoner who drew caricatures. The others I don't remember.[10]

The Comando Conjunto, for all its ruthlessness, did not succeed in destroying the Chilean Communist Party, which officially reemerged in late 1988 as part of a new leftist multiparty entity. But the Comando Conjunto's incursion into the regime's dirty war brought it into ugly confrontation with the DINA, whose founder did not appreciate the competition. The animosity was mutual.

Valenzuela described how his unit executed one of its own members thought to have been recruited by the DINA, along with a Chilean communist-turned-informer. At the time, he said, the DINA offered "better economic remuneration, automobiles, and houses" than the Comando Conjunto, which suspected that its information was being leaked to Contreras's organization.

Valenzuela's superiors told his group that one of its members, Bratti Cornejo, had betrayed the Comando Conjunto by passing on information to the Communist Party, including a list of agents' names, addresses, and places they frequented to facilitate their murders. To ensure their cooperation in killing their former colleague, Valenzuela and the others were ordered to a house used by the Comando Conjunto and given pills (probably tranquilizers) before receiving instructions to take the blindfolded, handcuffed security agent to a valley outside Santiago for his execution. A few years later, in 1979, Valenzuela happened to be house-sitting for a superior when he discovered several tape recordings of prisoners' confessions, including that of Bratti Cornejo, which revealed that he had been killed not for leaking his fellow agents' names to the Communist Party but for allowing himself to be wooed by the rival DINA.

In the meantime DINA was expanding its operations so quickly that by mid-1974 Contreras had enough agents to keep not only regime opponents but much of the government apparatus itself under surveillance. Frederico Willoughby, the junta's press secretary, was outraged to learn that DINA agents had broken into his office in Diego Portales and stolen several press credentials. After he complained to Pinochet, the credentials reappeared. Willoughby also found himself helping Chilean journalists menaced by the DINA, and when they approached him for help he would attempt to verify whether the security forces were indeed seeking the reporter in question.[11] If they were, Willoughby discreetly warned the intended victim.

The regime's interior minister, General Oscar Bonilla, became another Contreras enemy when other documents began disappearing from government ministries. Contreras, who attended cabinet meetings, attributed the thefts to "leftist infiltrators" within the government, but refused to offer any proof of this or to show Bonilla, his military superior, any deference. According to a former regime official present at this meeting, Contreras infuriated the interior minister by commenting that "certain things can't be said in front of strangers."

DINA's operations outside the country were also expanding, and some of these would qualify as terrorist activities. A copy of a letter from Contreras to Pinochet, dated September 16, 1975, obtained by the Chilean Catholic Church's Vicaría de la Solidaridad, requests an additional $600,000 in funds for increasing DINA personnel at Chilean diplomatic missions in seven different Latin American and European countries and for "neutralizing the junta's principal adversaries abroad."[12]

The letter mentions Mexico, Argentina, Costa Rica, the United States, France, and Italy, all countries with sizeable Chilean exile communities that in the view of Contreras and Pinochet needed to be brought under control. The DINA would establish contacts with its Argentine counterparts (who later waged their own dirty war), along with military intelligence groups in Uruguay, Brazil, Bolivia, and Paraguay. Operation Condor, a cooperative effort among the military regimes in the continent's southern cone to combat subversion—very broadly defined, of course—was Contreras's brainchild. The DINA chief also enlisted the help of Italian neofascists and Cuban anti-Castro activists for operations in the United States and Europe. DINA's extraterritorial capabilities were soon known around the world, and eventually caused the downfall of Contreras and his empire.

The bomb explosion that killed former Chilean army commander Carlos Prats and his wife, Sofía, in Buenos Aires on October 1, 1974, did not cause a public outcry in Santiago, but it did produce a kind of muted shock among some regime officials. According to Frederico Willoughby, few officials in the regime doubted that the bomb assassination had been the work of the DINA.

"No one dared comment aloud or talk about it," he said. "What you would overhear would be, 'They have gotten out of hand,' or 'Why did they kill Senõra Sofía?' "[13]

Others seemed to approve of the assassination, making comments to the effect that the Prats killing had been long overdue. In either case, the assassination had had the intended intimidatory effect of cowing would-be dissenters within the military into silence and prompting more outward expressions of loyalty to Pinochet.

During our interview, Willoughby recalled discussing the DINA's power with General Oscar Bonilla, whose seniority in the Chilean army made him next in line for Pinochet's job as service commander. Bonilla, who had been one of the coup's chief advocates within the army, was proving to be a popular figure among regime supporters and showed a populist touch when he visited several slum neighborhoods around Santiago as the regime's interior minister. In mid-1974 he had been shuffled to the post of defense minister. Bonilla, along with senior army generals Sergio Arellano Stark and Augusto Lutz, protested about Contreras and the DINA in a private communication with Pinochet, but to no avail. Two of these three officers, who were the coup's principal conspirators within the Chilean army, died under suspicious circumstances within one year. Lutz, a former director of the army's intelligence service, suddenly fell ill the day after attending a reception. He was interned in a military hospital where physicians erroneously diagnosed the teetotaling Lutz as having swollen blood vessels in his esophagus—a malady common to heavy drinkers—and operated, leaving him with septicemia.

For the next twenty days Lutz was kept under armed guard at the hospital while physicians subjected him to a series of exploratory operations that revealed no abnormalities. Finally, on November 28, 1974, Lutz died of septicemia. He had managed to scribble a terse note asking to be released from the hospital, and passed it on to his family, who demanded an investigation. Officials at the military hospital took statements from Lutz's widow and children, but months later when the family asked about the investigation these same officials professed ignorance of any such inquiry.[14]

On March 3, 1975, an army helicopter carrying Bonilla mysteriously crashed near Curicó, in southern Chile, killing Defense Minister Oscar Bonilla. The subsequent military investigation of the accident did not assuage suspicions of sabotage. Two French helicopter technicians in Chile to negotiate an aircraft sale visited the scene of the crash a few hours later, along with Chilean air force officials. The helicopter's rotor blade was discovered an unusually long distance from the wreckage. The Chilean army then took over the investigation from the air force, but the results were never made public. The two French technicians who had inspected the crash site were killed in another helicopter accident, and the lone survivor of the accident that killed Bonilla, a young corporal, was sent to France for a mechanic's course he had already taken.[15]

General Sergio Arellano, another coup instigator within the army, was beginning to have doubts about not only Contreras but also the regime's direction. Arellano had been ruthless when political prisoners were executed during his tour of army bases in northern Chile following the coup, but even this hard-line officer was concerned about the burgeoning strength of the DINA, calling it a "veritable Gestapo" in a private letter to Pinochet (a letter that probably wound up in Contreras's hands). Even worse, in Pinochet's eyes, were Arellano's ties to the Christian Democrats, whose party had become openly critical of the regime, and his expressed admiration for former president Eduardo Frei, Allende's predecessor.

By late 1975 Arellano's relationship with Pinochet had soured to the point where he was offered the post of ambassador to Spain. Arellano refused: another senior army general had gone to Belgium as ambassador and once out of the country was retired from the army. In a final, furious confrontation Pinochet demanded that Arellano hand in his resignation within twenty-four hours; Arellano whipped out an envelope from his pocket. "There you have it. I'm going." A few days later the military academy held a ceremony attended by hundreds of Chilean army officers who dutifully made a pledge of loyalty to Pinochet.[16]

The DINA's overseas operations had only just begun with the killing of former army commander Carlos Prats and his wife in Buenos Aires. On October 6, 1975, Italian neofascists working in behalf of Contreras shot and critically wounded Bernardo Leighton, who had been interior minister during the Frei government, and his wife, Anita, in Rome, where they were living in exile. An unsuccessful attempt was made on the life of Gabriel Valdes, another prominent Christian Democrat and former foreign minister under the Frei government, who was working at the United Nations in New York. The DINA also tried and failed to kill the MIR guerrilla leader Andrés Pascal Allende, living in exile in Costa Rica, and Carlos Altamirano, former secretary general of the Chilean Socialist party, in Spain. Then on September 21, 1976, a car bomb planted by American mercenary Michael Townley, acting on orders from DINA, killed former Allende government cabinet minister Orlando Letelier and his American co-worker Ronni Moffitt in Washington.[17] Letelier, who had once worked for the Inter-American Development Bank, had been lobbying the multilateral lending agencies to suspend loans to Chile and had successfully campaigned in Holland for the cancellation of a $62.5 million mining investment in Chile by a Dutch firm.[18] Worst of all, in the view of the Chilean military, he had received a sympathetic hearing from influential members of the U.S. Senate, which passed a bill cutting off arms sales to Chile on June 16, 1976.

Letelier's activities infuriated Pinochet, who felt he had done the former Allende government official a favor by releasing him from the Dawson Island concentration camp two years earlier. Less than two weeks before the assassination, the regime had stripped Letelier of his Chilean citizenship.

"The general wants this guy killed because he is good friends with Kennedy and they're going to form a government in exile. And all the funds that would have gone to Chile will go to that government in exile and people here will starve." Michael Townley, the American DINA agent who placed the bomb under Letelier's car, told his wife of his mission before leaving for the United States on a falsified Chilean passport as "Kenneth Enyart." Townley's Chilean wife, Inés Callejas, who now uses the first name Mariana, was an ex–Patria y Libertad activist who had also worked for the DINA but had grown increasingly disenchanted with the people in the organization. They had been obliged to entertain the anti-Castro Cubans and Italian neofascists who came to town, and Callejas, who had once lived on a kibbutz and was a staunch supporter of Israel, was disgusted by their rabid anti-Semitism as well as by their rough-edged manners.[19]

"Don't tell me they're sending you to do this," she said. "Well, not exactly," Townley replied. "They're sending me to tell the Cubans to do it." The bomb was placed by Townley and detonated by remote control by anti-communist Cubans. The Letelier-Moffitt killings, which occurred in the center of the capital, happened to take place in front of the Chilean embassy located on the route to Letelier's office at the Institute for Policy Studies, a left-wing think tank. The case marked the beginning of the end for Contreras, although not for the regime's human rights abuses.

The regime was quick to issue statements denying any involvement in the murder, but the circumstances raised eyebrows even within the government. The air force commander, General Gustavo Leigh, and the naval commander, Admiral José Merino, along with a few ministers, raised the subject during the first cabinet meeting held in the wake of the assassination. Pinochet asked Contreras to appear before the officials and asked him whether the DINA or the regime had been involved, and if not, who he believed had killed Letelier. Contreras denied any official involvement, and said it had been the work of the CIA.[20] "You see? This is the truth," Pinochet told the officers and ministers present. "Thank you, Colonel, you may leave."

Although his terror tactics and close relationship with Pinochet initially protected him from his enemies within the country, Contreras proved far less adept at handling U.S. Justice Department investigators on his trail. When first meeting with the FBI agent Robert Scherrer after the murders, Contreras offered the theory that Michael Moffitt had killed Letelier, arguing that the fact Moffitt was sitting in the back of the car and his wife in front with Letelier proved that the two victims were having an affair. Also, Contreras asserted, the assassination was undoubtedly part of a Marxist plot to damage the Chilean government.[21] The silliness of Contreras's explanation, presented to Scherrer with great seriousness along with an offer to help U.S. officials investigate this "lead," suggests a lack of sophistication on the part of the DINA chief, and perhaps a growing desperation. Contreras had carefully put together his network of anti-Castro Cubans, but it was far from clear they would protect him.

At the beginning of the investigation, however, many U.S. officials were reluctant to believe that the DINA was behind the Letelier-Moffitt murders: they were apparently unaware that Contreras's organization had expanded to the point where it could undertake overseas operations. One State Department cable, written a few days after the killings, said, "The reach of DINA—cited as responsible—almost certainly (80 percent) does not extend to the United States. Chilean image-building received a severe setback by the killing, *something that the planners of the attempt would have foreknown and considered*" (italics added).[22]

The cable shows a certain naïveté about the workings of military regimes, which tend to shoot first, ask questions later, and attempt to cover their tracks with censorship. Whatever forethought Contreras and Pinochet may have given to eliminating Letelier, it is doubtful they even considered the effect a car-bomb assassination in the heart of Washington would have on U.S.-Chile relations. Placating foreign governments was a job left largely to right-wing civilians in the regime, many of whom simply did not believe their government was committing such atrocities. The lines of communication between Pinochet and Contreras, and between Contreras and his trusted operatives in the DINA, were so tightly sealed as to let in no concerns other than the continuing war with suspected leftists and regime critics.

But after following several dead-end leads involving Letelier's promiscuous personal life and contacts with Chilean exiles living in Cuba, the FBI was beginning to identify the anti-Castro Cubans involved in the assassination, as well as Michael Townley, the American expatriate working for the DINA. Feeling the end was near, Contreras began casting about for ways to shore up his position in Chile and to justify the DINA to his enemies within the military.

In early 1977 the Chilean capital was rocked by a series of bombings, mostly minor explosions that damaged street lamps or shattered windows. Some of the bombings consisted of small explosives placed late at night in metal garbage dumpsters, producing tremendous reverberating blasts that caused little or no property damage but sparked public panic and fueled fears of a new wave of left-wing terrorism. But more than one Chilean official suspected the DINA: Germán Campos, formerly the carabineros' intelligence chief and now a general, was back in the capital as prefect after a posting in southern Chile.

Campos had been disgusted by the conduct of carabineros recruited to the DINA's ranks, where under the command of young army lieutenants of twenty-two or twenty-three they seemed to turn into bandits. In one case the Santiago prefecture had received a report of a Citröen stolen at gunpoint from its French owner, who had been tied up and thrown into a gutter by the thieves. The case was turned over to the carabineros' stolen car unit, which checked garages

and various neighborhoods, listening for the sounds of thieves dismantling a car. The unit found a Citröen being taken apart by three men,
who were arrested. The three turned out to be two army officers and
a carabinero, all working for the DINA, and they in turn charged the
arresting police officers with assault. It developed that the DINA
agents' immediate superior had owned a Citröen like the one they had
stolen, and when his car had broken down he instructed his men to go
out and get him another like it.

Then there was the robbery at the Farmacia Benjerodt in downtown Santiago. The drugstore clerk had managed to trigger the alarm
as the thieves were leaving, and a carabinero lieutenant who was coming off duty intervened and arrested three men—two carabineros and
an army officer, all working for the DINA.

"The DINA would send its men out to commit robberies, or leave
them free to collect whatever money they wanted," Campos recalled.
" 'Go out and collect your salaries,' " they'd say. They were veritable
death squads.[23] Campos ordered his carabineros to watch carefully for
any signs that DINA agents were placing the bombs, and to make the
arrests, pick up the shells and bomb fragments, and to note times,
places, and physical descriptions of people leaving the scene of an explosion. On April 27, 1977, he and junta member César Mendoza, a
carabinero general, were at a formal dinner held at the Club de Carabineros to commemorate the institution's fiftieth anniversary, with
representatives of foreign police departments also in attendance.
While dessert was being served, a senior carabinero official was called
away for a message and returned a few minutes later looking pale. He
whispered to General Mendoza that the capital was being rocked with
bomb explosions. Campos, who was seated next to Mendoza, told his
superior that he knew who was behind the bombings and that he
would ratify the accusation at headquarters the following day if Mendoza wished.

Mendoza telephoned Campos the next morning to tell him he need
not come in, for other carabinero officers on duty had confirmed his
accusation. More bombings followed, including one placed at an electricity pylon that caused a partial blackout in Santiago. Each time
Campos insisted to his fellow officers that it was the DINA, not any
new terrorist group, behind the blasts. The time had come for a direct
confrontation with Contreras.

A meeting was held at the defense ministry with the military governor of Santiago, the commander of the Santiago army garrison, Contreras, and Campos. Campos stated his position, citing what his men had reported, and Contreras responded with a series of denials: that the carabineros were mistaken, that they had not in fact witnessed DINA agents at the site of the explosions, that leftist extremists were indeed at large and had even disguised themselves as soldiers and security agents.

Campos said his men had recovered bomb fragments just moments after one bomb blast and that the parts were identical to those used by the Chilean army in its training programs. Chile's arms-control statutes were strict enough to prohibit the possession of gunpowder, detonators, or other explosives without permission of the army. Contreras continued his denials, and the other army generals at the meeting seemed reluctant to challenge the DINA chief, even though as a colonel he was their subordinate. Defense minister General Hernán Brady ended the meeting with a call for reconciliation, noting that such disputes could only harm the government. Campos and Contreras were quiet. But at that point neither man had any intention of backing down, and the two would collide again.

The kinds of prisoners the DINA were still picking up were political dissidents, not guerrilla bombers. Jaime Troncoso, a member of the Chilean Socialist party's youth wing, had managed to avoid arrest during the massive wave of repression immediately following the coup while maintaining some party activity: keeping in touch with other members, trying to recruit new ones, and occasionally scattering pamphlets. Troncoso, who had polio as a child and walked with the aid of crutches, was an economics student at the University of Chile; I interviewed him at his apartment in Santiago.

On May 2, 1977, Troncoso was on his way to meet another socialist friend at the corner of Diez de Julio and Arturo Prats streets in central Santiago. As he approached the prearranged meeting place, five men in civilian dress emerged from a car without license plates and grabbed Troncoso, who threw his crutches into the air and shouted his name and that he was being arrested by the DINA. There were witnesses to his arrest—a newsstand operator, a fruit vendor, and passersby—but the climate of intimidation in Santiago was so pervasive that no one dared intervene even to protect an unarmed man on crutches. When the friend he was supposed to meet reported his disappearance, Troncoso's family visited the corner of Diez de Julio and Arturo Prats streets, looking for clues. But no one in the area admitted to having seen anything.

Troncoso's captors put him on the floor of the car with a pistol against his back and his jacket pulled up over his head to prevent him from seeing their faces or where they were headed. The DINA car had been moving for about twenty minutes when Troncoso heard a gate open and the sound of wheels driving over gravel. The agents walked their disabled prisoner from the car down a flight of stairs and deposited him in a chair, handcuffing him and blindfolding him.

The first interrogation began; they wanted to know exactly where he lived. Troncoso had recently moved from his parents' home in Las Condes, an upper-income suburb in east Santiago, to an apartment with his wife, but he thought it prudent to tell his captors he still lived at his old address, since that was the one marked on his Chilean identity card. The DINA sent a squad of at least fifteen armed men to his parents' home and ransacked the house, looking for information on his activities. Finding nothing, the DINA agents came back in a rage and began to torture him.

Troncoso was kicked and beaten for about forty-five minutes, then taken to another room where he was stripped and tied to a chair. Electrodes were fastened to his ears, mouth, feet, and genitals, and his captors began interrogating him about his entire history, beginning with his parents, who were apolitical and had nothing to do with their son's activities in the Socialist party. The interrogators told Troncoso they had all the time in the world, that they had authority to do what they were doing, and that they had Pinochet's full support. "We can make you disappear," they said. "We suggest you behave yourself and answer all our questions."

When Troncoso yielded an answer, the torture would stop momentarily. After a particularly rough session, he would hear the voice of a seemingly friendly interrogator, who urged him to think of his family and cooperate. Troncoso was never asked about any bombings, any arms, or any terrorist incidents, and it soon became obvious that the DINA agents did not even believe he might be involved in such activity. What they were after was information on the workings of the Chilean Socialist party and what the party knew about the regime. Troncoso was also asked about the party's relationship with the Catholic Church, and his interrogators spoke in crude terms about Cardinal Raúl Silva Henriquez and other ecclesiastical leaders.

A political prisoner undergoing torture has to pick some middle ground between telling his captors nothing—in which case he might be killed—and betraying his associates. But Troncoso was perhaps better equipped to handle himself in this situation than most, having heard accounts of what happened to other prisoners and steeled himself to face interrogation. In addition, his disability seemed to distract the DINA interrogators. They apparently thought it was a special area of vulnerability when in reality it gave Troncoso a hidden reserve of toughness. When his captors lifted him to his feet at the top of the stairs and pushed him, Troncoso fell. But falling was not as painful as the electrodes, so when he collapsed at the bottom of the steps he screamed as theatrically as possible, trying to give the DINA agents the impression that this was the worst thing they could do to him.

After nearly four weeks of confinement and intermittent torture, Troncoso was handed his jacket and his orthopedic brace and told by his captors that they were all going out. The young socialist did not know whether he was about to be killed or released. He was wrapped in a blanket, put into a car, and forced to lie on the floor. Troncoso had the distinct impression that not all the DINA officers involved in his case had agreed on what to do with him. At one point the car stopped, he was leaned against a wall, and some men on the other side pulled him over. Troncoso found himself in a ditch when he heard the car leave, and after a few tense minutes he ventured to remove the blindfold he had worn since his arrest. His eyes were badly infected. It was about midnight.

Crawling out of the ditch Troncoso managed to find his crutches some fifteen yards away. A taxi suddenly appeared, probably driven by a DINA agent, and Troncoso gave him directions to his mother-in-law's home, where he spent the next few days recovering. Helped by the Catholic Church and the United Nations Intergovernmental Committee for Migrations, friends and family began a desperate attempt to find him asylum in another country. Sweden offered him and his wife a visa, but the interior ministry balked at giving him permission to leave the country, claiming he posed "extreme danger to the state's internal security." Troncoso was finally allowed to leave eight months later, and spent nearly seven years in exile.[24]

The winds blowing from Washington were distinctly chillier now that Jimmy Carter was in the White House. In addition to the pressures for cooperation in the Letelier investigation, there were messages from the U.S. embassy that Washington wanted some indication that the regime did not intend to hold onto power indefinitely. Pinochet's reaction to such overtures was usually hostile and defensive, but civilian advisers such as Jaime Guzmán made a case for "institutionalizing" the regime, making arrangements to carry on the anti-Marxist government should anything happen to Pinochet, who was then sixty-one. On July 9, 1977, the anniversary of a Chilean independence battle, Pinochet spoke at a candlelit gathering of young people, drawn from the ranks of government-sponsored youth groups. The speech, written by Guzmán, was a virtual outline of his neofascist political views, in which he described a transition to "constitutional normalcy," guided by the Chilean military but with civilian collaboration.

The speech also promised that Chile would never again fall to the Marxists, and used terms like "authoritarian" and "protected" to describe the brave new order the country was building. The State Department immediately praised this "advance" toward democracy, then backtracked a few days later with a statement to the effect that the Carter administration remained concerned about continuing reports of human rights abuses in Chile.

Pinochet, along with other Latin American heads of state, was invited to Washington to attend the signing of the Panama Canal treaties in September. It was one of his very few trips abroad, and inevitably drew public attention to his regime and the Letelier case. On August 13, 1977, the regime announced that the DINA was being dissolved and that a new security organization, the Central Nacional de Informaciones (CNI) would operate in its place. The decision was made without Contreras's backing, though he was to remain as its director. Human rights groups rightly pointed out that the changes were largely cosmetic, for the CNI would continue the DINA's tradition of terror and torture.

Contreras, who felt his power base slipping, remained with the CNI for three months before Pinochet promoted him to general and assigned him to the army's engineering department. The heat generated by the Letelier case had provided an opening for a Contreras rival, General Odlanier Mena, to gain access to Pinochet, who instructed him to draw up plans for a restructured security service.

And, over Contreras's objections, the regime had acceded to U.S. demands for the expulsion of Michael Townley. It sought to dissociate itself completely from Letelier's assassination. Townley, as an American citizen, could be presented in the Chilean press as a CIA agent. The Cubans indicted in the case could also enhance the desired impression of a complicated Havana-Washington plot to discredit Chile. But Contreras had promised Townley Chile would protect him, and had even told him he would be made an officer in the Chilean army at some future date. Townley, who had lived in Santiago since his early teens, had believed Contreras.[25] Now in the hands of the U.S. Justice Department, with an offer of reduced charges in exchange for his testimony, Townley was going to sing.

Pinochet was also furious with the Americans, in part for a *Washington Post* editorial calling for his resignation. The editorial prompted regime supporters to demonstrate in the streets of Santiago, burning an American flag. This fury boiled over in an unusual confrontation with U.S. ambassador George Landau at a formal dinner Pinochet hosted for ambassadors on June 22, 1978.

According to authors Taylor Branch and Eugene Propper (who almost certainly received this account from Landau himself), Pinochet took the American ambassador aside and began ranting about how the United States had betrayed him many times and how Chile had many enemies inside the U.S. government. Pointing to the Chinese ambassador across the room, Pinochet told Landau, "Believe me, Chile can go to China. We are not married to the United States. I could even turn to the Soviet Union. They would help. They would do anything to hurt you. . . ."

"Excuse me, Mr. President," said Landau. "I want to make sure I understand you. Do you really mean that last statement? Do you really mean that you could become an ally of the Soviet Union?" "Absolutely!" said Pinochet. "I would do it to protect my country. The Soviet Union will always intervene against American interests. It is unfortunate that you Americans always fail to comprehend this."[26]

Nine days later the U.S. Justice Department announced grand jury indictments against seven men in the Letelier-Moffitt case: four Cubans and three Chileans. The Chileans were Manuel Contreras, Colonel Pedro Espinoza (who had headed the regime's prisoner service after the coup), and Armando Fernandez Larios, a young army officer who had entered La Moneda the day of the coup and also accompanied General Sergio Arellano Stark, "the butcher of the north," on his murderous helicopter tour of northern Chile. Ambassador Landau, who had just completed a hasty trip to Washington for consultations, requested that the three DINA officials be arrested.

Contreras, Espinoza, and Fernandez were interned at the military hospital in Santiago. But Contreras had taken steps to protect himself. Days earlier he had traveled to Punta Arenas, in Chile's extreme south, with bodyguards and twenty-three suitcases that airport authorities were not allowed to examine. The baggage, containing detailed files on DINA, the regime, and Chilean officials, were loaded aboard the German freighter *Badenstein,* which sailed to Europe. With his most volatile data now safely out of the country, Contreras felt reasonably certain the regime could not afford to turn him over to the Americans.[27]

On September 20 Ambassador Landau brought the extradition documents to the regime's new civilian foreign minister, Hernán Cubillos, a former *El Mercurio* executive who had joined the government five months earlier. The sealed documents were to be transferred to the Chilean supreme court. Yet within days stories appeared in *El Mercurio* and other proregime media saying that the evidence presented in the extradition request was weak.

Chile's supreme court president, Israel Borquez, lived down the street from a former Chilean president, Gabriel González Videla. The elderly ex-president was celebrating his birthday on November 22, 1978, and requested carabinero protection for his guests that night. The carabinero colonel in charge of his area agreed, but then decided to move the officer who kept permanent guard over the supreme court president's home to the ex-president's home. There was a shortage of policemen, and since the carabinero guard could still see Borquez's house from this vantage point, the colonel decided to risk moving him for this one evening.

It was a serious mistake. A bomb exploded near Borquez's home, shattering windows and spraying glass all over the magistrate's living room. The carabinero colonel in charge of the area hurried to the scene, trying to calm the elderly Borquez. The next day Santiago prefect Germán Campos defended the carabineros' actions to his commander César Mendoza, insisting that Manuel Contreras's men must have been watching the supreme court president's house for days and seized the chance to place the bomb when the guard had to perform double duty that night. Mendoza at first seemed to agree, but then relieved Campos of his duties as prefect.[28]

Borquez, for his part, was not about to act against Contreras. Six months later the judge formally denied the U.S. extradition request, stating that Townley's testimony had been inadmissible as evidence. Asked about the U.S. court's decision to sentence Townley to ten years' imprisonment, Borquez ridiculed the court itself, noting that both Judge Barrington Parker and the jury were black, "so maybe they could not show their blushing when they heard the evidence."[29] This foolish, racist remark further worsened the regime's image in the United States and abroad.

On December 16, 1977, the United Nations General Assembly had approved a resolution condemning the Chilean military regime "with special concern and indignation" for its failure to correct human rights abuses. There had been 96 votes in favor, 14 against, and 25 abstentions. The news infuriated Pinochet, who began to plan a plebiscite in which Chileans would be asked to reject the United Nations resolution and support the regime. At a junta meeting on December 21, the air force commander, Gustavo Leigh, and the navy commander, José Merino, objected to the entire plan, arguing that there was no legal framework for such a vote and that the outcome could be disastrous for the regime. After the meeting Leigh and Merino asked their staffs to prepare formal and detailed objections to Pinochet's proposal.

But Pinochet's plans were going ahead with or without the agreement of the other junta members, and that evening he announced on government-run television that on January 4 Chileans would be asked to back him in his defense of the country's dignity and to reject the

United Nations' meddling. He also criticized the Carter administration, though not by name, charging that the United States was working "closely with Castro's Cuba" in attacking Chile's human rights record, and warned that his government would reassess its relations with the United Nations should the present situation continue.[30]

The following day presidential security guards cleared several blocks of a pedestrian walkway and positioned regime supporters along the route, preparing the way for Pinochet to walk past cheering crowds while the television cameras rolled. Chilean newspapers, most notably the government-owned *El Cronista*, had already been building up an indignant case against the United Nations resolution; one proregime editorialist had even gone so far as to urge the expulsion of U.N. personnel in Chile (which would have meant dismantling the massive Santiago headquarters of the U.N. Economic Commission for Latin America, as well as smaller branch offices of such entities as the Food and Agriculture Organization). Regime-organized groups such as the secretariats of youth and of labor, as well as a number of progovernment private organizations, quickly issued statements expressing their outrage, all serving to muster support for Pinochet.

Meanwhile, Leigh and Merino completed their formal replies to Pinochet's plebiscite, which was now being called a "consultation." Merino's letter expressed his "total disagreement" with the referendum, while Leigh made a more extended argument, charging that Pinochet's actions had excluded the other military commanders from the most important political decision the regime had made.[31] Although the air force commander's language was elaborately formal, addressing Pinochet as "your excellency," the letter delineated the power struggle between the two men. Leigh was not willing, he wrote, to go along with any more regime decisions undertaken without the junta's participation. Copies of Leigh's letter were distributed to the air force's twenty generals, and additional copies were leaked to other regime officials. When Leigh was presented with a decree law formalizing the referendum he refused to sign it (an act of defiance that made little difference).

Though the junta had misgivings about the referendum, other regime officials favored a strong response to the U.N. resolution. The U.S. embassy, which had been the target of at least one proregime street demonstration, reported that "working-level foreign ministry contacts, who say they are urging moderation, tell us that senior officials are enraged."[32] Ambassador George Landau paid a courtesy call on naval commander Admiral José Merino two days before Pinochet's televised speech, suggesting that "a bristling reaction might not be in the best interests of [Chile-U.S.] relations." Merino, according to the embassy cable, responded that Pinochet was forced to take a strong stand by "strong domestic pressures."

On Wednesday, January 4, 1978, over five million Chileans went to polling sites set up around the country by local authorities. The electoral registries had been destroyed during the coup, and to get around this technicality any Chilean over age eighteen could cast a ballot by simply showing his or her identity card. The text of the proposition, printed on translucent paper (which made it possible to see how the ballot was marked after folding), read: "In view of the international aggression unleashed against our country, I back President Pinochet in his defense of Chile's dignity and reaffirm the legitimacy of the government of the republic as the sovereign head of the country's institutional process."

The "Yes" box was marked with a Chilean flag; the "No" box with a black square. To no one's surprise, the official results showed an overwhelming victory for the regime, with 75 percent of the more than five million votes marked "Yes," 20.2 percent marked "No," and 4.7 percent declared null because they were left blank, mismarked, or defaced.

Even before the first results were announced, regime supporters began to congregate outside the Diego Portales building. Pinochet was inside, having an extended luncheon with the junta and the cabinet, when the early returns showed the "Yes" vote was winning. Pinochet, accompanied by Admiral Merino and carabinero commander Mendoza, appeared before the crowd, while Leigh made a point of leaving.

"Señor politicians, it is over!" Pinochet told the crowd. "Because I have the backing of the citizenry." Chile sent the United Nations a letter responding to the resolution, and no representative of the U.N. Human Rights Commission was allowed to enter the country "if he does not comply with our rules." Pinochet also said the regime's foreign ministry would be restructured and its foreign policy overhauled, making it "more aggressive and more pragmatic."[33]

Pinochet had managed to turn a U.N. resolution condemning the regime into a personal triumph, but Leigh's increasing obstructiveness was still a problem. The air force commander had many admirers in the regime and in pro-regime circles, and he also seemed to get along with the Americans, despite the fact that the arms embargo badly hurt the largely U.S.-equipped Chilean air force.

Inside the air force, more than one general would have liked to see Leigh replace Pinochet as the head of the regime, and a plan involving a show of force by the institution was hatched—but never attempted. The plan called for air force officials to take over the defense ministry, backed by air power that could conceivably overpower any resistance by the Chilean army. The plan presumed that Merino's navy would remain passive in such a scenario, but that carabineros might side with the air force.[34] Had the air force gone ahead with this scheme, the confrontation would almost certainly have been far bloodier than the 1973 coup. Their reasons for abandoning the plan are not clear, but it is known that the CNI, Pinochet's newly restructured security service, learned of it.

"The DINA and the CNI were used to spy on the military as much as on the opposition," Leigh said in an interview eight years later. "Imagine, I found out that one of the men in my own office worked for the DINA."[35]

But the incident that ultimately precipitated Leigh's removal from the junta was an interview he had granted to the Italian newspaper *Il Corriere della Sera*. Leigh's statements during the interview, which appeared on July 18, 1978, seemed innocuous. He did not, he said, believe the regime was involved in the Letelier assassination. In response to the question of whether he would reconsider his position in the junta if the regime turned out to be involved, Leigh answered affirmatively. "I do not believe that improving [the country's] image should begin from external actions, but from within Chile," he said. Leigh also asserted that the country needed an itinerary for an eventual return to civilian rule, and that Chileans "have an old tradition of freedom and democracy and cannot be kept indefinitely under a negation of freedom."[36]

The interview infuriated not only Pinochet, but also Merino and Mendoza, whose nationalistic sensitivities were irritated because Leigh had made such statements to a foreign journalist. When questioned about the interview by a progovernment radio station, Leigh simply confirmed his views. The day after the interview appeared, Leigh met with the other junta members, who demanded that he retract his statements. He refused. A cabinet meeting was also in session to discuss the ramifications of the Italian newspaper's article, and the ministers drew up a four-page letter decrying Leigh's statements.

The internal tension continued to build. Pinochet, Merino, and Mendoza met in private and decided to ask for Leigh's resignation; the air force commander sent back a message that he would not resign. Finally, on July 24, 1978, the four junta members gathered at the defense ministry for a final confrontation. Pinochet showed Leigh a decree providing for his resignation from the junta. Leigh refused to sign the decree. "Then we'll fire you," Pinochet told him. "And with what charges, under what law, are you going to do this?" Leigh asked him. "Don't worry, we have enough legal powers," Pinochet replied, and left the room.[37]

The decree removing Leigh from the junta indicated that the air force commander had been relieved of his functions, and that a replacement would be appointed. There were nineteen other generals in the Chilean air force at the time; all but two left the institution in protest. General Fernando Matthei, the health minister, was sworn in as the new junta member and air force commander. The year was turning out to be a very good one for Pinochet's presidency: during 1978 he had thumbed his nose at his critics abroad, and now one of his biggest rivals was out of the way.

Chapter Five

The New Institutionality

*By the year 1985 or 1986 each worker will be able to have
a house, an automobile, and a television.*
—General Augusto Pinochet, February 1979

After five years in power the regime was rewriting Chilean history,
along with the country's constitution. The Diego Portales building's
principal auditorium, used for most government ceremonies, now had
a gilded backdrop bearing the inscription "1810 Chile 1973" behind
the podium and stage. The first date is the year of Chile's independence from Spain. By association, 1973, the year of the coup (or "military pronouncement" as the regime's supporters dubbed it) was supposed to represent another turning point in the nation's history. The
Chilean central bank had minted five- and ten-peso coins depicting a
winged figure triumphantly breaking chains, with the words "Septi-
embre 11, 1973" and "Libertad." The regime had even added a second verse to the Chilean national anthem, glorifying the military:

> Thy names, valiant soldiers
> who have been the support of Chile,
> We carry them in our hearts
> and our children will know them as well.
> Let them be the cry of death
> that we hurl as we march to fight
> and dreaming of the door to the fortress
> always makes the tyrant tremble.

There were new right-wing civilian ministers, leaving military officers with only eight of the eighteen cabinet-level posts. Two admirals

had held the post of foreign minister before Hernán Cubillos, a former navy officer and executive with the *El Mercurio* newspaper chain, took the job. Chilean foreign policy seemed headed for disaster. The territorial dispute with Argentina in the Beagle Channel, off Tierra del Fuego, had brought the two countries to the brink of war. Argentina's military rulers could count on some support from Peru and Bolivia, which had never forgiven Chile for the territories lost during the 1879 War of the Pacific, a conflict whose centenary anniversary was approaching. The United States, which had already cut arms sales to Chile, was considering additional sanctions in the wake of the Chilean supreme court's refusal to extradite Manuel Contreras and other DINA officers, while American labor groups were about to organize an international boycott of Chile over the regime's ban on union activity. Great Britain had recalled its ambassador in the wake of the arrest and torture of Dr. Sheila Cassidy, a British physician working in Santiago, and had suspended arms sales to Chile. Sweden, Italy, and Holland had also recalled their ambassadors after the coup.

"I had only met Pinochet once, socially, and he suddenly called me and said, 'Well, you've been very critical of our foreign policy. I'd like you to take over and handle it.' Those were his exact words," Cubillos recalled. "He started telling me he didn't understand foreign affairs, but he knew I was well-connected abroad and knew about these things."[1]

The pragmatic modesty of this exchange may seem uncharacteristic of a dictator, but Pinochet was shrewd enough to understand that the regime's survival depended on reaching some grudging accommodation with the outside world, especially if the nation faced war against Argentina. Buenos Aires had just rejected a British arbitration awarding the disputed islands to Chile, and had staged practice air raids and mobilized troops along the two countries' 2,600-mile-long border. Pinochet and Argentina's General Jorge Videla had met twice to discuss the dispute, but little progress had been made toward a settlement, in part because military dictators are unaccustomed to making concessions and are unskilled in the art of diplomacy. Had Chile been under a civilian-elected government, it might have received some international sympathy, but few governments were eager to defend Chile's military regime.

Cubillos managed to boost the spirits of Chile's demoralized foreign service and set about smoothing out relations with Argentina, a task complicated by the Argentine military's ever-shifting policies. Pinochet at least allowed him a free hand in the negotiations, whereas Cubillos's Argentine counterparts were forced to clear every move with the different branches of the military. The Vatican offered to mediate the dispute, and on January 8, 1979, the two regimes signed an agreement renouncing the use of force while negotiations were under way.

"Pinochet was very much the military man, but he was a good listener, and took notes of everything said," Cubillos said. "He had an excellent memory." Buoyed by the general's support, Cubillos set off on a European tour, visiting Great Britain, Switzerland, France, Germany, and Spain. The trip yielded some improvements in these countries' relations with Chile (although France's foreign minister refused to be photographed with Cubillos), and Great Britain agreed to send a new ambassador to Santiago.

Cubillos was also trying to build up Chile's ties to Asia and the Pacific, and in 1978 had become the first Latin American foreign minister to visit Beijing. Despite Chile's virulent anti-Marxist stance, the People's Republic of China did not break the relationship it had with Chile since the sixties; officials in both countries talked of Pinochet possibly visiting China. But no matter how skilled the newly revamped Chilean foreign ministry was, Pinochet's image remained an embarrassment.

On March 23, 1980, Pinochet was scheduled to arrive in Manila for an official three-day visit to the Philippines. The LAN-Chile flight carrying Pinochet, his wife and eldest daughter, Cubillos, and three other cabinet officials departed Santiago on March 21, refueling on Easter Island and in Tahiti. As the plane approached Fiji, where Pinochet and his delegation were due to spend the night as official guests of the Fijian government, a message from Chile's ambassador to Manila came over the radio network that the regime's secret police, the CNI, had set up for the presidential plane: without giving any explanation, President Ferdinand Marcos had canceled Pinochet's visit, saying he could not guarantee his security. When the Chilean embassy officials asked if Imelda Marcos could receive Pinochet, Philippine authorities told them that the Chilean dictator was not to land in the country. No, President Marcos was not available for consultation; he had just left Manila to "attend to an urgent matter."[2]

Upon landing in Fiji, Pinochet and his committee were faced with more diplomatic insults. The official reception to be given by Fijian governor Ratu Sir Kamisese Mara was canceled, along with the overnight stay at the governor's residence in Suva. When the plane touched down at Nandi airport, it was surrounded by Fijian security agents, and a workman in overalls boarded the aircraft and proceeded to fumigate the interior with Pinochet and his delegation still in their seats. Immigration officials at Nandi proved surly and uncooperative, insisting on opening and thoroughly inspecting every piece of luggage. Outside the airport, demonstrators pelted the motorcade with eggs and tomatoes along its route to the Hotel Regent, where Pinochet and his officials spent the night.[3]

Once inside the hotel, Pinochet called a meeting to analyze the situation. Cubillos, who had planned to travel from Manila to Japan once Pinochet's visit had concluded, wanted to proceed with his own trip. Pinochet curtly ordered him to stay with the rest of the group.

What had gone wrong? Pinochet detected a conspiracy and suspected that the Carter administration was involved.[4] The United States, after all, had a massive presence in the Philippines, and could easily pressure Marcos to cancel the Chilean dictator's visit. But how could Chilean officials, who had spent months preparing for Pinochet's Pacific trip, have failed to detect anything? Unless, of course, some of them were involved? Pinochet's old distrust of diplomats resurfaced.

Back in Santiago regime supporters held a rally in front of the Diego Portales building, where Pinochet announced Chile was breaking relations with Manila. "I cannot accept a slap in the face of my country," he told the crowd. Cubillos was fired the following day and replaced by René Rojas, a career foreign-service officer. But from now on, Pinochet declared, he would manage Chile's foreign policy. After the Philippines debacle, Pinochet attempted no more trips outside Chile while in office.[5]

But if even another dictator like Ferdinand Marcos did not want to receive Pinochet, the regime was discovering the public relations advantage of the turnaround in the Chilean economy. "An Odd Free Market Success," a *Time* story on the Chilean economy, was one of the first of many laudatory articles to appear in the U.S. press. The article was accompanied by a photo of people crowded along the Paseo Ahumada, a pedestrian walkway stretching four blocks through the center of downtown Santiago, with the caption, "In an important area of life, much less restriction."[6] The *Wall Street Journal* cynically editorialized that Chile ought to lend the United States its economic team, if Washington ever stopped its political lectures. The University of Chicago–educated planning minister, Miguel Kast, the finance minister, Sergio de Castro, the central bank president, Alvaro Bardón, and the regime's Harvard-educated labor minister, José Piñera, were praised for their boldness and innovation in transforming the Chilean economy from an inefficient state-controlled model to one of streamlined laissez-faire modernity.

Many of Chile's economic indicators showed improvement: inflation fell to 31.2 percent annually in 1980. The economy grew by 6.8 percent in 1978, 6.5 percent in 1979, and 5 percent in 1980, and per capita income edged back up to the level it had been when Allende took office.

Chilean exports had been diversified to the point where copper, which had accounted for 80 percent of the country's foreign-exchange earnings, now made up less than half of this figure, making Chile far less vulnerable to fluctuations on the world copper market. A U.S. embassy report on the Chilean economy noted that the shock treatment applied in the mid-seventies had "ushered in a period of steady growth at above-average rates even by world standards. . . . Chile appears in the vanguard of a worldwide neo-conservative response to the menace of growing inflation. From an isolated beginning in 1975, Chile has seen variations of orthodox monetarist-fiscal policies take hold in several other countries."[7]

Foreign business travelers arriving in Santiago during this period were often pleasantly surprised by the economic environment created by the regime, as well as by certain Chilean idiosyncrasies: appointments were kept, usually on time, and there was none of the petty bribery required to facilitate transactions in other Latin American countries. A foreign-investment statute decreed in 1974 removed limits on the remittance of profits and capital and provided for equal treatment of Chilean and foreign companies. By 1980 there were 554 foreign-investment projects involving $4.1 billion either in the planning stages or already under way. Most of this authorized investment—83.3 percent—was in mining projects whose eventual development depended on the results of lengthy feasibility studies, but the mere presence of new foreign investors with long-term, if tentative, plans boosted the regime's morale.

"Chile's rich are equivalent to the upper middle class in the United States; the poor in Chile would be upper middle class in India," commented the central bank president, Alvaro Bardón. Such a glib comparison made little difference to Chileans themselves, especially since the rich were getting richer, and the poor, poorer. Unemployment was officially reported at 12.5 percent at the end of 1979, about three times as high as it was during the Allende government. Regime supporters defended this figure, arguing that during the Allende years unemployment was kept artificially low because the government employed people in unproductive make-work jobs. But the 12.5 percent figure did not include another 5.1 percent of the Chilean work force enrolled in the regime's minimum employment program, which paid them less than the minimum wage for working full time at menial jobs. And many of these jobs, such as gardening, street maintenance, and garbage collection, had once been salaried positions under municipal governments and were subsequently eliminated during the severe cutbacks in public spending.

The official unemployment figure also did not include the armies of Chileans in new and servile activities. The *cuidadores de autos*, or car-minders, had become semipermanent fixtures on the curbs of Santiago, waving orange rags at motorists pulling into parking spaces and taking their coins to insert them into parking meters—in exchange for a small tip.

The planning minister, Miguel Kast, defended the existence of the *cuidadores de autos*, saying that they made a good living from collecting tips, and "with all the new cars we are importing, they will have more work than ever." Undoubtedly car-minding paid more than many jobs available to Chile's underclass, but Kast's logic could not dispel the sense that something was amiss with this picture: the well-to-do Chilean whose driving skills were so poor he could not park his imported automobile without assistance, and the *cuidador de autos* who received more money kowtowing than he would at a productive job (which wasn't even available). The question remained of what, or who, was paying for the imported car and for the car-minder's services?

The answer was a rapidly increasing foreign debt, which jumped from about $4 billion in 1973 to $11.2 million in 1980. While the regime had placed tight restrictions on public spending, which helped bring down inflation, the civilian economic team had opened up Chile's financial markets to the waves of petrodollars sloshing through the western banking system in the late seventies. The gap between what Chile could sell abroad and what it imported was filled by foreign loans, and the current deficit had reached $1.6 billion in 1980. Much of the increase in this deficit, according to a U.S. embassy report, was caused by rapidly rising imports of consumer goods.[8] Import duties had been lowered to 10 percent on most goods. Officials had hoped this measure would make Chilean industries more efficient by subjecting them to a blast of foreign competition and would allow them easier access to parts and machinery from abroad.

The practical effect of lower duties, however, was to flood the Chilean market with cheaper and better consumer goods. A walk down Avenida Providencia, in Santiago's upper-income eastern zone, had the feel of a stroll in a European city, with boutiques bearing French or English names and offering clothing either imported or presented to look like foreign goods. The illusion of prosperity, however, was broken by the presence of beggars and the ubiquitous *cuidadores de autos.*

"We easily learn to drive around in a Mercedes Benz, but we are incapable of making a decent can opener," Chilean sociologist Pablo Huneeus wrote. He described a "highly developed consumer mentality superimposed upon an extremely backward productive structure."[9] Yet by making more consumer goods available to middle-class Chileans, the regime also helped shore up its political support. The effect was rather like donning a designer suit when one hadn't bathed for several days, but the first, superficial impression was positive.

With little sense of urgency, a regime-appointed commission had been studying a new constitutional project since late 1973. Chile's constitution of 1925 had been suspended after the coup, and the junta proposed reforming the charter by whatever means necessary to prevent a Marxist government from ever coming to power again in Chile. The commission's members, mostly right-wing civilian lawyers, finally delivered an entirely new draft constitution to Pinochet's desk. A regime advisory council pored over the draft, arguing about such issues as whether elections should be held at the end of the century, if ever, and which Chileans should be allowed to vote. One minority opinion within the council was to restrict voting to property owners, who presumably would not vote for leftist candidates. Carlos Cáceres, a council member who later served as finance minister, central bank president, and interior minister, was among those opposing universal suffrage, arguing that such a provision "could destroy the very system applying it." A popular vote would mean the inevitable formation of political parties, and "would not give any additional support to the President." Pinochet, Cáceres argued, had already received "impressive and massive expressions of support," including the results of the 1978 referendum and the proregime demonstration following his aborted trip to the Philippines. Cáceres's report was very critical of the U.S. political system, citing the "anguish of a nation whose political parties make it impossible to exercise freedom of choice."[10]

The 1979 Soviet invasion of Afghanistan, which Leonid Brezhnev had justified as an attempt to avoid "another Chile," proved that communist aggression was a continuous threat, and that efforts to fight this menace were "frequently destabilized by the United States, or its Congress, or by the campaigns of deceit in the communications media." Therefore, small countries like Chile must assume their own defense, the report said. Brezhnev's comment, widely publicized in Santiago, provided the regime with a terrific propaganda tool, with television advertisements showing Soviet tanks and flashbacks to the Allende years.

Although there were enough variations of this defensive, insular mentality to produce arguments among the advisory council, these disputes over the content of the new constitution suited the regime, for they further delayed the imposition of any limits, however vague, on its rule. The civilian-dominated cabinet of 1979 sought nothing less than the complete transformation of Chile's political and economic structures, an effort known as the "seven modernizations," and the longer the debate over the new constitution, the longer Pinochet's regime had to bring about these changes.

The areas to be modernized were industrial relations, agriculture, justice, public administration, health and the social services, the economy, and political institutions. Labor minister José Piñera had managed to head off an international boycott against Chile by granting trade unions some limited rights to organize, to engage in collective bargaining, and even to strike following unsuccessful contract negotiations. But after thirty days employers could still lock out striking workers and hire temporary replacements, and after sixty days strikers were considered to have fired themselves and lost social security benefits. The labor code outlawed the closed shop, prohibited industry-wide strikes, and in some strategic areas, such as Chile's largest copper mine, Chuquicamata, strikes were banned altogether.

High unemployment levels and the climate of intimidation played at least as important a role in preventing labor unrest as the regime's labor code did. One diplomat described to me off the record how he had "made the mistake" of using the telephone to set up a lunch appointment with a Chilean trade unionist, a regime critic with middle-of-the-road political views. The two men had barely sat down at their table at El Parrón, a popular restaurant, when a man in civilian dress entered the room and from the dozens of empty tables chose the one next to theirs. The diplomat and the labor leader proceeded with their meeting, but after a few minutes of strained conversation the unidentified man leapt from his chair and began screaming at the trade unionist, berating him for "telling the gringo lies about Chile."

For the Chilean business community, fear also shored up support for the regime. Many local companies were badly hurt by some of the regime's policies, such as the reduction in import tariffs, but bad memories of mass labor militancy and firms seized by the government during the Allende years prompted many business leaders to think twice about openly criticizing the regime.

"There is little question that class conflict dominated Chilean politics at the time of the military coup, and this fact set the tenor of the experience that followed," Jeffry Frieden wrote in *Debt, Develop-*

ment, and Democracy. "Class fear eclipsed sectorial concerns, class fear drove business to support a ruthless military regime."[11]

On August 10, 1980, Pinochet announced that the junta had approved a new constitution, and that a plebiscite to ratify the charter would be held a month later, on the tenth anniversary of the coup. Chileans once again would be asked to cast "Yes" or "No" ballots, and the latter choice would mean returning the country to chaos and ruin, he said. The text of the new constitution was not published until the following day, and the decree officially convoking the plebiscite appeared the next day.

The new constitution was not as authoritarian as Pinochet (who reportedly favored Carlos Cáceres's views) would have liked, but it awarded him broadened presidential powers that discomfited even some regime backers. A "transitional period" of eight more years was added to Pinochet's term of office, after which another plebiscite would be held in which a regime-nominated candidate would stand in a one-man presidential election. If that candidate were approved in the presidential plebiscite, he would serve eight years. Congressional elections could be held in 1990, but one-third of the senate seats would go to regime appointees, and a three-fifths majority in both houses would be needed to amend the constitution. This last provision was designed to help the regime's legal apparatus withstand any tampering by future civilian governments.

During the eight-year transitional period, the junta, with an army representative to replace Pinochet, would act as a four-man legislative body under Pinochet's presidency, but all laws passed would have to be approved unanimously. The role of the military in this brave new order was paradoxical, for while they enjoyed far more power than they would have had under a civilian, democratic government, the Chilean armed forces had definitely been subordinated to Pinochet's leadership. In addition, they had to compete for influence with civilian mandarins like finance minister Sergio de Castro and interior minister Sergio Fernandez, in a kind of hybrid civilian-military government.

Pinochet's handling of the Chilean army during this period illustrates how the institution was both pampered and kept strictly in line, with officers favored by Pinochet brought to the forefront and potential troublemakers kept at bay (though the absence of a tradition of coups meant that Pinochet, who came to power in one himself, would be unlikely to ever be ousted in one). The number of generals increased during the regime's first seven years from twenty-five to thirty-nine, and a new rank, that of lieutenant general, was given to the two most senior officers. The addition of this new rank increased the distance between Pinochet as commander in chief and the corps of generals. This system of promotions was gradually altered to allow trusted army officers to reach the rank of general more quickly. Older generals who enjoyed Pinochet's confidence could be kept on past the normal retirement age under a 1976 decree allowing them to keep their army rank while serving in a government post, a measure that also put to rest any awkward questions about Pinochet's own retirement plans.[12]

If the United States had hoped to weaken Pinochet's grip by undermining his support within the army, it found few tools to work with. The cutoff in military assistance had also distanced U.S. officials from contacts with the Chilean military, narrowing the flow of information about what was happening inside the armed forces. While the Central Intelligence Agency presumably still had some informants within the army, the termination of the above-board relationship afforded by U.S. military aid and arms sales could only have made the CIA's work more difficult. And there was Pinochet's own deep suspicion of the United States, whose links to those responsible for the 1970 assassination of the former Chilean army commander, René Schneider, had been revealed during Senate hearings on the U.S. role in destabilizing the Allende government. If the United States could act against one Chilean government, was it not logical to assume it could do the same to his regime? As a result, Chilean army officials were strictly limited in their outside contacts, while such fringe benefits as housing, loans, and educational grants were improved and expanded to keep them content. Entire neighborhoods in and around the military academy, in the affluent Las Condes municipality in eastern Santiago, were almost exclusively inhabited by military officers and their families. Several tenement-like buildings housed the most junior officers, while nicer apartments with balconies or ranch-style houses, built and constructed with the military's credit union loans, were reserved for higher-ranking officials. Military wives were encouraged to work with the different volunteer organizations headed by each commander's wife, thus strengthening the social ties among army families.

Lucía Hiriart de Pinochet's group, the Centro de Madres (CEMA)-Chile, had an extensive network of mothers' centers throughout the country, where low-income women were offered courses in basic domestic skills and child care, along with a proregime indoctrination. This last element meant that not just any woman could take advantage of CEMA-Chile's services: one Santiago woman I interviewed had approached her local CEMA-Chile center to enroll in a ceramics course, only to be told she would have to be "investigated" before her registration could be approved. CEMA-Chile also dominated the Chilean handicrafts market, with stores selling copperware, lapis lazuli jewelry, wood carvings, rugs, ponchos, and sweaters in most cities and towns. Its offices and store in Santiago, located in a Spanish colonial building, were a stop on most travel agencies' tours of the Chilean capital.

The new constitution further enhanced Pinochet's personal rule with the discretionary powers attributed to him under the new constitution's transitory article 24. This provision, which could be invoked in times of "danger of perturbation of internal peace," allowed Pinochet to order people arrested without charges and held for up to five days in their homes or "in places that are not jails" (that is, mass detention centers or secret-police stations).

In addition, article 24 provided for restrictions on the right of assembly and freedom of information ("the founding, publishing, and circulation of new publications") and banned from entry into Chile, or expelled from the country, anyone who was connected to prohibited doctrines such as Marxism ("or those who act against the interests of Chile") or who "constitute a danger to the internal peace." For those dissenters neither expelled from the country nor banned from entering, article 24 provided for internal exile, "the obligatory presence of certain persons" in remote parts of Chile.[13] The aforementioned powers had all been used since the coup, but now they were laid down in a constitution and specifically awarded to Pinochet.

With the announcement of a plebiscite and the publication of the new constitution, the regime unleashed a massive propaganda offensive urging Chileans to vote "Yes, for the Constitution of Liberty."

Once again, there would be no electoral registry; voters would simply be allowed to approach the voting station (staffed by regime officials and supporters) and present their identity cards.

This lack of safeguards prompted expressions of concern from foreign governments, but the regime felt itself riding high on the tide of economic success. It looked as though the Carter administration would be voted out of office, and the regime felt it could count on some support from a U.S. government headed by a staunch anticommunist like Ronald Reagan. And even if Chile was still a cause célèbre for many people of influence around the world, worse atrocities seemed to be going on elsewhere—in El Salvador, in Iran, and in Cambodia. After seven years of military rule, Chile had become a situation, not an event, and the country was slowly sliding into the backwaters of world attention.

In Antofagasta, the port city in Chile's northern Atacama desert, the pre-plebiscite atmosphere was even more repressive than it was in Santiago. In the capital two radio stations—one operated by the Catholic Church, the other backed by the Christian Democrats—at least gave listeners a view of events outside the regime's official line. In Antofagasta there were no such independent sources, and few people who privately opposed the notion of extending Pinochet's rule for eight to sixteen more years were willing to confide their fears and criticisms to anyone outside a small circle of trusted friends.

The city's former mayor, Floreal Recabárren, was one of these dissenters. A Christian Democrat and educator, he and other likeminded Antofagasta residents had discussed the mechanics of the plebiscite vote and the apparent lack of safeguards against fraud: no electoral registry—only an easily removable stamp affixed to the Chilean identity card and the voter's thumb dipped in indelible ink. Fliers showed former president Eduardo Frei, who had opposed the regime's constitutional project, in gross caricature, while other leaflets bore the hammer and sickle and equated a "No" vote with support for communism.

Early on the morning of the plebiscite Recabárren went to a voting site at the Antofagasta campus of the Universidad del Norte where he taught, showed his identity card, had the seal attached, and received a ballot with the words: "National Plebiscite, New Political Constitution of the Republic of Chile. 1980." The "Yes" choice was designated with a star, the "No" with a black circle. He marked the ballot "No," deposited it into the vote box, signed a list at the voting table, had his thumb marked with dark blue ink, and made a fingerprint next to his signature.

As he left the building, Recabárren happened to brush his hand against some shrubbery and noticed that the ink on his thumb, which was supposed to be indelible, was starting to smear. He went home and washed his hands with soap and water and saw that the ink completely disappeared. Pondering how best to draw attention to this irregularity, Recabárren proceeded to the local office of *El Mercurio*. He had not been allowed to vote, Recabárren lied to the editor in charge. Intrigued, the editor assigned a photographer to accompany him to the voting station, providing the former mayor a witness to what would follow.

Recabárren returned with the photographer to the same campus and selected a voting table near the site where he had cast a ballot only a few hours earlier. He showed his Chilean identity card, with the electoral seal removed, and asked if he could vote. Of course, the officials told him, and handed him a ballot. Recabárren began to move in the direction of the voting booth, then stopped and announced that he had already voted and wanted to demonstrate that the supposedly indelible ink was easily washed off and that it was possible for a voter to cast more than one ballot by going to more than one voting site. There were regime officials at the polls, including two men whom the photographer later told Recabárren he had recognized as CNI agents. One of these men approached the former mayor, but the other signaled him to wait. The former mayor of Antofagasta was sufficiently well known in the city for his arrest to cause an outcry. So the officials told him to go to the court building to make a sworn statement about what had happened.

The lone magistrate on duty that day seemed taken aback by Recabárren's denunciation, but seemed too intimidated to take any action to change the voting procedure. Instead he ordered Recabárren jailed for "attempted fraud."

Recabárren, badly shaken, was taken to the public jail but removed a few hours later and sent to a hospital. The judge, it seemed, wanted to ascertain whether Antofagasta's former mayor had been drunk or drugged at the time. After undergoing several tests and physical examinations, Recabárren was taken back to the jail. He spent three days there before the court released him on probation after he paid $450 bail. As a condition of this probation, Recabárren had to appear at the courthouse every Friday for a year. He was also fired from his teaching position at the Universidad del Norte.[14]

In Santiago the U.S. embassy was closely monitoring the pre-plebiscite campaign and trying to gauge public attitudes toward the vote. Ambassador George Landau, in a confidential cable sent to the State Department a few days before the plebiscite, predicted that the Pinochet regime would win 60 to 65 percent of the votes (including the blank ballots which officials planned to count as "Yes" votes) but doubted that the government victory would result from significant fraud. At the same time, he noted that the plebiscite was combining three issues into one: the new constitution, the extension of Pinochet's presidency for eight more years, and the transitory articles broadening his powers. "If voted separately it is likely that the constitution would be accepted by a handsome majority while the transitory articles might be rejected," he reported.[15] (A passage immediately before this sentence was deleted by State Department reviewers before releasing the document to me; the missing text very likely refers to what Landau thought of Pinochet's chances of winning the plebiscite if prolonging his presidency for eight years were subject to a separate vote.)

A systematic study of irregularities during the 1980 plebiscite was made by the Chilean sociologist Eduardo Hamuy, who gathered data from observers at roughly one-tenth of the 10,552 voting tables operating in greater Santiago that day. The study, financed by a Catholic research group, discovered gross fraud at almost 40 percent of the polling sites studied.[16] "No" votes, including those with anti-regime slogans scrawled on the ballots, were sometimes counted as "Yes" votes, and blank votes were counted as "Yes" votes. At one voting table, witnesses reported that a young man in blue jeans showed a credit card with eleven voting stamps, and an identity card with another four, and said he would continue to vote. He departed on a motorcycle, presumably heading for another polling place.

El Mercurio published a list of instructions for poll workers on September 10, 1980, the day before the plebiscite, which said that each voting table could accommodate no more than three hundred voters. Many voting tables delivered more ballots than this allotment, and researchers noted that in these cases the percentage of "Yes" votes was significantly higher than it was at tables receiving fewer than three hundred votes, suggesting that ballot-box stuffing had taken place there.

At approximately 7 P.M., Interior Minister Sergio Fernandez announced that the "Yes" vote had won by 70 percent (the official tally released later was actually 67 percent), and a crowd of regime supporters gathered in front of the Diego Portales government building. Pinochet, looking jubilant and accompanied by his wife Lucía and the other members of the junta, told the crowd that Chile did not need instruction from abroad on how to hold an election; instead, "we have taught the world a lesson."[17]

The streets of downtown Santiago were filled with proregime youths waving Chilean flags and honking their car horns in a staccato show of support for Pinochet that would last until curfew. After finishing work for the evening I managed to find an unoccupied taxi in the throng of proregime motorists, one whose driver waved a flag and occasionally added his horn to the cacophony. As we approached the area around Diego Portales, the proregime demonstrators in the cars ahead of us slowed, wanting to prolong their passage in front of the seat of government. The cab driver leaned out the window with his flag and called to the demonstrators, who waved and motioned for us to pass.

The fare from downtown to my home came to three hundred pesos, and as the driver could not change the one-thousand-peso bill I had, he kindly offered to take a check. As I sat writing it I muttered aloud the day's date: September 11.

"Yes, the day of the great deceit," he said. "Because the fraud was just too great." Like so many Chileans, the cab driver had feigned support for the regime in order to get by.

The official tally of the plebiscite showed a total of 6,271,868 votes cast, a suspicious 12.6 percent increase over the number of votes cast in the January 4, 1978, referendum on the United Nations resolution. According to the government's own statistical institute, the Chilean population had increased by only 3.8 percent between the two plebiscites. The "No" votes totalled 30.19 percent, the "Yes" votes 67 percent, and the null votes 2.77 percent.

The day after the plebiscite Pinochet told the foreign press corps that he would not be the regime's candidate in the one-man presidential election eight years hence and that if the "No" vote had won, he and the rest of the Chilean military "would have gone back to the barracks"—a statement that surprised many of those present.

"I have said five hundred times that I do not aspire to reelection, because a man as old as I would be [in 1988] cannot adequately perform in a post like this," he said.[18] But the regime was far from embarking on a transition to democracy, and its victory in the plebiscite only magnified Pinochet's sense of personal power. One month later officials announced that Andrés Zaldivar, president of Chile's Christian Democrats, would not be allowed to return to the country. Zaldivar, a former finance minister under the Frei government, had been a persistent critic of the regime's economic policies, charging that the great majority of Chileans felt poorer and that the country was becoming "a giant marketplace of imported goods, with domestic production limited to a few basic products." He was traveling in Europe when the regime, using the pretext of critical statements Zaldivar made to a Mexican newspaper, announced his banishment. He would not be allowed back into Chile unless he signed a public statement promising to recognize and uphold the new constitution.

Protests against Zaldivar's exile rained in from around the world, but to no avail. With Zaldivar out of the country, the regime had effectively rid itself of one of its most troublesome opponents. The most tactful indirect appeals had no effect, either. The archbishop of Santiago, Cardinal Raúl Silva Henriquez, and the Vatican's representative in Chile, Monsignor Angelo Sodano, had a private audience with Pinochet—something that was becoming increasingly difficult to obtain—to invite him to the closing ceremonies of a Eucharistic conference. After Pinochet accepted the invitation, Sodano gingerly tried to broach the subject of exile, talking about the themes of reconciliation and brotherhood at the conference.

"Don't tell me you, too, are going to talk about this Zaldivar!" Pinochet interrupted. The Vatican representative replied that the Pope wanted to communicate his concern to Pinochet. "Don't say anything to me, Monsignor! This Mr. Zaldivar is not going to get back in, because he has said some very serious things. The government knows what it is doing," Pinochet said. As the two church officials got up to leave, Pinochet approached the cardinal, who had been the single most important human rights advocate under the regime.

"You know that this is an authoritarian government," he told the cardinal. "And I know you do not like authoritarian governments."

"That is so, General," the cardinal replied. "I do not like them."

"But authority comes from God, Cardinal," Pinochet said.

"Authority, yes. Authoritarianism comes from men," Silva Henriquez said.[19]

The November 4, 1980, edition of the Chilean government newspaper *La Nación* showed a cartoon of a snivelling Jimmy Carter being carried away in a wheelbarrow along with the baggage of his administration's "unfair treatment of Chile." There had been some cautionary signs that the Reagan administration might not be quite as friendly as regime officials had hoped. Roger Fontaine of the American Enterprise Institute had visited Santiago weeks before the U.S. election and drawn audible gasps from the staunchly proregime Chilean-American chamber of commerce when he said, "The situation in Chile does have me worried. There have been favorable developments [steps toward democratic transition] in Brazil and Argentina. I wish I could say the same about Chile."

But other American dignitaries were arriving in Santiago and praising the country's new order. At a press conference in Santiago in early November, David Rockefeller complimented the regime's economic team. When Tom Fenton, the bureau chief of the Associated Press, asked him what advice he would give a wage earner whose paycheck was eaten up by an inflation rate higher than the interest rate offered by most banks, Rockefeller replied that the wage earner should vote to elect officials who would improve the economy, "as the American people have done in voting for Ronald Reagan." Several Chilean reporters present reacted with immediate fury. "And what if you cannot vote?" they asked. Rockefeller hesitated, then quickly recovered from his faux pas: "That would be a problem for those countries to solve," he said.[20]

The Reagan administration quickly lifted some of the sanctions against Chile imposed by the Carter administration: Chile resumed participation in Operation Unitas, an annual series of joint naval maneuvers between the U.S. and Latin American countries, and financing by the U.S. Export-Import Bank was restored. These two measures, along with a reduction in personnel at the American embassy in Santiago, had been imposed in response to Chile's refusal to extradite the DINA chief, Manuel Contreras, and two other DINA agents in connection with the Letelier assassination. State Department officials said restoring Eximbank credits, which help finance purchases of U.S. goods overseas, would help American producers compete in Chile's booming market.

In February 1981 General Vernon Walters, the Reagan administration's polyglot special envoy, arrived in Santiago as part of a tour of several Latin American countries in search of support for U.S. policy in El Salvador. Officially, Walters's visit had nothing to do with U.S.-Chile relations, for he was carrying documents confirming Cuban and Soviet arms shipments to Salvadoran guerrillas. But the progovernment press, and even regime officials, viewed the visit as having much greater significance for bilateral relations. Much was made of the fact that Walters had met Pinochet before and had served as deputy director of the CIA shortly before Letelier was assassinated. As the agency's second-ranking official, he had contacts with other foreign intelligence agencies, including DINA, and had once met with Contreras during the DINA director's visit to Washington. Walters's background, and his visit to Santiago, were interpreted by many regime officials as a vindication of Chile's refusal to extradite Contreras and the other DINA agents. The foreign minister, René Rojas, who had replaced Hernán Cubillos following the Philippines debacle, even predicted that the U.S. arms embargo against Chile would be lifted soon— though such a move would require action by the U.S. Congress.

Even Eastern bloc countries seemed at times resigned to Pinochet's permanence in power, despite official rhetoric to the contrary. The former Soviet Union approached Chilean officials after the plebiscite to accept an offer to renegotiate $31.5 million in debts, mostly obligations contracted by the Frei and Allende governments. A statement by the Chilean central bank said it had reached the agreement on November 26, 1980, after negotiations with a Paris-based bank representing Soviet banking interests in Western Europe. East Germany opened a commercial office in Santiago, and according to the Chilean foreign ministry, the Soviet Union, Albania, Bulgaria, Poland, Hungary, and Czechoslovakia all made "sporadic" trade deals with Chile, while Romania and Yugoslavia maintained normal commercial relations with Santiago.[21]

The new constitution officially went into effect six months after the plebiscite, and on March 11, 1981, Pinochet held a ceremony in which he swore in air force commander Fernando Matthei, navy commander José Merino, and carabinero director César Mendoza in the junta members' new roles as legislators, along with General Raúl Benavides as the army's representative on the junta. Benavides was considered extremely loyal and unlikely to put forth any independent views: when Pinochet administered the oath, he enthusiastically shouted, "Yes, I swear, *mi general!*"[22]

After this ceremony Pinochet officially moved to the La Moneda presidential palace, whose restoration had dragged on since the coup, with serious work undertaken only after the constitutional plebiscite six months earlier. A door on the palace's east side, through which Salvador Allende's corpse had been carried, had been removed, and a special elevator to Pinochet's new offices on the second floor had been added. With a crowd of government supporters gathered below, Pinochet stepped out on the balcony last occupied by Allende and waved triumphantly.

That evening the regime held a reception at La Moneda. Diplomats invited to the gathering were startled to find no receiving line, as is the normal practice. Instead they were herded onto a chilly outdoor patio. Pinochet and his wife swept through the entrance to La Moneda without stopping to greet the assembled guests.

Part Two

Dictatorship's Demise

Chapter Six

Cracks in the Order

Not a leaf moves in this country if I am not moving it.
I want that to be clear!
— General Augusto Pinochet, October 1981

On March 10, 1981, employees at the Calama branch of Chile's state bank discovered that over $1 million was missing from the vault, and that a bank guard, Luis Martinez, and a teller, Sergio Yañez, had disappeared. A nationwide hunt for the two men and the money (part of which was destined for military payrolls in northern Chile) initially turned up no leads. Then, two months after the robbery, a civilian judge discovered the remains of two men off a road some thirty kilometers outside Calama. The remains were in small, scattered pieces, and it became evident that the two bank employees had been blown up with dynamite, probably by those who had stolen the money.

Just a few hours after the remains were discovered, the CNI, the intelligence organization that had succeeded the DINA, announced that two of its agents had committed the robbery and murder. According to the police group, Eduardo Villanueva, a CNI agent working in Calama, and Gabriel Hernández, the CNI's chief in Calama, had kidnapped the two bank employees, killed them, blown up their bodies with dynamite, and taken the money. The CNI quoted a confession from Villanueva, who said that Hernández had ordered him to kill the two men: "First I shot Martinez in the head. Then I moved in closer and aimed at Yañez. He asked me not to do it. He said, 'Please don't kill me.' Then he started praying—and I shot him."[1]

One can only speculate as to how the CNI obtained this confession; nevertheless these revelations caused a sensation in the Chilean press, and officials reported that Villanueva and Hernández had implicated other CNI agents as well. But the trail seemed to come to an abrupt end when the CNI chief in Arica, a city near the Peruvian border, was found dead in his car, with a bullet hole in his temple. Officials said Major Juan Delmas, who had disappeared two days earlier, had committed suicide, an explanation almost no one believed. No bullet had been found in the car when the police discovered the body, and Delmas's car looked remarkably clean for a vehicle parked for forty-eight hours in the Atacama desert.

CNI officials scrambled to produce explanations: a second search of the car turned up the missing bullet, and Delmas's car, they said, had been parked in a "crusty" area of the desert, where there was little ground dust and sand to be blown around. Villanueva and Hernández faced a firing squad several months later (though many Chileans suspected the two CNI agents were released and other prisoners executed in their place).

The Calama case allowed Chileans a rare, brief glimpse into the regime's security forces, and despite the truncated investigation and official cover-up, one Chilean magazine managed to interview Hernández, who charged that he and Villanueva were being "sacrificed" in order to protect officials higher up in the CNI echelons who had planned the bank heist. Their commanding officer had explained that the secret police organization was facing a financial crisis of sorts and cutbacks were threatening the security forces' operations. The expenses of CNI agents attached to Chilean embassies abroad would no longer be paid for by the regime's fiscal budget and would have to be absorbed by the CNI itself, the monthly budget for provincial operations had been halved, and a freeze on new hiring and transfers, "among other measures," had been imposed.[2]

The revelations of CNI involvement in blatantly criminal activity caused a considerable outcry, and human rights activists renewed their call for the CNI to be disbanded. The head of the Catholic Church's human rights department in Chile, Monsignor Juan de Castro, expressed satisfaction that such abuses had come to light. "This is the first time that the lid has been removed from the pot," he said. "Things are now seen as they really are."[3]

But if Delmas had been killed to prevent him from naming other CNI agents involved in the Calama bank robbery, the bloody cover-up had only begun. Four other men, all with ties to the CNI or to Delmas, died in strange circumstances over the next two years: the cadaver of a retired noncommissioned officer was found floating in the ocean, a CNI informant was discovered dead with a bullet in his forehead, a lieutenant who had worked with Delmas perished in an odd car accident, and Delmas's brother-in-law died in an apparent suicide.[4] The Calama case was an embarrassment for the regime, but it did not cause Pinochet to swerve from his hard-line tactics, and human rights groups in Chile began to report a new wave of repression.

The regime was troubled by what was happening in other Chilean banks—most notably the private financial institutions that had grown fat on a diet of international lending—and cracks were starting to appear in the Chicago Boys' version of laissez-faire capitalism. While the regime itself had cut public spending and improved tax collections to the point where it was able to enjoy a modest fiscal surplus, Chile's private-sector borrowing had boosted the country's foreign debt to the highest per-capita level in the region, according to the United Nations Economic Commission for Latin America. Central bank figures for 1981 indicate that while Chile's public-sector debt increased by just over $300 million, to $5.623 billion, the private-sector debt rose from $6.021 billion to $10.077 billion. But Chile's foreign creditors would not be willing or able to maintain this flow of credits into the country indefinitely.

In May 1981 executives from one of Chile's biggest food processing corporations, the Viña del Mar Sugar Refining Company (or CRAV, the Spanish acronym), announced they were shutting down the firm's operations, pending approval from the finance ministry. CRAV had attempted a multimillion-dollar sugar speculation that resulted in $70 million in losses during the first few months of the year. Subsequent examination of CRAV's records showed unpaid accounts of almost $100 million. Twenty-five banks had lent the company over $230 million without adequate guarantees. The outcry over the CRAV case caused a two-month suspension of foreign lending to Chile, even as the country's trade deficit increased fourfold, to $2.2 billion, during the first three quarters of the year. The regime began drafting a new banking law designed to prevent similar bankruptcies.

The liberalization of Chile's financial markets had allowed the country's private banks easy access to foreign loans, and in the late seventies business conglomerates, usually centered on a financial institution, underwent a major expansion. The conglomerates' flagship banks typically extended a good part of their credits to their own companies. The Cruzat-Larrain group accounted for 17.1 percent of all loans granted by the Chilean banking system and controlled three of the country's largest banks, including the Banco de Santiago (whose director was the former regime finance minister, Jorge Cauas), in addition to holdings in construction, agriculture, and industry. Its assets were valued at $1 billion, and its debt at $739 million. Another conglomerate, the BHC group, controlled the country's largest private bank, the Banco de Chile, and accounted for 24.9 percent of loans. Its assets were estimated at $520 million and its debts at $437 million.[5] Economic liberalization was supposed to produce economic diversification, yet the regime's policies, intentionally or not, led to a massive concentration of resources in the hands of a few business groups.

The decree established stricter guidelines for bank lending and gave greater enforcement powers to the government's banking overseers. Specifically, the law sought to reduce lending from banks to companies within the same business conglomerate, the kind of financial inbreeding that could trigger a dangerous chain of collapses if a single company went bankrupt. Chilean bankers, including some economists who had served on Pinochet's economic team, were quick to attack the new regulations. Alvaro Bardón, the central bank president who was educated at the University of Chicago, questioned the wider powers granted to the banking superintendency, as did Pablo Baraona, a former economy minister for the regime. Like former finance minister Jorge Cauas, both men had joined private banks after leaving the government. Javier Vial, a Chilean conglomerateur and president of the country's association of banks and financial institutions, called the new regulations "a black mark against the government." But foreign bankers in Santiago had a more jaded view of the practices of their Chilean counterparts. "I cannot tell you how many times we've turned down a loan request, only to learn a week later that the applicant had managed to get three offers from Chilean banks," an executive at an American bank in Santiago told me. Cronyism, and even outright corruption, seemed to pervade many Chilean lending institutions.

"A Chilean banker is under tremendous social pressure to grant loans to friends and relatives," a diplomat revealed in our interview. "That is something many foreigners fail to understand." From the time of the coup until mid-1981, according to central bank figures, Chilean financial institutions had borrowed over $5 billion. That many of these loans were wasted on imports of luxury goods and speculative business ventures did not seem to worry some Chilean economic officials, who all too often combined their free-market economic philosophy with an elitist arrogance toward their fellow Chileans and a rather ingenuous view of the world economy. "We really thought these lenders, who were very conscious of what they were doing and had great market experience, would monitor our institutions themselves," one official said. "They should not just expect the banks here to be monitored by the government."[6] The outside world, however, proved not to be as laissez-faire as the regime's economic team had envisioned.

The new banking regulations did not cause Chilean financial institutions to change their ways. On November 3, 1981, the regime seized administrative control of four banks and four finance companies, arrested two officials of one of the banks on charges of fraud, and prohibited seven other bank executives from leaving the country. The banking superintendency cited "administrative deficiencies" and other violations of the banking law, while the Chilean central bank (which under the regime's 1980 constitution was supposed to be downgraded into a less interventionist body similar to the U.S. Federal Reserve) stepped in to guarantee the deposits of banks and finance companies that were investigated. The Santiago stock exchange was ordered to halt trading of shares in the eight financial institutions seized, while policies issued by two insurance companies affiliated with one of the affected banks were canceled. Pinochet justified the tough actions, saying that even if they raised doubts about Chile's financial stability the measures were preferable to pretending that the problems did not exist. "He who breaks the rules will be punished," he warned.[7]

The regime also reacted swiftly to any sign of labor unrest. In June the Coordinadora Nacional Sindical, an umbrella organization of left-wing trade unionists, presented authorities with a petition signed by over four hundred labor groups. The petition carried thirty-one provisions, including a request for a 30 percent hike in the minimum wage to about $250 a month, increased union rights, protection for Chilean industry and jobs, and an end to political repression. Asked about the petition, Pinochet called the Coordinadora leaders communists, saying that "communists are not saints of my devotion." Police arrested the labor organization's two principal leaders—one of whom, Manuel Bustos, was a Christian Democrat—on charges of "misrepresentation of union activity," triggering protests from unions and labor leaders around the world, including Poland's Lech Walesa. The protests, of course, fell on deaf ears. Any effect they might have had was offset by the regime's improved relations with the United States, whose U.N. ambassador, Jeane Kirkpatrick, had visited Chile as part of a tour of South America.

Officially, Kirkpatrick met only with regime officials, although she did converse with Christian Democrats during a reception at the residence of the U.S. ambassador, George Landau. She described her discussions with Pinochet, whom she presented with a Steuben glass apple, as "most pleasant." "My conversation with the president had no other fundamental purpose than for me to propose to him my government's desire to fully normalize our relations with Chile, to have regular consultations with Chile, and to work with Chile in a variety of arenas: bilateral, regional, international," she said.

At the close of her trip, Kirkpatrick held a press conference at the Crowne Plaza Hotel, where U.S. embassy officials offered copies of her 1979 *Commentary* article, "Dictatorships and Double Standards." A reporter from Radio Cooperativa, a Christian Democrat–backed radio station, asked her what results the Reagan administration's "silent diplomacy" was having in Chile, given that in the past several months human rights groups had received reports of increasing numbers of abuses: two cases of torture in February, ten in March, and eleven in April. Kirkpatrick, somewhat angrily, interrupted to ask what was the question.

"The Reagan administration is as fully committed to human rights as any U.S. government has ever been," she said. "We believe that under the Carter administration the nations of Latin America were frequently singled out for discriminatory treatment, as though other governments in the world were democracies." Communism, and communist countries were the single biggest danger to individual freedoms in the world today, with the Soviet occupation of Afghanistan being perhaps the worst case of abuse, she said. Kirkpatrick also praised the regime's economic policies for controlling inflation and bringing about growth.[8]

The president of Chile's human rights commission, Jaime Castillo, and Fabiola Letelier, an attorney and the sister of the murdered exile leader Orlando Letelier, had unsuccessfully sought a meeting with Kirkpatrick during her visit and were instead offered an appointment with José Sorzano, ambassador to the U.N. Economic and Social Council. Sorzano did not show up at the meeting, although his wife— also a member of the U.S. United Nations delegation—and another Kirkpatrick staff member did arrive, along with a U.S. embassy political officer, Michael Durkee.

The two U.N. staffers did not participate actively in the meeting, according to Fabiola Letelier, but left that job to the U.S. embassy official. She and Jaime Castillo, who had spent months preparing an appeal of the Chilean supreme court's decision to reject the extradition of Manuel Contreras and two other DINA agents to the United States, presented their case to the Kirkpatrick staffers.[9] Asked about the Letelier case at her press conference, Kirkpatrick said she did not think that "outstanding questions" in the case would affect the normalization of U.S.-Chile relations.

Three days after Kirkpatrick left Chile, Jaime Castillo and three other Chilean opposition figures were arrested by agents of the regime's civilian detective police, Investigaciones, and transported to the Argentine border, where they were left without documents or personal belongings. The frontier was the site of considerable tension between the two countries. Only a few months earlier Argentine military authorities temporarily closed the 2,600-mile border after Chilean officials had arrested two Argentine army officers and announced they would be put on trial for espionage. So when Argentine border police saw the four men approaching their post from the Chilean side on foot, their suspicions were aroused and then heightened when the Chileans could not produce passports. After explaining their situation as best they could, and after the border officials had made several calls to their superiors, the four were allowed to pass through Argentina en route to political exile in other countries. "If you had shown even the slightest indication of being subversives, we would have shot you," one of the Argentine officials said to Castillo.[10]

Back in Santiago, regime officials announced the four men had been expelled for having "violated the political recess" in effect since the coup. The U.S. embassy was visibly embarrassed by the timing of the expulsions and made a point of being the first government to protest. Ambassador George Landau met with the Chilean foreign minister, René Rojas, on at least two occasions to discuss the expulsions and presumably to make known the displeasure of the United States. But given Pinochet's mindset and the structure of his regime, the decision to expel the dissidents was hardly made with any consideration of international relations. Kirkpatrick herself tried to ameliorate some of the damage by meeting with Castillo in New York a few weeks later. And then–vice president George Bush, who earlier had announced his intention to visit Chile at some unspecified date, pointedly did not include Santiago on a Latin American tour later in the year. If the Reagan administration indeed still sought a "full normalization" of U.S.-Chile relations, it was not going to involve any more visits to Santiago by cabinet-level officials.

On January 22, 1982, former president Eduardo Frei, one of the few surviving symbols of Chile's democratic past, died in a Santiago hospital at age seventy-one. Although the regime's propagandists had vilified Frei during the 1980 plebiscite, he was entitled to the honors customarily given to an ex-president, such as a state funeral attended by government dignitaries. Pinochet sent his condolences to Frei's family and indicated that he and other regime officials would attend the funeral.

Unfortunately for Pinochet, the funeral arrangements were made by two organizations he considered enemies of his regime: the Catholic Church and the Christian Democratic Party. Despite years of official suspension, persecution, and the exile of such leaders as Andrés Zaldivar and Jaime Castillo, Chile's Christian Democrats had managed to preserve enough of their organizational structure to fill the plaza outside the cathedral with thousands of supporters and put together a crowd-control network of young, arm-banded marshals.

When Pinochet arrived at the funeral he was forced to confront a mob of antigovernment mourners. Amid cries of "Murderer!" the scowling general climbed the steps of the cathedral and coldly greeted Frei's widow and family. The funeral was the first time Pinochet had had to face mass antigovernment sentiment.[11] "That crowd actually scared the regime," a diplomat who had attended the funeral services commented to me afterward. "There must have been at least one CNI agent in the crowd for every ten people, and still they shouted 'Murderer!'" Over thirty people were arrested during Frei's funeral.

A few weeks later I received a telephone call from an official at the Chilean state copper company, CODELCO, who spoke nervously in English, saying he had to speak to me urgently. Somewhat taken aback, I asked him what he wished to discuss. "Not on the phone!" he said. Intrigued as to why a regime official would be afraid of his own government's telephone tappers, I agreed to see him the next day at CODELCO headquarters in downtown Santiago. The official, a retired naval officer, growled that he wanted to discuss something I had recently written, and showed me a telex he had received from CODELCO's office in London. There had been a rumor in the London financial markets that Chile was about to devalue the peso, which had been set at thirty-nine to the U.S. dollar in 1979, and CODELCO officials were trying to determine how the rumor originated in order to kill it. They had decided an article I had published in the *Financial Times* describing Chile's deteriorating economic conditions was to blame. The article, which appeared February 18, 1982, ended with the following sentences: "Chilean officials fear that devaluation, while possibly aiding local producers, would spur inflation and undermine confidence in the economy. Yet if Chile's recession continues, the Pinochet regime may be forced to take some drastic steps such as this to prevent a further economic decline." The article had not even mentioned CODELCO, or the Chilean copper industry, and yet this official had taken it upon himself to call me on the carpet.

"But you know the president has said he will not devalue," the CODELCO official said, raising his index finger in the air. "Yes," I said, "and the article says this." The CODELCO official wanted to know the names of any sources I had who might have predicted there would be a devaluation. Forcing a smile, I said that many bankers and economists were forecasting this, and then attempted to change the subject by asking him a question about CODELCO. "You are looking at me with a saint's face," he said disgustedly, and I left.

This Chilean official, who seemed to believe economic forces could be controlled by a combination of censorship and intimidation, was not unlike many hard-liners in the regime, who were adopting even more rigid positions as the country's macroeconomic indicators deteriorated. The year-end figures for 1981 included the highest number of bankruptcies in nineteen years, a decline in industrial production of 8.1 percent, and a fall in copper exports of 23 percent due to declining prices (Chile's total exports fell by 18.4 percent). But imports continued to increase, with the largest jump in the category of consumer goods (22.6 percent). The cheap U.S. dollar encouraged imports, and a U.S. embassy economic report noted that speculation about devaluation of the peso only encouraged more imports.[12] Yet regime officials knew that this same speculative atmosphere would give way to inflation once the peso was devalued. The regime's economic team was understandably proud of having brought about a steady decline in consumer price inflation, which had reached the triple-digit level in the seventies. Now inflation had finally dipped down to the one-digit level, from 31.2 percent in 1980 to 9.5 percent the following year. It was important to the regime's sense of control that inflation, along with troublesome opposition and labor groups, be kept in check.

Tucapél Jiménez, president of Chile's public employees' union, ANEF, had worked as a taxi driver since losing his civil service job for backing the "No" vote against Pinochet and the new constitution in 1980. Although Jiménez had supported the coup and even traveled to Geneva to defend the new military regime at an International Labor Organization conference, he and other ANEF leaders had clashed with the regime over salaries, union rights, and general economic policy. The regime's civilian economic team had sought to overhaul the country's seemingly entrenched civil service, with mass firings and a new promotion system that did not sit well with ANEF leadership. And as relations with the regime deteriorated, the public employees union found itself the object of harassment and surveillance by Pinochet's security forces. At times, the surveillance was comically blatant.

"These guys would follow us everywhere, even stand directly in front of the window, just staring," recalled Hernol Flores, who succeeded Jiménez as ANEF president. "A few times we even went up to them and asked, 'If you're going to watch us, why don't you at least come inside and have a seat?' But they would say nothing, just continue to watch. They wanted us to know we were being watched."[13] Nevertheless, as head of a union with two hundred thousand members, Jiménez enjoyed a certain amount of influence.

The civilian economic team had recently unveiled an innovative new social security plan in which pensions were administered by private investment companies. Under the plan, employees contributed 10 percent of their income into individual retirement accounts managed by a private pension-fund company of their choice. Another 3 percent of income went to disability and life insurance; another 4 percent went to health insurance. These contributions were less than the paycheck deductions for social security under the state-run system and gave most employees slightly more take-home pay. The legal retirement age was raised to sixty-five years for men and sixty for women, and the government guaranteed a certain legal minimum pension if an employee's private retirement savings failed to reach that level. Beyond that minimum, however, the amount of retirement benefits depended upon how much the employee had contributed to his or her individual pension fund. Employees switching from the old state-run system to the new private pension plan received interest-bearing bonds in recognition of past pension contributions, and were allowed to switch from one private pension-fund company to another if they were displeased with the company's performance.[14]

The regime's economic team hoped the new social security plan would give Chileans a more personal stake in the country's economic performance and perhaps stimulate employment by slightly reducing the cost of social security. The new private pension-fund companies launched a massive advertising campaign designed to attract new participants; one cleverly made television commercial showed an elderly Chilean couple vacationing in Rio de Janeiro.

By the end of 1981 Chile's new private social security system had attracted over 1.5 million participants. But many Chilean labor leaders, even those who grudgingly switched over to the new system, were skeptical of letting the country's private sector manage pension funds, especially since most of the new pension-fund companies were affiliated with business conglomerates whose financial practices were being exposed as questionable at best. Critics also noted that Chile's armed forces were exempt from the private social security plan; under a military government such a policy hardly inspired confidence in the new system.

One of the new pension fund companies offered Tucapél Jiménez the equivalent of $150,000 to deposit his pension funds in the company and allow them to publicize his membership.[15] A private Santiago bank offered him a management job. Both offers were refused, for Jiménez was committed to his union work and had begun talks with other Chilean labor groups about ways to press for change in the regime's economic policies. He had made contact with the left-wing Coordinadora Nacional Sindical, with whom he had had serious differences in the past, and had met with former regime officials such as General Nicanor Díaz, the former labor minister, and General Gustavo Leigh, a former junta member and air force commander.

On February 18, 1982, Tucapél Jiménez publicly called for the formation of a national coalition to oppose the regime's economic policies. The following day *El Mercurio* printed a tiny item reporting that eight Chilean labor unions had supported his proposal. On February 25, Jiménez's taxi was stopped by at least three men who pointed a gun at his head and commandeered the vehicle to a back road on the outskirts of Santiago. Jiménez, the president of the Chilean public employees union, who had opposed the Allende government and had publicly defended the new military regime before a United Nations labor conference, was shot five times in the back of the head.

Publicly, the regime condemned the killing and promised a full investigation. At the same time, Interior Minister Sergio Fernandez warned that the government would not tolerate any political use of Jiménez's death. As if to underscore this warning, carabineros arrested about fifty people in the aftermath of the union leader's funeral.

The official investigation, not surprisingly, failed to identify the murderers. The regime's propagandists spread the rumor that Jiménez, who was married, had been killed over a domestic dispute involving another woman. But several months later Galvarino Ancavil, a computer programmer working for the Chilean army's armaments and explosives department, nervously approached the French embassy in Santiago and requested asylum. Two weeks before Jiménez was murdered, Ancavil had delivered two guns to the CNI, and one of them, a .22 revolver, had been used to kill the ANEF leader. Ancavil was sent to France early in 1983. Eight months later he was in the Paris Métro when he was accosted by CNI agents who offered him five hundred dollars, a plane ticket, and guarantees for his safety if he would simply return to Chile and keep his mouth shut. Ancavil did not accept the offer, but later testified before a French court, which questioned him in behalf of lawyers for the Jiménez family. Ancavil named four CNI agents, who in turn were interrogated by the Chilean judge investigating the Jiménez murder, but no legal action was taken against them.[16]

On July 12, 1983, Juan Alberto Mundaca, a thirty-three-year-old carpenter, was found hanged in his home in Valparaiso. A suicide note found in the room in Mundaca's handwriting confessed to the murder of Tucapél Jiménez. The note said that Mundaca had killed Jiménez while robbing him, and after learning the identity of his victim he was overcome with guilt.

Chile's progovernment press duly reported that the Tucapél Jiménez murder had been solved. But a subsequent investigation into Mundaca's death ruled that he had been murdered. His killers apparently had not been able to decide how the carpenter should commit suicide. His wrists had been slashed before his body was hanged, and the investigating magistrate determined that with the tendons in his wrists severed Mundaca would not have been able to grasp or lift anything, much less hang himself.[17]

The killing of Tucapél Jiménez may have eliminated one regime critic and frightened others into a temporary silence, but the economic crisis that produced the new wave of antiregime sentiment was worsening. The month after Jiménez was killed, the University of Chile's economics department reported that unemployment had reached 19.1 percent in greater Santiago and 18.4 percent nationally, not counting another 4.5 percent in the government work program for the unemployed. The visible signs of hard times were everywhere: at most major intersections motorists were approached by street vendors hawking fruit, candy, ballpoint pens, and other goods. The vendors displayed their wares on buses, jumping on quickly at bus stops and marching down the aisles waving their goods at the passengers before jumping out from the back door at the next stop. The numbers of buses and taxis circulating in the city had also multiplied, as out-of-work Chileans began working as drivers in a virtually unregulated public-transportation industry. In the center of Santiago over half the vehicles on the streets were taxis, while buses carrying as few as four or five passengers clogged the capital's main avenue, the Alameda. The city had a new, French-built underground railway that extended beneath the Alameda (a project begun under the Allende government), and the original planning called for bus routes to be confined to areas not served by the Metro. The regime's planning ministry, under the control of the Chicago Boys, had unsuccessfully argued against continuing such an ambitious public works project during a period of budgetary austerity, but succeeded in eliminating any controls on privately owned mass transit. As a result hundreds of roving taxis and nearly empty buses crowded the downtown streets.

Meanwhile, street vendors had virtually taken over the Paseo Ahumada pedestrian mall in downtown Santiago, spreading their goods on blankets, paper, or the bare ground along the walkway. Despite complaints from local store owners, Chile's carabineros made only token efforts to clear the walkway. They usually began a slow stroll at one end of the Paseo Ahumada, allowing the vendors to shout or whistle warnings to each other as the police approached, and to snatch up their wares before disappearing into the crowds of pedestrians.

The numbers of beggars also multiplied: women with babies, shabbily dressed men, older children, and the handicapped stood on street corners or in front of stores asking passersby for coins. Beggars were not unknown in Chile prior to this crisis, and many were professional panhandlers, like the singing blind woman positioned near the central bank whom I saw everytime I went downtown. She was a permanent fixture for all the nine years I was there, but now she was joined by hordes of the newly impoverished, like the thin youth who timidly approached when I carried a copy of *Time* and asked me, in fluent English, for "help to get something to eat."

On April 19, 1982, a noticeably strained-looking Pinochet appeared on television and announced he had asked his ministers to resign, with a reshuffled cabinet to be sworn in later. He reaffirmed the regime's commitment to its laissez-faire economic policy, and added that the Chilean peso would not be devalued. But Pinochet's statements were offset by his own worn appearance and the removal of Finance Minister Sergio de Castro, the University of Chicago–educated economist who had headed the regime's economic team. Although the new cabinet retained other free marketeers like Miguel Kast, assigned to head the central bank, the reshuffle was correctly interpreted as a sign of policy changes to come.

Within the regime Kast and other civilians argued against a devaluation of the peso, and urged that the problem of joblessness be tackled by either reducing or eliminating the minimum wage.[18] Given the fact that in real terms wages had only crawled back to 1971 levels the previous year, such a move would have been harsh indeed, and undoubtedly would have sparked more of the unrest that had begun. The dogged devotion of Kast and other Chicago Boys to the fixed exchange rate was rather odd, for a free exchange rate would have been more in keeping with their professed philosophy of economic freedom, and in fact some members of the economic team had urged the regime to adopt a sliding exchange rate back in 1976. But now devaluation would almost certainly trigger inflation and undermine confidence in the regime. The Chicago Boys were having some success in cutting back the country's trade deficit, with the central bank reducing the availability of relatively cheap foreign financing for imports and extending the coverage period for Chilean export financing. The central bank also heeded local manufacturers' complaints of unfair market competition from imported goods by agreeing to investigate cases of alleged dumping of foreign goods, or imports directly subsidized in their country of origin. The Chicago Boys could point to the latest monthly trade figures, which showed a near-balanced import-to-export ratio, arguing that their economic model contained self-correcting mechanisms. A reduction in the minimum wage, they maintained, would have allowed Chilean businesses to curb some of their losses through payroll cuts.

In the end, Pinochet opted for devaluation. On June 16, 1982, while the central bank president, Miguel Kast, was in West Germany telling bankers there that the Chilean peso would remain fixed at thirty-nine to the dollar, the cabinet's new economy minister, General Luis Danus, went on television and announced that the peso was to be devalued by 15.2 percent and periodically readjusted in relation to a basket of international currencies. General Danus said that other economic measures would be announced the following week, and that the devaluation had been revealed first in order to avoid speculation and a run on imports.

The announced devaluation surprised even some of the regime's civilian officials. One mid-level official in the economic ministry indicated to me that he had known nothing of the devaluation prior to General Danus's announcement. Miguel Kast, returning from Europe, tried to resign but was persuaded to stay on a few more months, despite his loss of professional credibility.[19] Less than eighteen months later, Kast, considered one of the economic team's best and brightest, died of cancer.

The devaluation exacerbated Chile's economic crisis, for the banks had extended dollar-denominated loans at interest rates lower than peso-denominated loans, and much of the domestic private-sector debt was in dollars. Thousands of borrowers had taken the regime at its word when Pinochet and other officials had insisted there would be no devaluation. Overnight, these borrowers saw their financial obligations increase as the Chilean peso kept sliding downward against the U.S. dollar. The central bank decreed new restrictions on the purchase of dollars for Chileans traveling abroad in an effort to stem the outflow of the country's foreign reserves, and within a year Chile had what to all practical purposes was a black market for U.S. dollars (officials called it the "parallel market"). Semi-clandestine exchange houses, offering rates far higher than the official bank rate of exchange, sprang up around Santiago. In the central business district, street hawkers touting favorable peso prices for dollars joined the crowds of sidewalk vendors, accosting any affluent or foreign-looking passerby and offering to change money. If interested, the hawker would negotiate a price for the amount of dollars offered, then accompany the customer to a small storefront office for the actual transaction, collecting a commission in the process. The seedy ambience of Chile's new parallel market contrasted sharply with the modern atmosphere of the country's banks during the boom period just a few years earlier.

Meanwhile, the Chilean banks' unpaid debt portfolios had swollen to nearly $1.5 billion, a figure representing more than half the financial system's capital and reserves. The outstanding debts had mounted as Chilean companies continued to go bankrupt, with 363 firms folding during the first six months of 1982 (compared with 206 bankruptcies during the same period the previous year). The twelve largest banks were the most vulnerable; the Banco de Chile had at least eleven major debtor companies who belonged to its parent conglomerate, the BHC group.

The central bank was forced to bail out the troubled Chilean private banks via a peculiar accounting exercise in which the institution purchased the banks' bad-debt portfolios in exchange for nontransferable bonds that would be paid back over ten years.[20] In exchange, the banks would have to reduce their lending to affiliated companies to 2.5 percent of their total loan portfolios within five years—which, authorities would later discover, was a goal too ambitious for many of the troubled banks to achieve.

The regime's response to the economic crisis had been delayed partly because any reactive measures would have been tantamount to admitting that its laissez-faire model had failed, that the free-market mechanisms that were supposed to automatically adjust disequilibria would not work in time to prevent the regime from losing crucial support in Chile's business community. But the crisis had already caused the regime's relationship with this sector to deteriorate, with Pinochet blaming some of the conglomerate owners for the crisis and business leaders criticizing the regime for its handling of it. Javier Vial, the U.S.-educated head of the Banco de Chile and its conglomerate, the BHC group, became a target of special hostility. Vial had survived the anti-business climate during the Allende government, which had tried to nationalize a mortgage bank he controlled and at one point had even tried to jail him. Since the coup Vial had built up a business empire employing twenty thousand people and encompassing fifty companies, several of which had been purchased cheaply from the military regime when it denationalized private companies taken over by the Allende government. Now, under the shadow of a tattered free market, Vial was feeling a cold wind from the regime, which had issued an indirect warning that he could be expelled from the country if he continued to make negative predictions about Chile's economic performance.

Vial had balked at signing an agreement to transfer his banks' bad-debt portfolios over to the central bank, which would have allowed the entity to oversee much of his business empire's operations and curtailed his efforts to prop up ailing BHC-affiliated companies. In addition, the regime wanted him to resign from the Banco de Chile and separate the financial institution from the rest of the BHC conglomerate.

Official efforts to seize the assets of bankrupt companies were often met with fierce resistance from owners and labor alike, who at times forged alliances. In Valdivia, a port city in southern Chile, hundreds of protestors surrounded a bankrupt factory in a successful effort to keep it from being sold; the auctioneer arrived to find the door barred and a Chilean flag draped over the entrance.[21] Pinochet began to realize that Chilean capitalists could be almost as threatening to his regime as Marxists were. "I have been too soft, I should have expelled from the country one hundred to two hundred people who raised empires on paper," he said in a not-so-subtle allusion to the heads of Chile's conglomerates. Javier Vial was not deported in the end, but later faced charges that a Panama-based financial institution owned by the conglomerate, the Banco Andino, had illegally channeled funds to BHC companies.[22]

After replacing the finance minister, Sergio de Castro, with another University of Chicago–trained economist, Pinochet felt compelled four months later, as the economic crisis deepened, to change finance ministers once again. In August 1982, Rolf Lüders, a former executive with the BHC group, joined the government as "biminister" of finance and economy. On January 10, 1983, Lüders, who was considered more pragmatic and less rigidly orthodox than his predecessors in his economic views, announced that Chile had reached a two-year standby agreement with the International Monetary Fund. A few days later the regime seized administrative control of, or "intervened" in, five more banks, including the Banco de Chile. The regime also announced it was liquidating three other banks and was placing two other financial institutions under tighter official supervision. The move gave the regime control of 80 percent of Chile's financial sector, and given the tight relationship between the banks and their affiliate companies, the interventions gave the regime a greater degree of control over the country's economy than the Allende government had ever had.[23]

It was not the sort of control Pinochet had ever wanted, however, and the regime tried a number of measures to heal the ailing banks and companies in order to turn them back over to private management. These included sizeable subsidies to the banks and largest corporations, a more favorable exchange rate for borrowers with dollar-denominated loans, and central bank incentives to convert these same dollar loans into pesos. Between 1982 and 1985 the regime was forced to spend an estimated $7 billion on such programs. Worst of all, Chile's international creditors forced the regime to take responsibility for the private sector's debt, in view of the fact that Chilean officials were now administering much of this sector's holdings.[24] The IMF and other international financial institutions recommended to other Latin American debtor nations the kinds of free-market reforms the Pinochet regime had carried out years earlier in Chile: reducing the budget deficit, denationalizing state companies, and stimulating private investment. And yet Chile's private sector was largely responsible for the crisis. What had gone wrong? According to Carlos Cáceres, a former central bank president who later became the regime's finance minister, the economic team failed to recognize the extent of the international recession. If it had, it might have adjusted the exchange rate earlier.[25]

A different view is offered by Fernando Dahse, a Chilean sociologist who studied the rise of the country's conglomerates. According to Dahse, the failure of the regime's economic model had a distinctively cultural origin. "We Latins have a tendency to want to make a lot of money in the shortest time possible," he said. "The search for quick gains is very ingrained in the Latin American business executive. When they imposed this free-market model, the regime's economic team thought that Chilean businessmen would behave in the way British, American, or West German businessmen do."[26] Yet so many executives in the conglomerates had held posts in the regime's economic team that they could be said to have designed the very system they abused: Sergio de Castro was a board member on the Banco Andino, as was Boris Blanco, the head of the regime's banking superintendency, who was later jailed for the Banco Andino's illegal funneling of

funds to BHC companies. Rolf Lüders, the former BHC group executive, served as the regime's "biminister" of economy and finance for
five short months, and joined Boris Blanco and BHC president Javier
Vial in prison for his involvement with the Banco Andino's illegal activities. Viewed from a distance, the Chicago Boys and the business
and banking conglomerates their policies helped to create look a bit
like a pyramid scheme, with foreign banks playing the role of the gull-
ible investors. But the foreign banks were not willing simply to write
off their losses; they used their considerable leverage to get the regime to assume responsibility. The outside world turned out not to be
as laissez-faire as the economic team may have imagined.

At the same time, the economic changes brought about by the Chicago Boys never produced a completely free-market economic system
in Chile. The largest economic producer in the country, CODELCO,
remained in government hands as a strategic industry, despite efforts
by many civilian economists to convince Pinochet to privatize it.
CODELCO controlled Chile's four largest copper mines, and although it was relatively well managed for a Latin American state company, it was also, in the words of one foreign analyst, the "military's
cash cow."

Claudia Rosett, an economist who studied the Chicago Boys' policies while residing in Santiago in 1981–82, noted that the secretive
nature of the military regime made it difficult for investors to obtain
the political and economic information they needed to make decisions.[27] Censorship and other forms of political repression create a climate of uncertainty and do not help an economy to thrive.

Chapter Seven

Days of Rage

*The government is not going to open up for anyone, espe-
cially not in these times, because when Rome was facing
danger it looked for a man to rule it, when Rome had a
problem, when it had to confront enemy legions, they
looked for a single government to push things ahead without utopian discussions that did not lead to anything.*
— General Augusto Pinochet, December 7, 1982

In early 1983 Santiago, which normally is quiet during the southern
hemisphere's summer, was awash with rumors. Pinochet had announced that the economic crisis was too serious for him to take his
customary vacation that year, only to leave a few days later for Bu-
calemú, a resort southwest of the capital where he usually spent his
summer holidays. After several days during which Pinochet had not
been seen or even indirectly generated any government activity (such
as receiving other Chilean officials who would speak to the press afterward), rumors began to fly. The Chilean dictator was said to have
died, to have been placed under house arrest by the military, or to be
recovering from an assassination attempt.

The rumors reached Chilean exile communities abroad, and in
Washington a State Department spokesman could "neither confirm
nor deny" that a coup against Pinochet had taken place. I received at
least three calls from editors anxious to know if a coup had occurred.
Wasn't it possible, one of them asked me, that a coup could have happened without my knowing about it?—as if the overthrow of a dictator
could be accomplished so noiselessly.

The rumors, which contained an obvious element of wishful thinking, were unfounded. But their very existence demonstrated the climate of confusion within the regime at the time. A few weeks before
Christmas, Chilean authorities had deported three men arrested at

two separate "unauthorized" assemblies. Two of the deportees were trade union leaders, but the third was the avowedly anti-communist president of Chile's wheat producers' association, Carlos Podlech, who was detained, along with two sons and twelve others, when a group of farm, business, and labor leaders attempted to have a meeting in the southern agricultural town of Temuco. Shortly after Podlech's expulsion, two Temuco radio stations that had aired a commentary describing Chilean bankers as "usurers" were ordered to restrict their programming to music.[1] The regime's clampdown in a right-wing stronghold like Temuco disturbed regime supporters as well as some officials within the government.

On Valentine's Day, Pinochet reshuffled his cabinet for the third time in ten months. The new finance minister, Carlos Cáceres, who had been serving as central bank president, announced a new package of measures to reactivate the economy and provide for the renegotiation of $3.5 billion in foreign debt due that year and in 1984. The measures also included a rescheduling plan for domestic debtors whose obligations in dollar-denominated loans had swollen as the peso was devalued, some modifications in the sliding exchange rate, and a temporary hike in import tariffs from 10 to 20 percent. The Chilean business community, which had been urging a higher tariff increase than the one the regime adopted, reacted in a lukewarm manner, while middle-class anger and discontent continued to increase.

Among the victims of Chile's banking crisis were 130,000 people who had invested in mutual funds controlled by conglomerates such as the BHC group. When the Chilean banking superintendency took administrative control of the conglomerates' flagship banks, all accounts, including those of the mutual funds companies, were frozen. As a result, the funds' capital and reserves had fallen by 71 percent; those account holders who managed to withdraw their funds faced losses ranging from one-half to two-thirds their original investment.[2]

If middle-class Chile was hurting, the country's poor were worse off than ever. The government's statistical institute reported a 4 percent decline in the official unemployment figure, to 20.8 percent, but enrollment in the regime's work projects for the unemployed had risen to nearly 13 percent of the labor force, meaning that joblessness now affected one-third of the Chilean work force. Official figures also showed that those fortunate enough to have jobs saw their earnings fall by 16 percent over the previous year. Meanwhile, Chilean trade unions were questioning the official consumer price inflation calculations, arguing that poor families usually purchased fewer than 60 of the 348 items used in determining the monthly inflation figure, and that prices for typical purchases made by the poor had risen faster than the official figures suggested.

Against this background of political uncertainty and economic hard times, Chileans were criticizing the regime more openly than they had dared to in the past. A "march against hunger" called by left-wing labor and community groups in March attracted thousands of demonstrators who paraded through the streets of downtown Santiago, braving the carabineros' tear gas and water cannons. At least 250 people were arrested.

"The government is watching the Church and the labor unions like a hawk," a diplomat in Santiago commented to me after the march. Officials abruptly revoked the residency visas of three foreign priests—two Irish and one Australian—who were working in poor neighborhoods in Santiago, accusing them of running "politically oriented" soup kitchens. But repression could not eradicate the causes of the new surge of discontent, and leaders of the Christian Democrats and other parties saw an opportunity to restore their political organizations.

Since the parties were still officially "in recess," Chilean politicians had to work around regime restrictions, sometimes organizing purportedly nonpartisan civic entities. A group calling itself the Project for National Development (PRODEN) was among the first to emerge, with two former Christian Democratic parliamentarians, a trade unionist, and a senior citizens' activist among its leaders. PRODEN began holding press conferences to comment on regime activities, and boldly presented a proposal calling on the junta to assume executive power and to hold elections for a unicameral congress within six months. The group also sent letters to the four junta members— the navy commander, Admiral José Merino, the air force commander, General Fernando Matthei, the carabinero director, General César Mendoza, and the army's representative, General Raúl Benavides— requesting a meeting to discuss Chile's economic crisis and alternatives to the lengthy transition period stipulated by the 1980 constitution.

The junta's public response to PRODEN was a stony silence, but the fact that the regime, burdened with the financial crisis, did not try to crush the group encouraged more politicians to reemerge. On March 15 leaders of five political organizations ranging from socialist to rightist signed a statement called the Democratic Manifesto, announcing their intention to work together to promote a return to democracy. The manifesto's signers later officially formed a coalition, the Alianza Democrática, which publicly urged that Pinochet leave office.[3]

Meanwhile, Chile's most powerful labor union, the 23,000-member Copper-Mine Workers' Confederation, representing employees at CODELCO's four mines, elected a new president, Rodolfo Seguel. Seguel, a clerk at the El Teniente mine south of the capital, had been a compromise candidate during the union voting and perhaps more than any other Chilean opposition figure came to represent the anti-Pinochet movement that year.

Seguel had not always opposed the regime; he had in fact applauded the coup in 1973, volunteering to help with the distribution of foodstuffs by the military and right-wing groups after the takeover. "I didn't like the Allende government, especially the effect it was having on Chilean youth. Allende's Popular Unity government was holding courses in martial arts and the use of firearms," he told me in an interview. "There was so much violence. When the military first took over I was very happy. My boss at the time was a supporter of the Popular Unity government and fired me." He began working at El Teniente the following year, where he said he began to understand the significance of the regime's restrictions on labor rights. By 1976 he was "actively critical" of the regime.[4]

After his election as president of the Copper-Mine Workers' Confederation, Seguel joined the Christian Democrats, a move that linked Chile's largest political party with the country's biggest trade union. The copper-mine workers were urging a nationwide antigovernment strike, something the Alianza Democrática coalition and other labor groups sympathized with in principle but doubted would work. A compromise was reached: a national day of protest, on May 11, 1983, during which Chileans would be called on to leave their jobs early, keep their children out of school, refrain from making any purchases, and most important, to bang pots and pans at 8 P.M. in protest against the regime. The pots-and-pans protests, used before the coup by anti-Allende demonstrators, would be especially compelling used against the military regime.

The Copper-Mine Workers' Confederation issued a communiqué saying it was withdrawing its earlier call for a general strike because of implied threats of violence and the presence of army tanks in the mining centers. Neither the communiqué nor the call for the day of protest appeared in *El Mercurio* or other progovernment newspapers, which had received discreet telephone calls from regime officials suggesting the statements not be printed. But the Christian Democrats' radio station, Radio Cooperativa, whose listener ratings were among the highest in the country, broadcast the call.

On the morning of Wednesday, May 11, 1983, residents of the low-income neighborhoods ringing the capital found that fewer buses were running and proceeded to walk to work, some leaving before sunrise in order to arrive at their factory jobs on time. Traffic throughout Santiago was light, and carabineros patrolled the streets on foot with police dogs and Uzi submachine guns. Several schools closed; others reported absentee rates of 30 to 50 percent as Chileans kept their children home either in support of the protest or out of fear of violence. There were sit-ins on university campuses, and in the afternoon many businesses and stores in the center of Santiago began closing early to allow their employees to travel home on the reduced number of buses in service.

By nightfall the atmosphere in much of Santiago was one of subdued tension, with both regime authorities and protest organizers uncertain as to how many Chileans would dare to beat pots and pans. But at 8 P.M. the sounds of beating saucepans began, often with one timid metallic sound in an apartment high-rise followed by a cacophony of noisy banging as neighbors joined the protest. Bolder middle-class Chileans climbed into their automobiles and drove through the streets honking their horns. Carabineros tried to break up the carnivalesque demonstrations, firing tear gas canisters at some apartment buildings where the protests were loudest. In upper-middle-class areas of eastern Santiago, they dragged several drivers from their honking cars and clubbed them.[5]

In Santiago's poorer neighborhoods, youths erected barricades of trash, tree branches, and debris and set them on fire, while other residents stayed indoors. Witnesses reported seeing police and men in civilian dress fire indiscriminately at crowds of protesters from passing automobiles. Two Chileans were killed that night: a twenty-two-year-old taxi driver who was shot in the temple when he stepped outside his house following a cut in electrical power, and a fifteen-year-old boy killed by shots fired from a yellow truck. The following day Chile's detective police force, Investigaciones, said two of its agents had been arrested in connection with the latter shooting, but were later released because of a lack of evidence.

Over six hundred people were arrested that night, with about half released without charges. Rodolfo Seguel and nine other leaders of the Copper-Mine Workers' Confederation were charged with violating Chile's state security law, which carried penalties ranging from 541 days to five years internal exile or deportation. CODELCO, acting at the behest of the Chilean interior ministry, sought the removal of sixteen mineworker leaders from their trade union posts, accusing them of having violated the regime's labor code in organizing the protest. Authorities also ordered Radio Cooperativa to halt its news broadcasts indefinitely; a statement by the regime's communications agency, DINACOS, charged that the radio station had contributed to an "artificial climate of agitation and public effervescence" in its coverage of the protests.

The government newspaper, *La Nación*, barely referred to the protest, with an article in its May 13, 1983, edition headlined, "Workers Demonstrate That They Don't Want Politics." But *El Mercurio*, a regime backer, urged the authorities to take the protest seriously, saying that the events of May 11 "constituted the most serious challenge the government has faced in its almost ten years of existence." Noting that Seguel and other opposition leaders were planning a day of protest each month, the editorial warned that the regime faced difficult times ahead, and urged that the authorities look for ways to "resolve the social tensions and walk peacefully toward institutional goals."[6]

But resolving social tension was not something Pinochet had the skills to do, even if he possessed the inclination. It is interesting to examine his reaction to the protests in light of his past experiences. When the first "empty pots" protests began under Allende in 1971, Pinochet was commander of the Santiago army garrison. While the breaking up of demonstrations during this period was handled by carabineros, not the Chilean army, it is almost certain that Pinochet viewed protesters of any ideological bent as disruptive elements, possibly believing the Allende government was being too soft.

Since that time he had played down his early collaboration with the Allende government and reacted negatively, even violently, to any reminders of this past. Saucepan banging was a reminder, and in launching a crackdown Pinochet the military man was attempting to crush a movement that threatened him in more ways than one. At a meeting of cabinet ministers and senior military officials after the first protest, he delivered a furious speech against the political leaders involved in the protest and said that a Soviet-inspired plan to damage the regime's image was afoot.[7]

At daybreak on Saturday, May 14, troops from the Santiago army garrison cordoned off five of the capital's largest slums and ordered all the men and teenage boys to line up in soccer fields for questioning and identity checks. The soldiers also made house-to-house searches for weapons and any material that could be considered subversive, often destroying property in the process. Although most of the thousands of men detained in the roundups were released, the massive military operation terrified those who remembered the 1973 coup's violent aftermath.

Seguel and the other labor leaders, unintimidated by the regime's crackdown, went ahead with plans for a second protest on June 14. Although Chilean officials attempted to undercut the demonstrations by forbidding the news media from reporting on "illegal acts," this second protest produced a far greater response in provincial cities and towns than the May 11 protest had. Three people were killed and hundreds arrested, including Seguel, who had been staying in Santiago at the home of another Chilean labor leader when approximately one hundred security agents surrounded the house.

"At around 1:30 A.M. they broke the door down, dragged me out of bed, and drove me away in an automobile," he said. "I recall thinking I was going to be either killed or deported."[8] Seguel's arrest prompted labor leaders and PRODEN to call for a national strike July 12. The momentum was building, and the regime's security forces redoubled their efforts to thwart the protest, sometimes with comic results.

In late June a youth in the town of Villa Alemana, west of Santiago, claimed to have had a vision of the Virgin Mary, who, he said, had promised to speak through him again within the next few days. After attracting a crowd of would-be adherents, eighteen-year-old Miguel Angel Poblete had another "vision," in which the Virgin Mary was said to be bothered by the sound of pots and pans beating and issued warnings against protests and the aims of priests and the Catholic Church. The Chilean Church hierarchy conducted an inquiry into the youth's claims and concluded that there was no evidence of any miraculous apparitions. Nevertheless, Poblete and his followers continued their vigil for months before interest finally subsided.

A few days before the July 12 strike, I returned from a press conference held at the Copper-Mine Workers' Confederation headquarters with Raúl Montecinos, an Argentine cameraman, and Jorge Casals, an Uruguayan sound technician on assignment for ABC News. When our taxi pulled up in front of the Hotel Carrera, two men—who had evidently been ordered to go after foreign journalists—accosted Montecinos as he stepped out of the car and began haranguing him in English.

"You are telling lies about Chile! Let us see your press credential," they said to Montecinos, who spoke almost no English. "Come—we will take you to the police." When Casals climbed out of the taxi one of the security agents glanced at him, then asked Montecinos, "You are here with this Italian boy?" As the last to get out of the taxi I could overhear what was happening and broke in, saying that Casals and Montecinos did not speak much English, and asking if I could help. The two men looked confused, and quickly left. A Hotel Carrera doorman later told us the two men had been loitering around the entrance for some time before we arrived.

As a work stoppage the July 12 national strike was unsuccessful, especially in the copper mines, where a strong military presence and the threat of dismissal kept many workers from joining in. When I visited El Teniente that day, CODELCO officials were quick to offer a tour of the facilities in order to prove that normal operations were under way. But trucks of soldiers and armored tanks were driving up the hill toward the entrance to the mine and the foundry by late afternoon, about when second shift workers were due to arrive. Back in Santiago, authorities ordered a curfew from 8 P.M. until midnight, but once again the sound of clanging pots and pans rang out. Two youths were killed by gunfire.

The following month's protest, on August 11, was the bloodiest yet, with Pinochet announcing he had eighteen thousand soldiers ready to protect the capital. The precise number of army troops dispatched that day is not known, but almost certainly there were thousands, including soldiers moved to Santiago from other army bases around the country. Soldiers wearing the light-colored uniforms of regiments from the Atacama desert in northern Chile were positioned on bridges across the Mapocho River.

Trucks of army troops began moving into the center of the capital by early afternoon, after carabineros in full riot gear and armed with tear gas and water cannons broke up a demonstration organized by university students. The curfew was extended, beginning at 6:30 P.M. for two consecutive nights, and the death toll exceeded that of the first three protests combined: twenty-six dead, including several people who were killed inside their own homes by bullets penetrating the walls.

The day before the August protest Pinochet reshuffled his cabinet yet again, bringing in as his new interior minister and cabinet chief Sergio Jarpa, a former leader of the right-wing National Party who had been serving as Chile's ambassador to Argentina. Jarpa, who knew the leaders of the Alianza Democrática from his career as a member of the Chilean senate prior to the 1973 coup, thought that a dialogue could be arranged to defuse the tensions that threatened to tear the country apart.

Jarpa sought and received support from Santiago's newly appointed archbishop, Cardinal Juan Fresno, a conservative who, much to the delight of Pinochet and regime hard-liners, had just replaced Raúl Silva Henriquez, a dedicated human rights advocate and regime critic. He also sufficiently impressed U.S. ambassador James Theberge, a conservative academic and Reagan appointee who had arrived in Santiago the previous year.[9] Theberge, according to several political sources, was instrumental in encouraging Alianza Democrática leaders to accept Jarpa's offer of dialogue, despite their misgivings over the regime's intentions and the suspicion—which turned out to be well-founded—that Jarpa's overtures and even his appointment to the cabinet was an attempt by Pinochet to defuse the protest movement.

But the opposition movement was having problems of its own. The number of people killed during the August 11 protest disturbed many organizers, who felt at least indirectly responsible for the violence unleashed against the protesters by the military. The Chilean Communist Party, which had silently backed the protests and was still strong in low-income areas of the capital, now wanted to participate directly in the planning, especially in drawing up instructions to the public. The Alianza Democrática leaders, several of whom had been jailed briefly on charges of printing pamphlets and fliers for the protests, balked at this; the communists then began distributing their own instructions. The protest movement began to lose some of its cohesiveness.

On August 25, Cardinal Fresno hosted the first meeting between the Alianza Democrática and the regime's new interior minister. The opposition leaders brought a full agenda of concessions they were seeking: Pinochet's removal, restoration of civil liberties, and an accelerated transition to civilian democracy. The first item was rejected outright, but Jarpa could offer hope for the second and third proposals.[10] A date was set for a second meeting, and the following day, as a first gesture of political *apertura*, the state of emergency was lifted. Although Pinochet still retained broad discretionary powers under article 24 of the 1980 constitution, the end of the state of emergency did give the impression of a somewhat less restrictive regime.

Authorities also released a list of 1,600 Chilean exiles who would now be allowed to return, including Christian Democratic leader Andrés Zaldivar and the human rights commission president, Jaime Castillo, who were met by hundreds of supporters at the airport. The ending of the state of emergency also allowed Chilean book publishers to circulate new titles without having to first secure permission from the interior ministry, and dozens of new books, including some by former political prisoners describing their torture by the military, began appearing in bookstores. The protests, it was clear, had forced the regime to loosen the reins, and while new clampdowns would occur from time to time it would prove increasingly difficult to make new restrictions stick.

General Carol Urzua, military governor of Santiago, left his house in eastern Santiago with his driver and bodyguard at 8:30 A.M., August 30, when five people in a passing truck opened fire. Urzua and his two aides were killed as almost sixty bullets were discharged into his automobile, and his assassins, members of the Movement of the Revolutionary Left (MIR) guerrilla group, fled. Why they had targeted General Urzua is something of a mystery, for he had never been fingered as one of the regime officials responsible for interrogating prisoners or having been involved in other forms of political repression. But Urzua, as military governor, was an easily identifiable target and the MIR appeared to have selected him purely on the basis of his accessibility.[11]

The MIR had planned this assassination for months, and the timing was not necessarily intended to sabotage the Jarpa–Alianza Democrática dialogue. Pinochet, upon hearing the news of Urzua's killing, had immediately wanted to declare a state of siege and was only dissuaded from doing so by Jarpa and other cabinet members.[12] The next morning, as a demonstration of the regime's new openness, a group of foreign correspondents was invited to a breakfast at La Moneda with Alfonso Márquez de la Plata, who had just been appointed the regime's spokesman. I asked if the government was considering any special measures in the wake of the Urzua assassination, and the minister was quick to say no. "That is just what they [the MIR] would want us to do," he said.

The MIR organization had been seriously damaged after the 1973 coup, and most of its surviving members had fled into exile abroad. From the mid- to late seventies, according to an internal memorandum prepared by the carabineros intelligence department, fewer than fifty MIR members remained in Chile. But by 1980 the guerrilla group was beginning to rebuild itself, with its military wing surpassing its political organization.[13] That year the MIR shot and killed a young policeman standing guard over a monument commemorating the coup and also claimed responsibility for a series of bank and supermarket robberies. The killing of General Urzua, however, was the most serious attack the MIR had committed under the regime, and retribution came swiftly: on September 7, 1983, the CNI announced that five MIR members had been killed in two separate shootouts with authorities in Santiago.

Two days earlier the Alianza Democrática had its second meeting with Interior Minister Sergio Jarpa, and urged once again that

Pinochet's term in office be shortened and that the CNI be disbanded. Jarpa defended the security organization and said that in the coming year electoral registries might be opened and a law governing political parties could go into effect. These last two measures were under study by a regime advisory body, the Council of State, which perhaps some of the opposition leaders would consider joining? The Alianza Democrática members demurred, and the discussion turned to the protest planned for the next month.

The September 8 protest would be peaceful, both sides agreed. There would be no curfew and no army troops, only carabineros in charge of keeping order. The discussion ended on an optimistic note, and a date was set for a third meeting.

But when demonstrators gathered that day in a plaza in eastern Santiago to hear speeches by opposition leaders, carabineros almost immediately moved to break up the gathering, firing dozens of tear-gas canisters and spraying the crowd with water cannons. Genaro Arriagada, a Christian Democrat who was to address the gathering, was dragged on the ground and beaten by carabineros. The following day the Alianza Democrática, furious at the way police had treated the demonstrators, announced they would not meet again with Jarpa until the regime made its itinerary clear.

Pinochet and his supporters, meanwhile, were about to celebrate the regime's ten years in power. While carabineros were breaking up the opposition gathering, Pinochet was being declared an "illustrious son" by the Santiago municipality and awarded a medallion by the city's mayor on a balcony overlooking the Plaza de Armas. "Have you ever seen anything so ridiculous?" an elderly man in the crowd asked me.

The regime also held a massive parade for itself that evening, organized in part by a new progovernment party, the Avanzada Nacional, which was formed by CNI officials and collaborators. The Avanzada Nacional printed thousands of posters bearing Pinochet's image and distributed them to government employees and jobless Chileans enrolled in government work projects who were forced to take part in the parade.[14] But the progovernment demonstration, despite its composition, lasted for hours as group after group of supporters paraded past the grandstand where Pinochet and the three other military commanders stood watching, and boosted the regime's spirits.

At the end of the month the Alianza Democrática, reneging on their earlier statement that they were suspending the dialogue with the government, met once again with Jarpa and presented proposals for a new commission to study political reforms, an emergency economic program, and an end to the regime hard-liners' attacks on opposition politicians. Jarpa accepted their document for further study, but the dialogue was about to end: on October 2, 1983, Pinochet delivered an improvised speech in which he attacked the country's politicians and warned that "whatever it costs, the constitution will not be altered." Politicians, he said, "could just keep on conversing."[15] Pinochet's statements, with their indirect allusion to Jarpa, seemed to undercut his cabinet chief's efforts and confirmed suspicions in many quarters that the Jarpa–Alianza Democrática dialogue had been nothing more than a maneuver to distract opposition leaders. Yet Jarpa must have believed he had some backing from Pinochet for the talks when he first approached the opposition leaders.

On October 11, a sixth day of protest against the regime was organized, this time not by labor groups or the Alianza Democrática but by a new left-wing coalition, the Movimiento Democrático Popular (MDP), whose leadership included Communist Party members and the more radical wing of the Chilean Socialist party. Participation in this protest was markedly diminished in many middle-class neighborhoods, where the momentum was ebbing as opposition leaders appeared divided and confused over what course to follow. But six people were killed in violent incidents in poor and working-class areas, including a carabinero shot with his own weapon.

The summer months brought an uneasy calm to the country, and no new protests were attempted until the following March. Within the regime, however, tensions were building. The construction of a twelve-million-dollar presidential residence, ostensibly to house future Chilean heads of state as well as Pinochet, had been leaked to the press, and even regime supporters questioned the judgment behind such a project when the country was strapped for funds and renegotiating its foreign debt.[16]

Although in the nineteenth century the La Moneda presidential palace had housed Chilean heads of state and their families, in more recent years presidents had lived in their own private homes. An engineer who had inspected the building site told me that flooding problems caused by the construction of three subterranean floors were driving up the costs of the project, which Pinochet's wife was supervising personally. The house, located in a wealthy hill neighborhood in eastern Santiago, included an Olympic-sized swimming pool, two tennis courts, and a heliport. It was completed a few months later but never occupied after security experts determined that the residence was vulnerable to attack from the surrounding mountains.

There were other, equally uncomfortable reports surfacing in the Chilean press concerning the business dealings of Pinochet's son-in-law, Julio Ponce Lerou, who had served on the boards of several Chilean state companies that were being privatized and had ended up with sizeable share holdings.[17] Pinochet's oldest daughter, Lucía, had an insurance company of mysterious background while his oldest son, Augusto, officially an employee of the LAN-Chile airline office in Los Angeles, had been involved in a number of questionable business transactions. These included using his influence to convince CODELCO to sell 12,000 tons of copper to Westinghouse Corporation in 1985, a deal brokered by a small U.S.-based company with which he was associated and not by the sales agent CODELCO normally used.[18] "This is part of the left wing's campaign against me," he told *Newsweek's* diplomatic correspondent, Patricia Sethi. "It is so low that I don't even want to credit it with a reply. How do you answer calumny?"[19]

The white-elephant mansion could perhaps be explained away as bad judgment, and the dubious business dealings of his children and son-in-law might have been brushed aside as not Pinochet's direct responsibility. But another set of revelations was threatening to emerge, with more serious consequences for Pinochet's standing.

On March 20, 1984, Jorge Lavandero, a Christian Democrat and the leader of PRODEN, was forced to the side of the road by four vehicles whose occupants dragged him out of his car, beat him unconscious, and stole a folder of documents he was carrying. The documents showed that Pinochet had acquired a thirteen-hectare property outside Santiago from the regime at a fraction of the price the government had paid for it, using an army lieutenant colonel as his purchasing agent.

The attack left Lavandero deaf in one ear and unable to walk without a cane. The interior minister, Sergio Jarpa, denied any government involvement in the attack, and the proregime rumor mills leaked a story that the opposition leader had been beaten by the male relatives of a young woman with whom he was allegedly having an affair.[20] But authorities also ordered four Chilean newsmagazines and a weekly tabloid to submit their copy to censorship before publication in an effort to suppress the story of Pinochet's questionable property deal.[21]

The effort was unsuccessful. On May 5, 1984, twenty-four lawyers affiliated with opposition parties presented the Chilean supreme court with documents showing that Pinochet had purchased the property for 535,000 pesos from the government, which had paid 3.5 million pesos for the land. The court did not act against Pinochet, but the lawyers' gesture made the case public.

The regime reacted with a statement charging that the accusations against Pinochet were made by politicians attempting to return the country to pre-1973 conditions of chaos. The statement also said Pinochet had financed the property purchase by selling to the government a former country home whose market value had not been reported in the documents. Over the next few days Pinochet gave audience to the army corps of generals and other regime officials who "spontaneously" arrived at La Moneda to express their support. The revelations did not weaken Pinochet's power base within the Chilean army, but they certainly had touched a nerve.

The Raúl Silva Henriquez shantytown, named after Santiago's former Roman Catholic cardinal and human rights defender, was a squatters' neighborhood the carabineros seldom bothered to patrol. About twenty thousand people lived in flimsy wooden shacks without electricity, heat, or running water. Unemployment, by most accounts, affected at least 80 percent of the heads of households, with many families subsisting on tiny government subsidies or charitable donations.

Despite their hardships, the residents of the community held elections for a neighborhood council in June 1984. An electoral commission was formed, voting tables were set up, and candidates began to campaign under the aegis of Chile's traditional political parties. But disagreements arose over the voting procedures, with accusations from Christian Democrats that pro-communist candidates were rail-roading the election in their favor. And so what had been described to me as a rare exercise in grassroots democracy under the military dictatorship was marred by charges of fraud.[22]

The economic slump that had helped to spark a series of nationwide protests against the regime now seemed to have generated a political slump. By mid-1984 political discontent was as strong as it had ever been, but the opposition movement seemed nebulous and uncertain of its own direction. Labor groups, which had spearheaded the first days of protest, were continuing to press for more demonstrations and called for a new protest on September 4, 1984. Over 900 people were arrested, at least 150 injured, and 10 people killed. Among the dead was Father André Jarlan, a French priest working in La Victoria, an older, low-income neighborhood in Santiago. Bullets fired by carabineros in the direction of fleeing demonstrators had smashed through the walls of the modest wooden rectory where Father Jarlan lived, killing him as he sat reading in his room. Another priest with whom he worked discovered his body slumped over a table, a Bible in his lap.

Father Jarlan's untimely death was not the only violence the Catholic Church would face from regime officials in the next few months. On October 6, a bomb destroyed a church in Punta Arenas, in the country's extreme south. Human remains and an identity card belonging to a Chilean lieutenant working for army intelligence were found in the rubble. The army acknowledged the dead man's identity but issued a statement suggesting that Lt. Patricio Contreras might have been a victim of a terrorist explosion—perhaps he was trying to remove the bomb set by left-wing extremists or had been kidnapped and placed in the church just prior to the explosion.[23]

On November 6, Pinochet announced he was imposing a state of siege, claiming that it was needed to curb a growing terrorist threat in the country. In addition to the church explosion, there were 734 terrorist bombings throughout the country that year.[24] Responsibility for many of them was claimed by the MIR and a new offshoot of the Chilean Communist Party, the Manuel Rodríguez Patriotic Front, named after a Chilean independence hero. Other bombs were almost certainly placed by the security forces themselves. "This government and the guerrillas have a nice, symbiotic relationship," a diplomat com-

mented. After years of suppression, armed left-wing groups had returned to Chile and were providing Pinochet the army commander
with fresh pretexts for his continued rule.

On the same day the state of siege was announced, army troops surrounded the Raúl Silva Henriquez settlement and rounded up an estimated two thousand men. After checking their identities, most were
released but at least one hundred were found to have police records
(though not necessarily outstanding arrest warrants) and were sent to
Pisagua, a fishing village in northern Chile that had been the site of a
concentration camp after the 1973 coup. But the raid on the shantytown was only a dress rehearsal for an even bigger military operation
elsewhere.

On November 10, 1985, electricity and telephone service in the La
Victoria neighborhood was cut off at dawn as helicopters circled the
area. Army troops in combat gear sealed off the surrounding streets
and began conducting house-to-house searches.[25] "This is an operation under the state of siege," a voice shouted over the loudspeaker.
"Anyone who leaves his home will be taken as an agitator." The soldiers rounded up at least five thousand men and teenage boys, herded
them aboard trucks and buses, and transported them to a nearby soccer stadium. It was a scene that recalled the mass arrests in the National Stadium after the coup: soldiers with machine guns guarded
prisoners as they filed past tables for identification checks. Those with
police records were sent to an official who was wearing a ski mask, and
afterward they were marched through a tunnel into a dressing room
beneath the grandstands.

Most of the prisoners were eventually released and allowed to walk
the two-and-a-half miles back to La Victoria. But authorities retained
237 men, and announced that at least thirty of them had "subversive"
backgrounds. Officials also reported they had seized weapons, a de-
vice for making homemade explosives, and "propaganda," and that the
seven-hour military operation had yielded "quite positive results from
a security standpoint."

Many of La Victoria's thirty-two thousand inhabitants told a different story, of property damaged or destroyed and of radios and other
small appliances taken. One woman reported that three Catholic mag-
azines were confiscated by soldiers who told her that she was being
brainwashed by communists who had infiltrated the church.

For a poor community which had already suffered more than its share of repression and violence, the raid was devastating. "This was done to terrify and punish the population," said Father Pierre Dubois, La Victoria's parish priest. A few days later leaders of the Alianza Democrática visited La Victoria, and were confronted with angry residents demanding to know what they, the purported leaders of a democratic Chile, were doing to prevent the regime from committing further abuses against their community. The question was an uncomfortable one, and the opposition leaders' visit, which had been intended as a show of sympathy for La Victoria and a repudiation of Pinochet's heavy-handed crackdown, seemed to underscore the political stalemate.

The repressive tally for the new state of siege in 1984 included 257 Chileans sent into internal exile in remote parts of the country, a late-night curfew, the temporary detention of over 8,000 people in military raids in the slums, closures and restrictions on opposition news media, and the imprisonment of 421 men with police records in the Pisagua detention camp in northern Chile.[26]

The following month four members of the U.S. House of Representatives' Hispanic caucus visited Santiago and managed to meet with Pinochet. Although the congressmen—Bill Richardson of New Mexico, Henry González of Texas, and Esteban Torres and Tom Lantos of California—were Democrats and therefore suspect in the regime's eyes, Pinochet was persuaded to receive them after learning that Lantos had been born in Hungary and was present during the anti-Soviet uprising in 1956. According to a source present at the meeting, Richardson opened the conversation with a diplomatically worded expression of concern about the state of siege and received an unsettling display of Pinochet's temper. Chile did not accept foreign interventions in its internal affairs, Pinochet shouted at Richardson, who was visibly taken aback by the outburst. He later described the meeting to *New York Times* correspondent Lydia Chávez: "[Pinochet] is very isolated, everyone refers to him as 'His Excellency.' . . . We met him in an office where he was dressed in an impeccable white uniform and sat behind a huge desk that was set up in a configuration that looked like a throne."[27] Richardson also described the opposition as divided and leaderless, and suggested that the only person who might be able to persuade Pinochet to lift the state of siege was Ronald Reagan.

A few weeks after the congressmen left, Chilean authorities arrested and deported an American priest accused of "political activities." Father Dennis O'Mara, who had lived in Chile for six years, had given his parishioners Christmas cards calling for an end to torture in the New Year. On his arrival in Miami, he was cursed and insulted by a crowd of about fifty regime supporters, who shouted "¡Viva Pinochet!"[28]

On February 16, 1985, Interior Minister Sergio Jarpa left the regime, along with the finance minister, in the fourth cabinet shakeup in less than a year. Pinochet was unhappy over Jarpa's support for constitutional reforms and increasingly suspicious of his contacts with foreign embassies, especially the U.S. mission. Although the official dialogue with the Alianza Democrática leaders had been dead for months, Jarpa still communicated with opposition politicians, and had argued, unsuccessfully, for an end to the state of siege that Pinochet had just two weeks earlier renewed for another ninety days. His replacement was Ricardo García, a businessman who appeared a far less assertive figure than Jarpa, and the change seemed to signify a further hardening within the regime.

On February 11, 1985, the U.S. assistant secretary of state for inter-American affairs, Langhorne A. Motley, arrived in Chile and met with Pinochet, Chilean officials, and opposition leaders. To critics of U.S. policy toward Chile, the visit looked like yet another Reagan administration boondoggle: Motley spent one of his four days in Chile on a fishing trip with Ambassador James Theberge and told the Chilean-American Chamber of Commerce that there would be no dramatic change in U.S. policy toward Chile. Against the advice of the U.S. embassy in Santiago, he gave an interview to *El Mercurio*, in which he said the world owed Chile a "debt of gratitude" for overthrowing Marxists in 1973.[29] At an airport press conference before he left, Motley skillfully ducked questions about his views on the state of siege, press censorship, and the transition to democracy, saying that "the future of Chile is in Chilean hands, and from what I've seen those are good hands."[30]

But even if Motley's public statements dismayed critics of U.S. policy, Pinochet's reaction to the visiting State Department official was as belligerent as if he were being forced to meet with Fidel Castro. Motley later told Shirley Christian of the *New York Times* that Pinochet "was the toughest nut I've ever seen. He makes Somoza and the rest of those guys look like a bunch of patsies." While Pinochet received him cordially at La Moneda and stood beside Motley while pictures were taken, the pleasantries ended abruptly as the photographers were leaving:

He put his finger under my nose and said, "We're not a colony of the United States. Relations have not been very good between us for a long time. We almost went to war in the last century, and I don't take advice."

I told him I was not there to lecture but that I wanted to tell him what the reaction was outside, in Europe and the United States. . . . I told him that if he were writing the script for the communists, he couldn't write it better than he was doing then.

He responded with a long lecture about how he was the No. 1 communist target in the world. I said I agreed but that he was helping the leftists in places like Washington and Paris and that he ought to do something to let the air out of their balloon.[31]

A regime spokesman, Francisco Cuadra, later said that Motley "was in our country as a guest of the Chilean government." When I asked him if the visit had helped improve relations, he said rather drily that "anything that aids a better-informed view is always useful."[32]

The regime may have had a brief honeymoon with the Reagan administration, but by 1985 Pinochet had reverted to his earlier wariness regarding American governments, whether Democratic or Republican. He was not going to drop the war against his enemies, and if the Americans could not understand the Marxist threat, the regime would just have to fight its battles alone. On March 29, security agents kidnapped a teacher and a sociologist working with the Catholic Church's human rights department as the two men conversed near the entrance to the school where the teacher worked. Another teacher who tried to intervene was shot in the abdomen. The following day a retired painter was kidnapped. The bodies of the three men, all members of Chile's proscribed Communist Party, were discovered at the side of a road on the outskirts of Santiago, near the site where three years earlier labor leader Tucapél Jiménez had been found shot in his taxi. The three men's throats had been slit, and the body of one of the victims, the sociologist José Manuel Parada, bore a deep slash wound in the chest.[33]

Political murders were nothing new in Chile under the military regime, yet the case of the *degollados,* the slit-throated men, caused a far stronger public outcry than many previous cases of human rights abuse had done. The crimes had occurred after two years of antigovernment protests, and even though a state of siege was in effect, Chilean public opinion demanded a serious investigation into the crimes.

Because the kidnappings had taken place in the relatively affluent eastern end of Santiago, in broad daylight, there were many witnesses. The outbreak of protest against the regime had irrevocably changed Chile's political climate, and even if Pinochet had launched a crackdown, fewer of those witnesses could be intimidated into silence. And perhaps most important, the investigation happened to fall into the hands of a brave civilian judge whose four-month investigation indicted fourteen carabinero officials. Clearly, Chile was no longer the same country it had been during the military's first few years in power, and against the most repressive efforts of the regime some of the elements of a democracy were emerging: a judiciary that sometimes acted independently and a public opinion that was no longer resigned to unsolved crimes.[34] The regime's credibility was not helped by the indiscreet remarks of several senior military officials. The Chilean defense minister and two junta members blamed the grisly killings on leftists, and naval commander José Merino even suggested that the carabineros might have been infiltrated by communists seeking to discredit the police force.

The murder of these three Communist Party members boomeranged back at the regime, striking down a member of the junta. In the wake of the investigating judge's report, which was turned over to a military court for further action, carabinero director César Mendoza handed in his resignation on August 2, 1985, saying he did not want to give the regime's enemies a continued pretext to attack the carabineros.[35] His replacement was the institution's second-in-command, General Rodolfo Stange, who to Pinochet's frustration would prove to be a more independent operator within the regime than Mendoza ever was, slightly tipping the balance of power within the junta away from Pinochet.

Chapter Eight

Heroes and Villains

At eight in the morning of January 15, 1986, groups of right-wing Chilean youths gathered behind the Crowne Plaza Hotel in Santiago and climbed into buses provided by the regime's national youth secretariat. Some carried eggs and tomatoes, as they had been instructed to at a meeting the previous night by secretariat leaders. They did not need to make placards or signs; these were provided by two Santiago print shops that had produced thousands of posters bearing a reproduction of the famous black-and-white yearbook photo of Mary Jo Kopechne, Edward Kennedy's former secretary, who drowned when the senator's car crashed off a bridge at Chappaquiddick in 1969. Kennedy, the American most despised by the Pinochet regime, was scheduled to arrive in Santiago that morning, and the Chilean government and its backers were preparing what they felt was a suitable reception.

Pinochet had not even wanted to let Kennedy, the sponsor of legislation banning U.S. arms sales to Chile, into the country. Although Chile had found some replacement suppliers in South Africa, Israel, and other countries, and had begun to manufacture some of its own weapons, the U.S. arms embargo irked Chilean military officials perhaps more than any other sanction. The regime had been further angered when Washington had moved to lift a similar ban against Argentina, Chile's territorial rival, in 1983, following the departure of the military from government. The United States had tried to smooth things over with the regime: President Reagan sent Pinochet a personal letter advising him in advance of the decision to lift the embargo against Argentina, and special envoy Vernon Walters visited Santiago and held two meetings with Pinochet to discuss the issue.[1]

Kennedy's initial request to visit Santiago had been passed on to Pinochet by nervous Chilean foreign ministry officials, who received a brief and blunt "No" from the general. But in Washington the Chilean embassy was feeling the pressure of seemingly endless telephone calls and messages from the State Department and Capitol Hill. Pinochet finally relented after General Walters, one of the few U.S. officials for whom he had any respect, sent him a message to the effect that banning Kennedy from Chile would only enhance the senator's political standing.[2]

Kennedy and his committee landed at 10 A.M., and word of his arrival was radioed to the two hundred or so proregime demonstrators who blocked the highway leading from the airport to Santiago. U.S. ambassador Harry Barnes obtained a police helicopter to transport Kennedy and his group. But several Chilean opposition and human rights leaders who met the senator at the airport and attempted to leave in their own vehicles were attacked by progovernment demonstrators who hurled rocks, eggs, and tomatoes at them as carabineros stood and watched.[3]

Kennedy's first appointment was at a private children's rehabilitation center. The senator and his delegation then traveled by car to the Círculo Español, a restaurant club in downtown Santiago where he was to hold other meetings. The proregime demonstrators managed to regroup along this route, hurling eggs and at least one rock at Kennedy's car. But the Chilean police finally moved to control the crowd, keeping the demonstrators on the opposite side of the street from the Círculo Español, where they soon attracted the hostile attention of passersby and Chilean supporters of Kennedy. Fistfights broke out, and the suddenly outnumbered proregime demonstrators were forced to retreat.

When Kennedy's visit ended, Ambassador Barnes contacted the Chilean air force to obtain helicopter transport back to the airport for the senator and his committee, in order to prevent further incidents. An air force official sarcastically told the embassy that all its helicopters were grounded for lack of parts—a situation caused by the Kennedy amendment.[4] Once again, carabineros provided the necessary transport.

The regime was still seething even after Kennedy's visit ended. On Saturday, January 18, 1986, Barnes, the embassy's deputy chief of mission, and the embassy's labor attaché were having lunch at the country home of Máximo Pacheco, vice president of the Chilean human rights commission, whose automobile had been stoned by pro-regime demonstrators at the airport. While Pacheco was out of the city that day, his housekeeper of sixteen years, Rosa Espinoza, was abducted from a Santiago street at about 11 A.M., shoved into a car, blindfolded, and taken to a building, where for the next twelve hours she was interrogated about her employer's contacts with Kennedy, the U.S. embassy, and other American officials. Her interrogator was a young-sounding woman claiming to be a journalist, whose use of language was similar to that of an anonymous caller who had telephoned threats to the Pacheco household in the past.[5]

For Barnes, a respected career diplomat who had recently replaced the conservative James Theberge, a Reagan administration political appointee, the Pinochet regime's actions during the Kennedy visit were a harbinger of things to come, and in time he too was to find himself the target of official vilification. Barnes's predecessor, according to opposition sources, had rarely met with opposition politicians, and regime critics were usually only invited to U.S. embassy functions if a visiting American official specifically requested their presence. In addition, Theberge had urged that the Inter-American Foundation, a U.S. development agency, reduce or terminate its funding of four Chilean research institutes with ties to opposition groups such as the Christian Democrats.[6] The four think tanks had received $1.25 million from IAF between 1980 and 1983, and had provided a venue for research by Chilean academics unable to work at the country's military-controlled universities.

Since his arrival in Chile November 15, 1985, Barnes had set about meeting with as broad a spectrum of government, political, and community leaders as possible, and traveled extensively outside the capital to provincial cities and towns as well. But Barnes's widened net of contacts was viewed with increasing suspicion by Pinochet and hardliners in the regime. In its second term in office, the Reagan administration was proving to be far less friendly to Chile than during its first four years: the United States had abstained during the voting on three loans to Chile from multilateral lending agencies such as the

IADB and the World Bank (which were approved) to protest the continued state of siege. (When Washington appeared set to block a badly needed World Bank guarantee of $150 million in private-sector loans, the state of siege was lifted.)[7] Then the United States backed a United Nations resolution condemning the regime's human rights practices. The resolution was based on a report by a U.N. special envoy who attributed the continued arbitrary arrests, torture, and other abuses to "a government not founded on the principle of self-determination of the people."

The regime was also infuriated by statements made by senior Reagan administration officials, including White House Chief of Staff Donald Regan. When asked if the United States was trying to destabilize the Pinochet regime, Regan responded: "No, not at the moment," adding that the administration was still hoping for peaceful change. The American official's remarks, widely circulated in Santiago, prompted Admiral José Merino, the naval commander and a junta member, to call Regan "insolent and meddlesome" and to charge that the Reagan administration had changed its policy toward Chile out of concern for Republican party setbacks in the 1986 congressional elections (as if Chile were a major campaign issue).[8] Pinochet was equally vehement, saying that the regime's constitution had been approved by the Chilean people (in the dubious 1980 plebiscite) but that the Americans' constitution had been imposed.

Pinochet, however, felt he had other reasons to be wary of Washington; the year was turning out to be a bad one for dictators in other parts of the world. In the space of a single month, the Philippines' Ferdinand Marcos and Haiti's Jean-Claude Duvalier had been toppled from power, with the United States playing a role in negotiating each dictator's departure from his country. Even NBC's *Saturday Night Live* comedy show had urged its viewers to send in predictions of when Pinochet would join Marcos and Duvalier.

Meanwhile, Chilean opposition groups seemed to remain stagnant. One promising exception, the National Accord, was a proposal sponsored by the Catholic Church calling for free and direct parliamentary and presidential elections, along with an end to restrictions on political activity. Eleven Chilean political parties had backed the accord, and air force commander and junta member General Fernando Matthei had called it "interesting." The newest member of the junta, carabinero director General Rodolfo Stange, was also thought to favor at least some parts of the opposition proposal.

Stange, who had replaced General César Mendoza the previous year, had proved to be a far more formidable man than his predecessor. Like Matthei, he was the son of German immigrants, and the two were often overheard conversing in German, much to Pinochet's uneasiness. Stange also spoke English and was considered to be, in the words of one regime insider, "of a very high IQ." The changes and reforms he initiated within the carabineros, after the force's involvement in the murder of three Chilean Communist Party members, had raised the hopes of many human rights activists, who reported that detainees arrested by carabineros received far better treatment after Stange took over the force.[9] The carabineros still used tear gas and water cannons to break up most demonstrations; yet with two of the four Chilean military commanders now approachable on the subject of political reforms, there was hope for a peaceful change.

But Pinochet, who commanded the army, the most important military branch, was having none of it. At a meeting of the junta members and other senior military officials on November 7, 1985, Pinochet instructed General Santiago Sinclair, one of his most trusted army officers, to read the document before him. It was the text of the Argentine navy officer Emilio Massera's defense for his actions in that country's dirty war against left-wing guerrillas, which the admiral had presented in Buenos Aires only a week earlier:

> The war against terrorism was a just war. In spite of this, here I am being prosecuted because we won this just war. If we had lost it we would not be here, neither you nor we, for in time the high justices of this court would have been substituted by turbulent popular tribunals, and a fierce and unrecognizable Argentina would have replaced the old country. But here we are, because we won the war of arms and lost the psychological war.

After Sinclair finished reading, Pinochet looked around sharply at the other junta members. Their Argentine counterparts had made the mistake of doubting their own mission, he said, and allowed their institutions to be judged and scrutinized. Matthei, feeling that this odd presentation was directed at him, tried to argue that the situations in Chile and Argentina—which had lost a war with Great Britain—were very different. But Pinochet cut off the discussion with the surprise announcement that the army representative on the junta, General Raúl Benavides, who had joined the legislative body in 1981, would be replaced by General Julio Canessa, the army's vice-commander. Benavides, who had not been advised of the move beforehand, looked stunned.[10] He was the general closest in age to Pinochet, the last of those army officials holding a senior rank at the time of the coup to retire from the regime. Benavides's removal meant that, with the exception of General Canessa, there were no army generals remaining of Pinochet's generation.[11] The abrupt move to replace Benavides, without advising him or even consulting the other junta members, was intended to show the other officers who was boss.

The backers of the National Accord had begun collecting signatures from the public to demonstrate the popular backing for the multipartisan agreement. According to Sergio Molina, a Christian Democrat who had been a cabinet minister under the Frei government, as many as eight hundred thousand signatures had been collected. But with the possibility of a dialogue with the regime blocked, the initiative began to lose momentum. "The truth is that there was never a systematic collection of signatures," Molina said in an interview. "It was a pretty dispersed effort and there was never a nationwide tally. We stopped this campaign because what was really important at the time was making the National Accord known publicly."[12]

For the time being, the opposition initiative seemed to be dying, although it was undoubtedly a useful political exercise that would serve the same politicians well in planning their strategy for the 1988 presidential plebiscite. Meanwhile, another group calling itself the National Civic Assembly had sprung up. An umbrella organization of professional organizations and special interest groups, the assembly called for a protest on July 2, 1986. The protest call was met with mixed reactions in some opposition circles, where some felt that it was not the right time for such a move—there would not be much support in middle-class neighborhoods, and there would almost certainly be violence and deaths. As it turned out, the July 2 protest would give way to one of the most flagrant human rights abuses in the Pinochet regime's history.

Rodrigo Rojas, age nineteen, had returned to Santiago only two months earlier. The son of a political refugee, he had grown up in Washington, D.C., and attended Woodrow Wilson High School be-

fore dropping out and taking up photography. He had always felt himself to be a Chilean, despite the English syntax that crept into his
Spanish, and dreamed more than anything of returning to his native
country and working as a photographer.

"I told him he should get himself some sort of credential," Marcelo
Montecino, a Chilean-American photographer who had been one of
his mentors in Washington, said later.[13] Rojas was working for *APSI* on
a freelance basis, but had no press card with him on the morning of
July 2 when he went to General Velasquez street to shoot the building
of a barricade by slum dwellers.

Carmen Gloria Quintana was eighteen, an engineering student
from a poor family living in the Los Nogales neighborhood where the
barricade was to be built that day. She had met Rojas a few days earlier, in a soup kitchen where she was a volunteer, but it was by accident that she and Rojas were in the same place that day. When Rojas
arrived at General Velasquez street, only two people met him there,
carrying tires, a jerrican of gasoline, and small bottles to be used as
Molotov cocktails.

First the barricade would be built, then one of the small soda bottles lit and thrown from a distance at the barricade. "Rojas forgot himself," lawyer Hector Salazar said later. The young photographer
helped carry the materials to the site, perhaps not thinking of the professional distance he should keep from the events he wanted to
record. As he and the two men walked along, they ran into Carmen
Gloria Quintana and four other young Chileans who wanted to join
the protest.

Then a truckload of army soldiers in combat gear and wearing camouflage paint came down the street. The group scattered, and Quintana and Rojas, who according to his lawyer was probably still holding
the bottles, ran down together. According to witnesses, Quintana
slipped and Rojas stopped to help her up, a delay that probably cost
him his life.

It was not the first time that year Pinochet had dispatched army
troops to perform what was properly a job for the police, and the
carabinero director, General Rodolfo Stange, had locked horns with
Pinochet on this issue before. Two months earlier opposition politicians had hosted a conference of parliamentarians from Europe, Latin
America, the United States, and Canada at the Hotel Tupahue in

downtown Santiago, and Pinochet had responded to the threat of antigovernment demonstrations by filling the center of Santiago with army troops. One surprised Norwegian parliamentarian, Tore Austad, told me he had not seen anything like it since the Nazi occupation of his country during World War II. "And let me emphasize that I am a conservative," he said.[14]

The truckload of soldiers that detained Rodrigo Rojas and Carmen Quintana that day was led by a young lieutenant, Pedro Fernandez Dittus. Like many of the younger officers in the Chilean army, he had never worked under a civilian government and had been trained to believe that Marxists posed a constant danger to the country. Fernandez Dittus did not have an exemplary record despite the image his lawyer tried to project of him: a few years earlier he had been accused of driving while intoxicated after his car was involved in a fatal accident.

Now Fernandez Dittus and about two dozen other soldiers had captured two of the enemy—a university student and a young man whose slightly accented Spanish betrayed the fact that he had spent years outside the country and therefore was almost certainly a returning political exile. According to witnesses, the soldiers led Rojas and Quintana to a dusty, unpaved street and began beating them with their rifle butts and interrogating them.

Jorge Sanhueza, a factory worker who lived in the area, was on his way to work that morning when he saw the soldiers arrest Rojas and Quintana, whose family he had known for years. Hiding behind a wide utility pole he watched as the soldiers took a jerrican of gasoline from the truck, poured it over the two teenagers, then set them on fire with one of the Molotov cocktails.

"The young people both tried to put out the fire on them but the girl was hit in the mouth with a gun by one of the soldiers, and the boy [was struck] on the back of the head until he lost consciousness," Sanhueza later recalled. "After a while the soldiers wrapped up the bodies in blankets and threw them on the back of the truck like parcels."[15]

The army truck drove for about half an hour to the outskirts of Santiago, toward the airport, and left Rojas and Quintana for dead in a ditch in the same vicinity where the body of labor leader Tucapél Jiménez was found in 1982 and the three Chilean Communist Party members' bodies were discovered the previous year. Rojas's and Quintana's bodies were blackened; third-degree burns covered two-thirds of their skin, which was falling off in scraps. Their hair had been burned off. But they were still alive and managed to crawl out of the ditch and stagger down the road until they were spotted by workmen who called the police. An ambulance was called but never arrived. Finally a passing motorist agreed to take Rojas and Quintana to the hospital, and they ended up at the Posta Central, a public hospital with few facilities to treat them.

The next day the proregime newspaper *El Mercurio* published a brief story headlined, "Investigation Requested in Case of Two Burn Victims." After stating that two young people had been burned in "unclear circumstances," the newspaper reprinted an army communiqué that denied that the institution had anything to do with the case.[16]

Rodrigo Rojas died on July 6, 1986, in the Posta Central hospital. Efforts by family and friends to get him and Quintana transferred to another medical establishment, the Hospital del Trabajador, which had better facilities to treat burn victims, were blocked by hospital officials, who were probably acting out of fear or under pressure from the regime.

Rodrigo Rojas's case provoked a storm of outraged protests. About five thousand people attended his funeral, including Ambassador Barnes. Chilean police commandeered the hearse carrying Rojas's casket to the cemetery. Tear gas was fired into the crowd, but the mourners finally regrouped and the funeral was allowed to continue. The young man who had spent half his life outside Chile had become, in death, a martyr whom every political group wanted to appropriate, including the Communist Party, which posthumously claimed him as a member.[17]

Carmen Quintana was finally transferred to the Hospital del Trabajador several hours after Rojas died. But before the Posta Central hospital officials allowed her to leave, they demanded a check for an equivalent of $2,500, an impossible amount for the daughter of a semiemployed father and a mother enrolled in a government work project. Rojas's mother, who had flown to Santiago from Washington when she learned of her son's burning, gave the Quintana family the check demanded by the hospital, which was supposed to give free medical attention to the poor.[18]

Dr. Jorge Villegas, a respected burn surgeon at the Hospital del Trabajador, thought Carmen Quintana might have a 6 percent chance of survival when he first examined her. But support for the young woman was pouring in: people who did not even know her were offering to become donors for skin grafts and were lining up to give blood. Negotiations were under way to move her to an even better facility outside Chile.

"I kept asking about Rodrigo. And the young man? And the young man?" Quintana said. "They told me he was in the United States being treated."[19] It was not until months later, when she arrived at Montreal's Hospital Dieu for more advanced treatment, that she learned he was dead. The shock sent her into a depression that lasted for days. "She said that Rodrigo had insisted they keep walking, not to go weak, after they were abandoned by the military," Quintana's aunt said. "He encouraged her, saying that they would be found soon and it would all be over. And afterward, when they were waiting for the ambulance, he had her rest her head in his lap."[20]

While Carmen Quintana hovered between life and death in the Hospital del Trabajador, the Pinochet regime's propaganda apparatus went to work to stem the damage from the case and to launch a counterattack. The government newspaper, *La Nación*, reported that the arrival of Ambassador Barnes at Rojas's funeral "encouraged the violent groups present in the area" (as if Chilean extremists would rally around an American diplomat). Regime spokesman Francisco Cuadra said that Rojas's death was being used in a "systematic campaign against Chile in the United States." On July 10, 1986, the government television station aired a videotape that it claimed had been taken the previous month by its reporters covering a demonstration by university students. The blurry videotape showed a young, dark-haired woman handing bottles to other students; the narration identified her as Carmen Quintana and said that she and the other students were preparing to throw acid-based Molotov cocktails at carabineros. The television report was picked up and re-reported by the rest of Chile's progovernment news media. But the broadcast of the videotape, which had been prepared by the CNI and not by any television crew, disturbed even the proregime staff at Channel 7, and several of the journalists prepared a letter disclaiming any responsibility for the material. The Channel 7 staffers never released the letter, however, out of fear for their jobs and other possible reprisals.

The case made the already tense relations between Chile and Washington deteriorate even further. But then the regime received a boost of sorts from North Carolina senator Jesse Helms, who arrived in Santiago on July 10. Helms had been invited by Chile's National Agricultural Society, whose membership had bitter memories of agrarian reform programs under the Frei and Allende governments and whose political views could be said to range from conservative to fascist. Upon his arrival at Santiago's airport, the Republican senator praised the Pinochet regime, saying that Chile was one of only two countries in Latin America resisting communism.[21]

Although his visit was not an official one and he was cold-shouldered by the U.S. embassy in Santiago, Helms was granted an immediate audience with the Chilean foreign minister and several other cabinet-level officials, and on that evening of July 11 he met with Pinochet for two hours in La Moneda. Helms did not divulge the content of his conversation with Pinochet, who rarely received foreign visitors for anything more than a short protocol greeting, but upon leaving the presidential offices the senator attacked the U.S. press for its "biased" view of Chile. The *Washington Post* and the *New York Times,* he said, "never met a socialist government they didn't like." That evening Chilean officials said they were considering filing a lawsuit against certain U.S. news media for "injury and slander" against the country.[22] (Chilean foreign minister Jaime del Valle, when asked about the planned suit by Chilean reporters, indicated he knew nothing about it.)

Helms, who described Rodrigo Rojas and Carmen Quintana as "communist terrorists," continued to press the regime's case on his return to the United States. He urged panelists on ABC's *This Week with David Brinkley* to visit Chile and listen to the pro-regime views of the same people he had met.

"Talk to the American Chamber of Commerce, to the American head of the United Nations computer department," he said.[23] Many U.S. residents of Santiago shared Helms's views of the regime; his statement in Santiago that Chile was one of two Latin American countries resisting communism was recycled a few weeks later by the president of the local American Association, who was the wife of a Bechtel

Corporation executive. She told an ABC television crew that Chile "was one of two countries in Latin America moving toward democracy. All the others are socialist."

The American business community in Santiago had been uncomfortable with the increasingly negative tone of U.S. policy toward the regime, and earlier that year sent a delegation to Washington to lobby against any possible sanctions against Chile. The group, which included three American executives heading the Santiago offices of Exxon Corporation, the Sydney Ross pharmaceuticals company, and Chemical Bank, held meetings with members of Congress and officials at the Department of Defense, the State Department, and the National Security Council. The group argued that Chile was recovering from recession, had cooperated with international lending institutions in renegotiating its foreign debt, and was generally an attractive country for U.S. investors. Reported human rights abuses, they argued, were sensationalized in the press—a position not shared by many of the officials they met. According to one observer familiar with the American Chamber of Commerce group's trip, the delegation's members were somewhat taken aback by the extent of negative sentiment in Washington toward the regime.

"There is the strong sense that any instance of torture in Chile is one too many," the president of the American Chamber of Commerce in Chile, Lawrence Hayes, wrote in the organization's magazine, *The Journal*.[24] The death of Rodrigo Rojas and the reaction in the United States and elsewhere was a setback for their lobbying efforts, and several AmCham officials adopted the Chilean army's position, claiming that Rojas and Quintana had set themselves on fire accidentally. One AmCham employee routinely told visitors to their Santiago office that the U.S. press had "gotten the story wrong," that what really happened was that the two teenagers had been burned when Quintana kicked a Molotov cocktail at the army patrol, which then hit the jerrican of gasoline, ignited, and somehow engulfed them both in flames.

But although the Chilean-American Chamber of Commerce demonstrated ignorance or cynicism on the subject of the regime's abuses, it could argue convincingly that the Chilean economy was indeed on an upward course. The country's gross domestic product, which had contracted by 14 percent in 1982 and another 0.7 percent in 1983, had grown by 6.3 percent in 1984, 2.4 percent in 1985, and 5.7 percent in 1986, according to the central bank. There were still problems: unemployment remained very high, with 18.8 percent of the labor force out of work in 1984, 16.3 percent in 1985, and 13.9 percent in 1986, according to the University of Chile's economics department, and inflation remained a serious problem (although not by the standards of many other Latin American countries): 19.8 percent in 1984, 30.7 percent in 1985, and 19.5 percent in 1986. But Chile's external accounts were improving. After a trade deficit of $89 million in 1984, the central bank reported a surplus of $536 million in 1985 and $763 million in 1986. Even more impressive to foreigners was the way Chile was handling its external debt burden, at a time when much of the rest of Latin America seemed to be teetering on the edge of default. The International Monetary Fund had approved a two year standby loan of $500 million in 1983 and a three-year credit of $750 million in 1985. The World Bank, despite U.S. abstentions on some petitioned credits to Chile, approved three structural adjustment loans to Chile, each worth about $250 million, from 1985 to 1987. Commercial banks had agreed to lend the country $1.3 billion during 1983–84 and $785 million in 1985–86.[25] After the freewheeling borrowing in the seventies and the multiple changes of finance minister in the early eighties as the country's economic crisis deepened, Chile had become a relative model of financial propriety.

In the meantime, Chile's central bank had become one of the first entities to offer debt swaps, which allowed promissory notes from foreign-creditor banks to be converted into Chilean pesos. International banks had been trading foreign debt notes among themselves, usually at a discount, for a few years before the Chilean central bank devised a way to turn this activity to the country's benefit. In addition, the central bank used debt-equity swaps to encourage more foreign investment, allowing investors to use the converted pesos for projects within the country if the funds remained in the country for at least ten years. By the end of 1988 some $6 billion of Chile's foreign debt had been eliminated through debt-equity swaps.

The regime was also pushing ahead with its privatization program, turning twenty-three state companies over to the private sector (although CODELCO, the state copper company, remained in government hands) as well as a similar number of formerly private companies intervened in by authorities between 1981 and 1983 to prevent their collapse. The state companies included the Chilean steel company, the telecommunications company, the power company, the nitrates company, the explosives company, a pharmaceutical company, and the national telephone company. Chilean authorities converted the firms into stock companies and offered some of the shares to company employees at reduced prices. Foreign investors were also allowed to buy shares, and some used the central bank's debt-equity programs to finance the purchases.[26]

But although the economy was improving, the regime's human rights record was deteriorating. On July 17, 1986, the Chilean army, which had been so quick to deny any involvement in the burning of Rodrigo Rojas and Carmen Quintana, issued a statement repeating the official claim that the two teenagers had accidentally caused their own burning, but that three officers, five noncommissioned officers, and seventeen conscripts had been detained as part of the official investigation into the incident. The statement was read by General Carlos Ojeda, commander of the Santiago army garrison, who allowed no questions afterward.[27]

The civilian judge assigned to the case, Alfredo Echavarría, seemed to accept the army's version of events, despite eyewitness testimony from civilians like Jorge Sanhueza, Quintana's neighbor, who had viewed the two teenagers' burning from behind a utility pole. After Sanhueza gave his testimony to the court, he was accosted by two men who forced him into a taxi where he was blindfolded and threatened with death if he did not change his testimony. "They stopped many times by the river and held a gun to my head saying, 'Shall we shoot you here and throw you in the river, or shall we kill you somewhere else?' " he said. "They told me that someone was with my wife and children at my home and would 'fix them up.' "[28] Sanhueza and his family were hidden by the Catholic Church for three months and then given political asylum in Australia under a special humanitarian program. The Rojas-Quintana case had nevertheless hurt the regime. Even some conservative Chileans backing the government found it difficult to accept the army's version of events. But the damage was soon offset by two related and, for Pinochet, fortuitous events.

In August 1986 the U.S. Central Intelligence Agency alerted the Chilean military that its satellite photographs had revealed large quantities of weapons stashed in the Atacama desert. The caches, unearthed in seven different sites in northern Chile and three other sites in and around Santiago, included over 3,000 M-16 rifles, over 200 rocket launchers, and an assortment of grenades, explosives components, and ammunition. A statement issued by the U.S. embassy on September 17, 1986, said that the arms constituted the largest quantity of illegal weapons ever discovered at one time in Latin America. The M-16 rifles had apparently been left in Vietnam by U.S. troops and later sold to international arms dealers.

The regime appeared stunned by the CIA information, and the government communications agency, DINACOS, contacted the Chilean press to request that the "events in Vallenar," a small city in the country's northern desert, not yet be revealed. Most of the local and foreign news media had no idea to what the DINACOS officials were referring. Neither, it seems, did the DINACOS functionaries or other Chilean officials, who had not yet had time to present the arsenals' discovery with the customary propaganda touches. A few days later the CNI announced the discovery of the first arsenal, with subsequent arms caches found over the course of the following week.

Officials said the arms had apparently been brought to the Chilean coast by Soviet ships and loaded onto Chilean fishing boats, which brought them to shore and stored them below ground in the desert. The deliveries, officials said, had taken place over a two-year period, with the last shipment on July 27, 1986. Junta member Admiral José Merino, asked about the arms deliveries, said that the Chilean navy was simply not able to control all activity along the country's lengthy Pacific coastline.

The CNI held a rare press conference at one of its offices in central Santiago, displaying rows of missiles and other weapons. A CNI official even answered a few questions, saying that six people (including four who had taken courses in "dialectical Marxist-Leninism" in Cuba) had been arrested.[29] Nevertheless, the official presentation left many unanswered questions. The armed left-wing groups operating in Chile, the MIR guerrillas and the newer Manuel Rodríguez Patriotic Front, were not thought to have more than a few hundred members at most, and the massive quantity of armaments greatly exceeded either group's capacity. In addition, the kinds of weapons found were more appropriate for rural fighting than for the urban guerrilla actions favored by the MIR and the Manuel Rodríguez Patriotic Front. Nor was it clear how either group could obtain and pay for such a massive supply of armaments. One hypothesis was that the arms were really intended for Peru's Shining Path guerrillas; another that the weapons were to be used in some future uprising undertaken after the Chilean military had left the government.

For many regime officials, the discovery of the arms caches was something of an embarrassment, for the military and police had been staging raids and mass arrests in the poor and working-class areas around Santiago, ostensibly for security reasons, and Pinochet had sent the army out into the streets to keep order during antigovernment demonstrations. Now here was a genuine threat to the country's internal security right under the regime's nose and it was the Americans, not the Chilean security forces, who had first noticed it.

Worse, many Chileans simply did not believe the reports. A Chilean morning tabloid, *Las Ultimas Noticias*, had printed random public comments on the news of the arsenals, and most respondents were more than a little skeptical of the regime's announcements. One university student interviewed called the displayed weapons "a circus." The story in *Últimas Noticias*, which belonged to the *El Mercurio* chain, infuriated the regime, and its editor, Hector Olaves, was fired at the request of Chilean authorities. Officials also seized the 25,000-copy run of an opposition newsmagazine that questioned the arsenals' discovery, and an army prosecutor jailed the periodical's editor on slander charges.

But by now the regime was beginning to understand how to use the discovery to its political advantage. Chilean television showed Pinochet leaving his upstairs office to greet a group of civilian supporters assembled in La Moneda's central patio, which included a former Miss Chile and her race-car-driver husband. The television report said the group was requesting Pinochet's permission to hold a parade September 9 in support of the regime and against terrorism, and amid their applause Pinochet told them he would authorize the demonstration.

As it turned out, the pro-regime anti-terrorism parade would have even more to celebrate. On Sunday, September 7, Pinochet was driv-

ing back to Santiago from his residence at El Melocotón, the contro-
versial property he had purchased from the government at a bargain
price. The motorcade consisted of his automobile, six other cars, and
a motorcycle that led the caravan along the mountain road toward the
capital. As the vehicles approached a bridge, their drivers saw a car
with a camper trailer stopped diagonally across the road, blocking traffic. The motorcade slowed, and a hit squad from the Manuel Rodríguez Patriotic Front emerged from the hill directly above the road
and opened fire with automatic weapons and rocket launchers. Five of
Pinochet's bodyguards were killed and ten others wounded, but Pinochet survived with only a cut to his hand. His car, the third from
the last in the motorcade, was armored, although it would not have
withstood a direct rocket hit. One of the projectiles even skidded over
the roof of Pinochet's vehicle, but his driver reversed and sped back
toward El Melocotón, a quick reaction that probably saved his passengers' lives.

The attempt to assassinate Pinochet had been planned for months,
with César Bunster, the son of a former Chilean exile, coordinating
the plans in Santiago. Bunster's father had been the Chilean ambassador to Great Britain during the Allende government and had been
allowed to return to the country just six months earlier. César Bunster
had been in Cuba, where he made contact with the Manuel Rodriguez
Patriotic Front, and returned to Chile with his father. Once in Santiago the younger Bunster obtained a respectable cover when he began working at the Canadian embassy. A large country house not far
from Pinochet's retreat at El Melocotón was rented where Bunster
and a woman posing as his wife could observe the movements of Pinochet and his security guards coming to and from Santiago. The
group rented vehicles similar to the ones habitually used by Pinochet's
entourage, and after the attack the guerrillas, dressed to look like CNI
agents, were even waved through stop signs and traffic signals by local
police as they sped back to Santiago.[30] At a press conference in Buenos Aires five days later, Front representatives said twenty-five guerrillas had taken part in the attack, and promised to strike again.

When Pinochet returned to Santiago that evening he quickly summoned the junta, and a new state of siege, with a curfew, was decreed.
Pinochet appeared on television that night, showing his bullet-marked

car to a reporter from the government television station, who inquired about the bandage on his hand and what he had seen, heard, and thought during the attack. One of Pinochet's young grandsons had been riding with him, and Pinochet said his first reaction had been to get out of the car, but he then realized the boy's vulnerability and covered him with his body.

Some Chilean television viewers also saw an odd little announcement on Channel 7 that night: "The Papillon Sports Club is called to a meeting."[31] With a strict curfew in effect, it was extremely unlikely that any Santiago sports club would be calling a meeting; the announcement was more likely a coded message to the regime's security forces. In the early hours of September 8, armed men in civilian dress dragged one Chilean Communist Party member and two other men with links to the MIR guerrilla group from their homes. A fourth man, a Communist Party member, was kidnapped the following night. The bodies of all four men were later discovered, riddled with bullets, in different parts of Santiago. The killings were almost certainly committed in revenge for the attack on Pinochet, and the victims appeared to have been selected from a previously compiled list of Chileans with left-wing connections.

Authorities also used the state of siege to arrest eight well-known opposition figures, to expel from the country three foreign priests working in slum neighborhoods, and to ban five opposition periodicals and one newspaper. I had interviewed one of the detained opposition leaders, Ricardo Lagos, a few weeks earlier for a back-page interview in *Newsweek*'s international edition. He had discussed U.S. votes against loans to Chile in multilateral institutions and predicted that the violence in the country would worsen with Pinochet's hard-line stance.[32] The day after the interview appeared, Lagos's house was stoned by a progovernment mob, and Chilean officials insinuated that his statements in the interview had prompted his subsequent arrest.

The U.S. State Department issued a statement that condemned the attack on Pinochet but also expressed concern for the renewed suspension of civil liberties under the state of siege. For Pinochet, however, the failed assassination attempt could not have come at a better time, for the regime went ahead with its previously planned progovernment parade on September 9. Thousands of Pinochet supporters and government employees marched past a pavilion across from the La Moneda presidential palace, where Pinochet stood waving triumphantly with the three other junta members. The general who had withstood international condemnation and countless diplomatic sanctions had survived a spectacular assassination attempt, which not only garnered him renewed sympathy in some quarters but provided the pretext for launching a new crackdown. It was one of the peak moments in his career.

Chapter Nine

Pinochetistas

I say to those bad Chileans who insult us on television because they know we are in a democracy and are not going to do anything to them: be careful, because patience has a limit and this limit can make itself known.

Now as we approach the plebiscite we are going to show this minority, which shouts and vociferates as if they were many but are only a few, we are going to show them, generously but proudly, we are going to wipe them off the map.

—General Augusto Pinochet, June 9, 1988

My general, know that the black berets will never permit that our brothers who fell in combat that September 11, 1973, to view from beyond an attitude of conciliation or treason, because our brilliant steel curved knives will be ready at the call of our leader, to defend the beloved Chilean people who have always been the victor and never the vanquished.

—Colonel José Zara, commander of the Chilean army's special forces unit, in a homage to Pinochet on March 31, 1988

Pinochet's bid for reelection in the one-man presidential plebiscite set down by the regime's constitution began in earnest on July 10, 1986, in the little town of Santa Juana in southern Chile, about six hundred kilometers south of the capital. He told a crowd that the regime was not going to hand over power "for the fun of it," and that its constitution set down a transition period of sixteen years, referring to the latest date at which presidential elections could be held. "The first eight years are for dictating laws. The next eight years are for applying these laws in earnest," he said. "If we don't apply these laws, the constitution will be lost."[1]

It was perhaps the first time Pinochet had openly admitted he would seek the junta's nomination, although the timing of his statement was not the best. The Rojas-Quintana case was still reverberating within the regime, and Pinochet was upset that his family mausoleum in Santiago's general cemetery had been spray-painted with antigovernment slogans during Rodrigo Rojas's funeral. But a few weeks later Pinochet backed down, saying that he had not declared himself a candidate. The other junta members had been irritated by Pinochet's premature gesture, for according to the terms of the constitution they would first have to decree one law providing for an electoral registry and another allowing political parties. Over the next few months the other three military commanders made vaguely worded public statements to the effect that the junta might choose a civilian as the regime's candidate, and many regime supporters wanted to believe this would be the case. The names of alternative candidates for the one-man election were circulated, with the former interior minister, Sergio Jarpa, frequently mentioned. A typical view was expressed by a Chilean businessman who insisted that Pinochet would not put himself up for reelection: "Pinochet is a savvy character; he is just going to tease all these politicians along until the last moment and then withdraw himself as a candidate," he said.

Of the three Chilean DINA officials the United States had unsuccessfully sought for extradition in the Letelier case, Major Armando Fernandez Larios was the most vulnerable to U.S. pressure. He had family in the United States: his sister Rose Marie was married to an American, and he had visited the country many times. Since the DINA's dissolution he had been dissatisfied with the bureaucratic jobs the Chilean army had assigned him and was often seen drinking in a piano bar in an affluent neighborhood in eastern Santiago. Fernandez Larios was also feeling threatened by revelations in Chile's opposition press linking him to the mass executions of political detainees in northern Chile after the coup. He had been a member of General Sergio Arellano's committee during the army officer's helicopter tour of military installations in northern Chile.

During an interview for a Chilean magazine, Fernandez Larios recalled a conversation he had once had with his father, a retired air force officer who had been proud of his son's military career. At the time, Fernandez Larios had let his hair grow for undercover work with the DINA. When his father noticed his somewhat disheveled appearance, he made inquiries through other military friends and learned Fernandez Larios was working with Colonel Manuel Contreras's new security organization. His father, Fernandez Larios later told his lawyer, hated the DINA. "Someday you'll go to jail for this, and I am going to help you, but I fear for what might happen when I am no longer here," he told Fernandez Larios.[2] His father had died before the Letelier assassination, and after the United States had delivered its extradition request, he, Col. Pedro Espinoza, and Manuel Contreras were placed under house arrest at the military hospital in Santiago.

Fernandez Larios, whose assignment in the Letelier assassination had been to find out where the Chilean exile leader lived, told his superiors he wanted to go to the United States to clear his name. He was then called to a meeting at the Chilean defense ministry, where Pinochet confronted him, saying, "I understand that you want to go to the United States."

"That is not true. It is not that I want to go to the United States, but that I am going to the United States," Fernandez Larios replied.

"Don't worry, I will order it so you have no more problems in the hospital," Pinochet told him. "Be a good soldier, be firm, and this problem will have a happy ending."[3] Fernandez Larios would have three more meetings with Pinochet in which he requested authorization to travel to Washington, and each time Pinochet refused.

For over a year Fernandez Larios had been in surreptitious contact with U.S. authorities, and an American lawyer, Axel Kleinboimer, who would represent him. At some point in late January 1987 he met with U.S. agents in Chile who helped him leave the country without the knowledge of his army superiors. On February 3 of that year, he appeared in U.S. Federal Court in Washington to give his version of events in the Letelier case. He was, he said, "overwhelmed by guilt."

Fernandez Larios had left behind a letter to Chilean army vice-commander General Santiago Sinclair, with additional copies of the missive to be leaked to the press by friends once he was out of the country. The eighteen-point letter described his previous attempts to clear his name and to be relieved of his army commission during the previous nine years, which were all unsuccessful. The letter, somewhat impertinently, ended with the hope that his departure from the Chilean military "helps so that in the future no subaltern officer is blamed for the actions of the army's high command."[4]

The regime's public reaction to the news of Fernandez Larios's defection was cool and measured, with a spokesman saying the case was being given "careful study" and that the government was prepared to "lend all its cooperation in establishing the truth of the case, in accordance with Chilean law." When asked by a group of Chilean reporters to comment, Pinochet said only, "For me, Fernandez Larios is a deserter." Behind the scenes, however, the regime was reeling from the news. That a promising young army officer should turn on Pinochet in that manner was bad enough, but there was the political fallout to consider as plans for the presidential plebiscite got under way. But the regime's well-developed propaganda apparatus launched a counteroffensive almost immediately.

In late 1986 a new weekly newspaper, *Negro en el Blanco*, had hit the Chilean newsstands. The publication contained no advertisements and cost a modest fifty pesos (about fifteen cents at the exchange rate then) even though it was published not on newsprint but on more expensive, magazine-quality coated paper. News vendors were "encouraged" to give *Negro en el Blanco* prominent display on their kiosks, although customer demand was extremely low. The newspaper's masthead bore the names of several columnists and journalists who had worked for the government television station, Channel 7, and the official newspaper, *La Nación*. When news of Fernandez Larios's defection broke, the *Negro en el Blanco* headlines proclaimed that the former DINA agent had been kidnapped and brainwashed by the CIA. One issue bore an unflattering drawing of U.S. ambassador Harry Barnes clutching a briefcase, with the title, "The Truth About What Barnes Is Hiding."[5] An accompanying story described Letelier's contacts with Chilean exiles in Cuba, while a separate item attacked the justice department investigator, Eugene Propper. As weeks went by, the attacks on U.S. officials became more virulent, with one *Negro en el Blanco* drawing showing Barnes surrounded by prostitutes bearing the faces of opposition leaders.

The regime did finally allow opposition groups to open a daily newspaper, *La Época*, whose publication had been delayed for three years by officials' refusal to authorize its circulation. *La Época*, whose majority owners were Christian Democrats, gave the opposition a voice at a time when violence from either end of Chile's political spectrum seemed to be increasing. The government had opened voter registration, and Pinochet himself had made a show of being the first Chilean to sign up (a workman who had made an all-night vigil outside the registry, hoping to be the first registered voter, was nudged aside). But after an initial flurry of progovernment public figures registering to vote, the numbers of newly inscribed voters had decreased to a trickle.

The one-man presidential plebiscite was not scheduled to be held for another year, and many Chileans opposed to Pinochet were wondering why they should bother to take part in what they suspected would be another regime circus. But while the country's opposition groups, who represented the political center, were stalled and demoralized, the regime's security forces and the left-wing extremist groups became more active than ever. Although the CNI managed to identify and arrest a dozen members of the Manuel Rodríguez Patriotic Front in connection with the assassination attempt on Pinochet, the Front continued to attack police stations and set off bombs. Explosions near electricity pylons caused massive blackouts in Santiago and other cities. On September 1, 1987, the Front kidnapped Colonel Carlos Carreño, deputy director of the Chilean army's munitions company, eluding a citywide police and military dragnet. They smuggled the officer across the Argentine border and then into Brazil, where he was finally released after three months' captivity.

A few days after Carreño was kidnapped, five Chilean youths, all members of the Communist Party, disappeared and were never seen again. The Chilean human rights commission reported that the number of reported death threats, kidnappings, instances of torture, and politically related killings had reached its highest level in seven years. The commission counted at least seven different right-wing groups, thought to be made up of off-duty military and police officers and pro-regime youth bands, making the death threats. These numbered nearly one hundred per month, compared to an average of thirty-five per month two years earlier. The likely explanation for the wave of threats was that the Pinochet regime and its hard-core supporters were trying to drive as many government opponents as possible out of the country before the plebiscite.

In some cases the death threats were followed by physical attacks. A Chilean pediatrician in Valparaiso was dragged from his car by men armed with automatic weapons, who beat him, tied him to a tree, carved a swastika on his forehead, and subjected him to a simulated execution before warning him to leave the country. The doctor had filed a court suit weeks earlier stating that he had received death threats and that men in a yellow Subaru had followed him, but judicial authorities had rejected his request for protection.[6]

A group of eighty Chilean actors, directors, and playwrights received warnings from a right-wing extremist group that if they did not leave the country within thirty days they would be killed. Their plight attracted attention from actors' organizations from around the world, and on November 30, 1987, the day the deadline expired, the actors put on a show in a Santiago theater to defy their would-be assassins. American actor Christopher Reeve, known for his role in the *Superman* films, traveled to Santiago to take part in the show. The image of Superman coming to the aid of politically persecuted Chileans delighted the actors and their supporters and angered the regime.[7]

If Pinochet seemed determined to prolong his rule past 1989, when his eight-year term ended, and opposition groups seemed stalled and divided, there were still those who thought an electoral effort worthwhile, even if it had to be played by the regime's rules. If the regime's lone candidate in the presidential plebiscite were defeated by a "No" vote, then, according to the regime's own constitution, free elections would have to be held the following year. The director of the newly opened electoral service, Juan Ignacio García, was a respected official who had worked for the service before the 1973 coup. There appeared to be a good chance the actual voting mechanism would be clean, in contrast to what had happened during the regime's 1978 and 1980 plebiscites. But in order for the "No" vote to win, there would have to be an organization capable of counteracting the regime's political and propaganda machine.

The National Accord, the multipartisan proposal for a transition to democracy, had withered as the different parties attempted to form a political coalition, something best undertaken when there are no restrictions on political activity. But Sergio Molina, the Accord's leader, had still managed to salvage the general principles behind the initiative and organize the Committee for Free Elections. The committee's fourteen members included Chilean novelist Jorge Edwards; a former regime ambassador to the United States, José Miguel Barros; and Molina and other political party leaders.

The committee's first task was to convince Chileans to take the plebiscite seriously and register to vote. The turnout in poor neighborhoods had been especially low, even though antigovernment sentiment was strong in such areas, for many low-income Chileans were reluctant to spend the equivalent of two dollars to renew their identity cards or even to pay the bus fare needed for the trip to a voter registration center.

An opinion survey by a Santiago social sciences research institute, FLACSO, released in mid-1987 showed that from 12.5 to 17 percent of those polled would vote "Yes" if Pinochet were the candidate, while 40 percent would vote "No" (the remainder either abstained or failed to respond). Measuring public opinion under a military dictatorship is difficult for obvious reasons, yet the relatively high number of potential "No" voters was encouraging to the opposition. Slowly voter registration began to increase, and two months before the plebiscite, scheduled for October 5, 1988, 7.4 million people had registered. The law allowed foreigners who had lived at least five years in the country to vote in plebiscites and municipal elections, so I also registered.

The regime was taking its own private polls, and their results suggested the vote might be close. The Chilean Communist Party had publicly called for a "No" vote rather than a boycott of the plebiscite, and this provided the regime with a propaganda asset: the Red Scare, the return of the Marxists. But the largest of the right-wing political organizations, the National party, looked as though its leaders might back a "No" vote as well, and if they did so the regime would be in serious electoral trouble.

In June 1988 the National party held a council meeting and took a straw poll of how its members might vote in the plebiscite. The results, according to National party sources, were 120 in favor of an outright "No" vote and 145 in favor of a "consensus" candidate, that is, someone other than Pinochet running in the one-man election. That night regime hard-liners decided to take over the party.

Dictatorship's Demise

A new membership drive began, spearheaded by two young businessmen with seemingly bottomless bank accounts. A National party youth congress was held in Santiago the following month, and the party's new benefactors brought in eighty people, paying for their plane tickets and hotel rooms. A few days later the National party president, Patricio Phillips, who had held a private meeting with Pinochet, made the bizarre announcement that *leftists* had been trying to infiltrate the party and that a new vote for a party council must be held.

To the National party's vice president, German Riesco, the call for a new party council was a hamfisted attempt by the regime to gain control of the organization. He and other council members scheduled a press conference at party headquarters to denounce the situation, but when they arrived at the building they found the door locked. "A group of youths in parkas began arriving, and we asked them where they had come from," said former National party council member Javier Díaz. "They told us they were from the 'Yes' campaign headquarters, and had been instructed to participate in a takeover. 'What takeover?' we asked them. 'This is the National party. Are you members?' "[8] The youths seemed embarrassed, and did not even know where they had been sent. "There must have been a mistake," they mumbled, and left.

At 3:30 P.M., a white truck with a large antenna pulled up to the National party headquarters and several heavyset men got out and strong-armed their way into the building, expelling the National party members who had managed to crawl through a back entrance. There were shouts of "¡Viva Pinochet!" and from that moment the National party joined Pinochet's reelection campaign.

Nevertheless, more and more one-time supporters of the regime were drifting into the opposition camp. In August, just weeks before the junta officially nominated Pinochet as the regime's presidential candidate, a Chilean journalist published a thin volume of interviews with five former regime officials, including the junta's former press secretary Frederico Willoughby. Willoughby, who had left the job when he developed serious kidney disease (and eventually recovered following a transplant), said in the interview that Pinochet's closest advisers had misled him into believing he could rule for sixteen more years under the terms of the 1980 constitution. "They deceived him, for when he divided it up into two eight-year terms, Pinochet's advisers knew that the political conditions of 1980 would have run their course by 1988," Willoughby said in the interview.[9]

Pinochet did not take kindly to his former press secretary's statements. A few weeks later he appeared at a luncheon for senior and retired military officers, and during an improvised speech cruelly attacked Willoughby and the other former officials interviewed in the book, although he stopped short of mentioning them by name. "There was one who came to me with a long face, and said he was dying," Pinochet said, referring to Willoughby's kidney failure. "Well, I wish he had died." Then the general dropped his guard somewhat and made a vague allusion to his nonparticipation in the coup plotting: "Some of you have said I wasn't with you in the beginning. Well, I did what I could under the circumstances."[10] It was a rare public acknowledgment of his true actions in the past, but this moment of candor was quickly swept away by the campaign.

Pinochet's comment regarding Frederico Willoughby caused an angry, protective stir in opposition circles and among Chilean journalists. At a press conference at the journalists' association a few days later, Willoughby responded to Pinochet's attack, saying that he forgave him and wished him a long life free of persecution. "I have the impression that when Pinochet makes one of these improvised speeches there is an alter ego at work, another self rebelling against the controls imposed on his person, what he may say and where and how he can say it," Willoughby said in an interview afterward. "So this unconscious rebellion will come out all of a sudden and naturally produces undesired effects."[11] Willoughby's moderate response to Pinochet's cruel comment earned him praise, while his decision to back a "No" vote against his former boss meant the beginning of a beautiful friendship between the former regime official and the opposition campaign.

On August 30, 1988, the junta met at the Chilean defense ministry and officially nominated Pinochet the regime's candidate in the one-man presidential plebiscite. After the ceremony Pinochet addressed a gathering of about six thousand supporters from the balcony of the La Moneda presidential palace. The progovernment press grossly overestimated the crowd at sixty thousand, while Chilean television stations avoided broad camera shots of the crowd, sticking mostly to close-ups and shots of Pinochet. The "No" command, a group of sixteen political organizations calling for a vote against the regime, called on Chileans to beat saucepans to protest the junta's decision to nominate Pinochet, and urged the public to remain indoors and avoid confrontations with Pinochet supporters.

But disturbances erupted in poor neighborhoods. Two people were shot to death, several others were wounded by men in civilian dress firing from moving cars, and over eight hundred people were arrested.[12] Officially, the plebiscite campaign had begun.

There were small concessions to the concept of fairness: although the regime tightly controlled the country's television networks, both the "Yes" and the "No" campaigns were allowed fifteen minutes each night to present their case. The regime's propagandists had not given much importance to this aspect of the campaign, for the brief programs were to be aired late at night and the government had the rest of the day's broadcasts during which to make its arguments. But for the "No" campaign those fifteen-minute programs were crucial, and each segment was prepared as though the entire vote hung in the balance—as in many ways it did.

To enhance the programs' credibility, the opposition campaign strategists decided to use a news anchor to open each broadcast. And, acting on the advice of media experts, they made the programs unrelentingly upbeat and optimistic in tone. The intention was to counteract the fear the regime used as one of its biggest tools. Many Chileans were unconvinced that the vote would really be secret, that reprisals would not be taken if they cast "No" votes. The subliminal message of the "No" campaign spots was that there was nothing to fear.

Nevertheless, many Chileans who worked on the programs were all too familiar with the regime's intimidatory tactics. Patricio Bañados was a Chilean Walter Cronkite, a telegenic broadcast professional with a square jaw and wavy silver hair who had for a time been one of the country's favorite newscasters. He had begun working for Channel 11, run by the University of Chile, but as a condition of employment had insisted that the texts he was to read contain no insults to other people or organizations, and that government announcements be presented as such and not as the truth.

Shortly after he began working at Channel 11, Bañados found that this pre-hiring agreement was being ignored. He was handed news texts with phrases like "a terrorist was arrested," instead of "an accused terrorist," or, more accurately yet, "a man accused of terrorist activities." So Bañados began making little changes in the texts he was to read each evening, with no apparent reaction from station officials.

During the 1980 constitutional plebiscite he was given a report covering an opposition rally at which former president Eduardo Frei spoke. The text contained two insulting sentences about Frei and a group of Chilean entertainers who appeared at the rally, and Bañados simply left them out. When the broadcast was over, station officials informed him he was fired. Bañados argued, and the station executives relented. A few months later, he was handed a news report about a new loan that the Chilean finance minister had just negotiated with Japan. The lead-in suggested that money was now going to rain down on the country. Bañados considered the text irresponsible and once again made a change. This time he was fired, and he also found himself blacklisted from Chilean television.

"I couldn't even appear on one of those lightweight talk shows," he said to me in our interview. "I was never, ever allowed to set foot in a television studio in Santiago."[13] Bañados survived by working for radio stations, and was hosting a political discussion program on the Christian Democrats' Radio Cooperativa when he was recruited by the "No" campaign to appear in its television programs. The first fifteen-minute program began with the image of a painted rainbow and the word "No," while the opposition campaign's theme song, "Chile, la alegría ya viene" (Chile, happiness is on its way) played in the background. Then the camera focused on Patricio Bañados: "Chile, happiness is on its way. Good evening. This is the first chance in fifteen years for those who do not share the government's thinking to express their views in their own program. For me, personally, this is an opportunity to return to this profession, from which I have been excluded. But as fifteen minutes, after fifteen years [of military government] isn't much, let's go immediately to our program."[14]

The program then went back to playing the campaign theme song, accompanied by video images of Chileans in a variety of settings showing their support for a "No" vote: a cab driver waving his finger back and forth in time with his windshield wipers, a baker turning around to show a "No" emblem on his back, a group of workmen clapping in time to the theme song. One of the last images was of two men using back-to-back public telephones; one a bearded younger man in jeans and casual dress, the other a balding, more conservative-looking man in a three-piece suit. The men suddenly spot each other and drop the telephone receivers to shake hands vigorously. The camera then cut back to Bañados saying, "We Chileans have been convoked to ratify, via a plebiscite, the single candidate for president designated by the commanders in chief. In democracies there are various candidates; here there is only one."

The program then showed footage of the junta members arriving at the defense ministry the day of Pinochet's nomination, walking up to the building on a red carpet and ceremoniously turning to salute before entering the building. Each of the military commanders had previously said that Pinochet would not be the candidate, and the narration cited the dates and publication of their statements, including Pinochet's own public declaration years before that he would retire by this time. As the junta members were presented, Strauss's "Blue Danube" waltz played softly in the background.

The choice of music had sly significance. A few weeks earlier, an eccentric Chilean pop singer, Florcita Motuda, had called a press conference to present his new single, a call to the Chilean public to vote "No," set to the tune of the "Blue Danube." The singer, who looked a bit like Groucho Marx, dressed in tails and wore a presidential sash across his chest. After playing a tape of his song, with the refrain, "No no no no no nooooo, no no no no no no noooooooo," Florcita Motuda led his audience to the entrance of the La Moneda presidential palace and tried to deliver a copy of the cassette to the guards, who refused to accept the offering. The singer then posed for photographs in front of La Moneda, waving his tape in the air.[15] "What I'm trying to do is alleviate the tensions of the plebiscite with a little humor," he said. Indeed, by daring to poke fun at the regime and apparently getting away with it, Florcita Motuda and his song did considerably more for the anti-Pinochet campaign than simply providing a comic outlet.

The regime was caught off guard by the slickness of the "No" program. The day after the first "Yes" and "No" programs were aired, Pinochet had lunch in the La Moneda presidential palace with a group of former officials and progovernment businessmen, who urged that the government improve the technical quality of its programs, which compared unfavorably with the "No" segments. The regime's later propaganda pieces were more virulent, with images taken from the "No" segments and voiceovers ridiculing the opposition's campaign slogans and songs; in one case a rainbow drawing used as a symbol in the "No" campaign was repainted in the black and red colors of the Manuel Rodríguez Patriotic Front while a chorus paraphrased the opposition's theme song to say that Marxists were on the way. Other regime segments included a garbled interview with the ex-wife of leftist opposition leader Ricardo Lagos, and a scene in which a young mother and her baby hid from a mob.

But the Pinochet campaign was scrambling to recover from the losses the "No" campaign was inflicting. After the turnout at the August 30 rally in front of La Moneda compared unfavorably with the massive attendance at an opposition rally a few days later, authorities announced they were suspending progovernment rallies and would concentrate their campaign resources in other areas. Repression was one of those areas: several peasant farmers who had appeared on one of the "No" programs were beaten up, along with a young Chilean man who appeared on the music video segment of the programs. A harpist who appeared briefly in that same portion of the program was fired from her job, and Bañados lost the sponsor to one of his radio programs.

During the thirty days the programs were broadcast, Bañados told me he felt such nervous exhaustion that most evenings he fell asleep at 8 P.M., and did not wake until morning. He avoided going out in public any more than was absolutely necessary. At the Apumanque shopping center in eastern Santiago, progovernment youths armed with clubs had marched past shoppers; in the center of the capital similar groups of young people, usually led by an older man in civilian dress but with the characteristic clipped hair of a military official, had chased and attacked "No" campaigners. A few days before the campaign officially ended, the Pinochet campaign staged a massive car rally through the streets of Santiago. The cars drove by Bañados's house for hours, honking as they passed. The regime, it seemed, wanted him to know that its supporters knew where he lived. The caravans also made a point of stopping by the Hotel Carrera in downtown Santiago, where most of the visiting foreign press were staying. I witnessed one man in dark glasses jump out of his car and gesture angrily in front of the hotel entrance, where other progovernment demonstrators had painted in huge letters on the sidewalk, "PINOCHET."

The "No" campaign organizers had asked Bañados, for security reasons, not to use his own car when driving to and from the studio. The campaign had contracted with a taxi company to take him back and forth, but one evening one of the taxi drivers began a strange conversation with the Chilean broadcaster, which he interpreted as a veiled threat. "Maybe you feel immune from danger, since you are a public figure," the taxi driver told him. Bañados replied that if one was going to die, it didn't matter whether it was by a bullet or because of pneumonia.

"But the thing is to die on your feet," the driver said.

"Well, if it's pneumonia I'm going to be lying down," Bañados said.

"I'm not talking about that. If you are beaten up by six guys, it is very different," he said. Bañados said nothing more to his driver.

Another night there was a telephoned death threat. "You son of a bitch, I'm going to kill you," the caller said to Bañados, who flippantly replied that it was very late to be making that sort of call. It would have been even better, Bañados thought later, if he had had the presence of mind to say, look, I only take death threats between nine and ten in the morning. But then the caller repeated his threat. "You son of a bitch, I'm going to kill you."

A few weeks later Bañados was crossing a street when a man in a car tried to run him over. The vehicle had been stopped in the road, waiting. Bañados saw that the car was not moving, but as a precaution decided to run across the street. His foot had barely hit the street when the driver gunned his motor and came straight at Bañados, shouting an insult as he raced past.[16]

Publicly, Pinochet was adopting a moderate, conciliatory stance, usually appearing in a suit and tie before the television cameras. His media advisers tried to present him as a kindly old grandfather, but Pinochet was a difficult product to sell and often appeared stiff and uncomfortable on camera. The "Yes" campaign's final fifteen-minute program, which I watched on October 1, included a relaxed interview with Pinochet, but during the transmission the sound and the pictures became somehow unsynchronized, with Pinochet's mouth moving out of sync with his own words. The effect was comic rather than compelling.

Pinochet announced that he would lift the state of emergency, impose a less-stringent special powers measure, and allow all of Chile's remaining political exiles to return to the country. Some of the returning exiles, including a former Allende economy minister, were filmed on their arrival at the Santiago airport. The pictures were used in regime propaganda spots in which viewers were asked to recall the inflation, shortages, and other economic hardships under the Allende government.

Although hard-liners within the regime emphasized the Marxist threat if the "No" vote won, many Chileans who had misgivings about Pinochet still supported a "Yes" vote. The return to civilian rule in neighboring Latin American countries such as Peru and Argentina had not been accompanied by economic improvement, and there was concern in many quarters, especially the business community, that the same fate would befall Chile. The country's gross domestic product had grown by 5.7 percent in 1986 and 1987 and by 6.6 percent during the first nine months of 1988. One business leader who favored the "No" vote explained the misgivings of so many of his cohorts: an elected civilian government would be more receptive to pressures from labor groups and would be more likely to adopt programs based more on populist than on economic considerations, just when the Chilean economy seemed to be getting back on its feet. There were some historical precedents for this concern: during the sixties and under the Allende government, political participation had expanded much faster than Chile's economy. The number of registered voters grew from 1.5 million people in 1958 to more than 3.5 million in 1970, with the percentage of voters in relation to the population doubling. Union membership had skyrocketed, with blue-collar membership increasing by 38 percent under the Frei government (1964–1970), white-collar membership by 90 percent, and peasant union membership from barely 2,000 to 114,112 adherents.[17] If the Frei and Allende governments were unable to satisfy the demands of Chile's newly enfranchised groups, according to this line of thinking, how would any other civilian president handle such a situation, especially after fifteen years of pent-up frustrations under the Pinochet regime? In the words of Ernesto Fontaine, a civilian leader of the regime's campaign, a "Yes" vote promised stability.

A less convincing case was made by Joaquín Lavin, an economist educated at the University of Chicago who directed *El Mercurio*'s economics and business section. In a book published by a government editorial house a few months before the plebiscite and distributed by Chilean embassies abroad, Lavin argued that the regime's economic policies had almost completely modernized the country. While recounting business developments throughout the country, Lavin argued that children in Santiago's slums were "more creative" than those in the higher-income districts: "Most of the time a six-year-old child from La Pincoya [a low-income neighborhood] must strive for his own food and clothing, and solve his daily needs for himself. This makes him much more creative."[18] Lavin also cited the cleanly wrapped foodstuffs in the country's supermarkets and the "sophisticated bacteriological control practices" for vegetables, ignoring the fact that fruits and vegetables in Santiago, which had no sewage treatment system, had to be carefully disinfected before eating.[19]

Yet even if Lavin's perceptions of the economic changes under Pinochet were skewed, his political views were shared by many affluent Chileans who were afraid of losing any progress, however lopsided, that had been achieved. For this sector, it was not Pinochet's candidacy but Chile's economic growth that was at issue. (The "No" campaign tried to address this concern with a newspaper advertisement entitled, "Kiwis or Democracy?" which referred to the boom in Chile's exports of kiwifruit and other new products, noting that economically advanced countries also had democracies.)

Chilean exiles who had not set foot in the country for over a decade were landing at Santiago's Pudahuel airport almost every day. Volodia Teitelboim, the Chilean Communist Party leader who had lived in Moscow for most of his exile, arrived a few days before the plebiscite and horrified the "No" campaign by advocating armed struggle to oust the regime. The Pinochet campaign was delighted by the public pronouncements of this political Rip Van Winkle, and quickly incorporated Teitelboim's statements in its propaganda.[20]

But other public figures from Chile's socialist past were also arriving and projecting more benign images of reconciliation. Allende's widow, Hortensia Bussi, returned to Santiago shortly before the voting and was greeted deferentially at an opposition rally October 1 by three right-wing politicians. They had once been among her husband's bitterest adversaries, but now had joined the "No" campaign. At that same rally, I watched, amazed, as Fanny Pollarolo, a Chilean Communist Party leader and psychiatrist who worked with torture victims, spotted former junta press secretary Frederico Willoughby in the crowd and kissed him in greeting. The "No" campaign had made some very unexpected political bedfellows.

That night a massive power outage blacked out Santiago. The timing of the blackout was suspicious and raised fears that the regime, faced with a Pinochet defeat in the plebiscite, would cancel the voting and cite a terrorist threat as the motive. To many the blackout seemed like a CNI maneuver. The U.S. embassy sent a ten-page cable to the State Department that evening, reporting that several loud explosions had been heard during the blackout, which cut electrical service for several hours in central Chile. No group claimed responsibility. The copy of the cable I obtained under the Freedom of Information Act was almost completely blacked out, save for one short paragraph and a subheading entitled, "security forces." Whatever its content, the cable prompted the State Department to call the Chilean ambassador to the United States, Hernán Felipe Errázuriz, to an unusual Sunday morning meeting to express, in the words of a State Department spokesman, "our serious concern."[21]

Back in Santiago, leaders of the "No" campaign had met with the military governor of Santiago, General Jorge Zinke, to discuss the planned activities for the day of the plebiscite, October 5, and with other regime officials, such as deputy interior minister Alberto Cardemil, who claimed knowledge of an extremist plan for October 5. Carabineros had told the opposition leaders that four buses, of the type the police institution used, had been stolen over the past few months, and the officials were concerned they might be used in some sort of terrorist plan. General Zinke, when he met with "No" campaign leaders that day, had not seemed worried about any security threats, but did mention that there would probably be a cut in power that night.

General Zinke was right, but what was going on? To many regime critics, it looked like a staged "extremist plot" by the security forces, who would then use the fabricated danger as an excuse to call off the plebiscite if it appeared that the "No" vote was winning.

The curtains of the wooden voting booth closed behind me, and I looked down at the words printed on the paper ballot in my hand:

Plebiscite President of the Republic
Augusto Pinochet Ugarte
__Yes   __No

I took my pencil and marked a vertical line crossing the horizontal line by the word No, folded the ballot, and sealed it by moistening the gummed edge along one side. I returned to the voting table, where an electoral service functionary detached a paper tab from my ballot and handed the ballot back to me. I hesitated a second before pushing the ballot through the slot, trying to savor the moment. My thumb was then rubbed into an ink pad, and I left a thumbprint in the vote book next to my name.

My assigned polling place was a girls' school in the Providencia section of Santiago, where women soldiers wearing camouflage fatigues and carrying weapons were patrolling the site. In Chile women, who did not receive the vote until 1946, vote separately from men. I arrived at the school at 8 A.M., but some of the women in line ahead of me had been there since 7 A.M. There was another hour's wait as the women in charge of our voting table—electoral service functionaries and poll watchers from both the "Yes" and "No" campaigns—argued over the ballots, the ballot box, and the voter registration book. When the voting finally began, I was asked to show my voter registration card and my Chilean identity card; then I was given the registry book to sign.

A total of 7,236,241 votes were cast that day in Chile, with 3,959,495 (54.7 percent) "No" votes, and 3,111,875 (43 percent) "Yes" votes. The remaining 2.2 percent were either void or left blank. The turnout represented a higher level of voter participation than at any

previous election in Chilean history, according to electoral service officials, and Chileans by the thousands lined up patiently at polling
places, in some cases waiting for hours to vote.

Former Arizona governor Bruce Babbitt, one of the hundreds of
foreign observers who came to Chile for the plebiscite, said he asked
one elderly man how long he had been standing in line. "Four hours,"
was the reply. Babbitt remarked on his stamina, and the old man responded, "Four hours is nothing when you've been waiting fifteen
years."[22]

That morning the government television station broadcast an interview with a proregime pollster and retired navy captain whose agency
was called Gallup-Chile but had no relation to the U.S. Gallup organization. The pollster claimed that on the basis of his agency's early
exit polls the "Yes" vote was already ahead. But the actual vote tally
was painfully slow, with Chilean officials reporting that by 10:30 A.M.
only 38.8 percent of the voting tables were operating. By 11:30 the
deputy interior minister, Alberto Cardemil, who days earlier had spoken of the dangers of an extremist plot during the plebiscite, announced that 75 percent of the voting sites were operating.

The announced delay worried opposition leaders at the "No" campaign headquarters, where their own poll watchers had reported that
98 percent of the tables were already working. Also troubling were
the Chilean army's operations that day. Two weeks earlier, at the traditional military parade held during Chile's national holiday, spectators had seen one of the largest displays of army hardware, marches,
and homages rendered to Pinochet in recent years.[23] Interior Minister Sergio Fernandez stated then that a victory for the "Yes" vote
would constitute another victory for the Chilean army.

Officials had moved a six-hundred-man rapid deployment force to
the military academy the day of the plebiscite, and the director of the
army paratroopers school, Colonel José Zara, was ordered to prepare
a special unit of his men in eastern Santiago.[24] Zara, a hard-line officer, had frightened many Chileans earlier in the year when he told Pinochet that his paratroopers would defend the regime "with our
curved knives."

Pinochet arrived at La Moneda that morning and told journalists
that he had "twenty-five thousand men ready." The slightest incident,

it seemed, could set off a violent crackdown. Pinochet spent most of the rest of the day in his bunker built under the plaza facing La Moneda.

At 7:30 that evening, deputy interior minister Alberto Cardemil read the first official results, based on the reports from seventy-nine voting tables: the "Yes" vote had 57.36 percent, the "No" vote 40.54 percent, with .36 percent of the results reported. The regime's selective reporting of the results sparked some progovernment celebrations in Santiago's affluent eastern neighborhoods. The next results would be announced one hour later, and some officials were already in contact with proregime groups to organize more street demonstrations.

Independent tallies of the results, however, showed a strong lead for the "No" vote. The "No" campaign's manager, Christian Democrat Genaro Arriagada, quickly called a press conference to criticize the interior ministry's reporting, and announced that the "No" command would start releasing its own tabulations.

"The GOC [government of Chile] is obviously sitting on voting results and releasing them very slowly," the U.S. embassy cabled to Washington that evening.[25] Carabineros had detained several suspicious vehicles in Santiago and had been fired on from a passing car bearing CNI license-plate numbers. But the carabineros, along with the Chilean navy and air force, were also keeping their own tallies of the voting, and their commanders, General Stange, Admiral Merino, and General Matthei, had concluded that the "No" vote was winning. The three junta members were scheduled to meet with Pinochet at 8 P.M. but were forced to wait while Pinochet emerged from the bunker to confer with interior ministry officials. Speaking in a hoarse voice, Pinochet told reporters there had been "disturbing reports" of armed men wearing ski masks in Santiago.

The situation was becoming more volatile. In addition to the barrage of proregime propaganda being transmitted on the government television station, Channel 7, the Universidad Católica television station was reporting that the early returns favored the "Yes" vote. The "No" campaign leaders went ahead with their threat to release their own tally of the vote, which gave the "No" vote 58.7 percent, the "Yes" vote 41.2 percent.

The second official tally of the votes, which was to be read by deputy interior minister Cardemil at 8:30, was not announced until

10 P.M. According to Cardemil's figures, the "Yes" vote was still ahead with 51.3 percent, and the "No" vote had 46.5 percent. To the opposition leaders, it was obvious that the regime was fudging the results. Cardemil was scheduled to announce a third official tally at 11:15 P.M., but he never appeared. He was called to a meeting at La Moneda and given the unpleasant task of reporting to Pinochet the latest returns which showed the "No" vote winning at 53 percent. Pinochet, whose sycophantic supporters had led him to believe he would be reelected, was enraged.

There was still no official announcement, and regime supporters at the "Yes" campaign headquarters several blocks away were still releasing figures that showed Pinochet winning. But then Sergio Jarpa, the regime's former interior minister, arrived at the Universidad Católica's television station for a scheduled appearance on a talk show. Jarpa, whose right-wing party had backed the "Yes" vote for Pinochet, greeted his fellow guest Patricio Aylwin, president of the sixteen-party coalition backing the "No" vote. As the cameras rolled, Jarpa let the cat out of the bag: the "No" vote had a clear advantage.

Shortly after midnight Pinochet called his cabinet ministers to a meeting and informed them that the regime had lost the plebiscite, and that he wanted their resignations immediately. The ministers left the room in stunned silence. Then Pinochet called in the other three military commanders who had walked from the defense ministry to La Moneda. It was about 12:30 A.M., and air force commander General Fernando Matthei saw a group of Chilean journalists waiting in the outer patio for any official announcement. Leaving General Stange and Admiral Merino, Matthei walked over to the reporters and dropped a bomb: "For me it is pretty clear that the 'No' vote won, but we are calm," he said.[26]

Matthei later reconstructed the commanders' meeting with Pinochet for the Chilean press. The three junta members had found Pinochet in a rage, pounding on his desk and saying that he had been lied to and deceived. When the air force commander told him he had already informed the press that the "No" vote had won, Pinochet became even angrier, accusing him of consorting with the enemy. Interior Minister Sergio Fernandez, who had remained at Pinochet's side after the other cabinet officials left, attempted to describe the results of the vote in positive terms, saying that Pinochet's share of the vote still meant that he was the most important political figure in Chile.

"Very good!" Matthei said. "So where is the champagne? Because if what you say is true, then we should be celebrating." A shouting match between the air force commander, Pinochet, and the interior minister erupted but stopped when Pinochet's presidential secretary, army general Sergio Valenzuela, collapsed on the floor. Fatigue and the tension of the moment had caused the officer to faint, and he was quickly carried out of the room and stretched out on a sofa.

The interior minister then showed Matthei and the other commanders a proposed decree that would give Pinochet widened powers to "deal with the post-plebiscite political situation." Matthei, Merino, and Stange refused to sign the measure. Pinochet became angry again, warning that now every political group in the country would be attacking him and that the unity among the country's armed forces would be broken. He said he did not want to continue governing with his powers curtailed. "Do you want me to resign right here and now?" he asked. The other commanders tried to calm him, saying that the constitution had to be upheld, and that this would be best for the country. Pinochet finally calmed down, and the junta members left.

When Matthei had acknowledged the "No" vote victory to the Chilean press, there was an explosion of joy at the "No" campaign headquarters, located barely a block from the Diego Portales government building. Outside the headquarters, about two hundred campaign volunteers had gathered, fists in the air, singing one of the original verses from the Chilean national anthem:

> Sweet country, accept our oath
> which we have sworn for your sake
> that you will be the tomb of the free
> or a refuge from oppression.
> That you will be the tomb of the free
> or a refuge from oppression.

Many of the people in the crowd were overcome with emotion, sobbing as they embraced, while others were jumping up and down with unrestrained enthusiasm. I spotted Juan Pablo Letelier, the youngest son of the murdered Chilean exile leader, in the crowd and asked him what the opposition group's next step would be. "We are going to keep the sixteen-party coalition together and win next year's elections," he said.

There was a bus of carabineros parked on a side street nearby, which suddenly started its motor and pulled away down the avenue. "¡Adiós, muchachos!" the crowd shouted after them, waving. The long night of the generals was over. Against all odds Chileans had beaten back their dictator, winning the game by the enemy's own rules.

Chapter Ten

Twilight of the Dictator

I make up the night of the soldier, the time of the man without melancholy or extinction, the character carried a long way by the ocean and one wave, who does not know that the bitter water has cut him off and that he is growing old.
—Pablo Neruda, "The Night of the Soldier"

The crowds outside La Moneda began to gather around noon the day after the plebiscite, watching the presidential palace for some clue as to what the defeated dictator would do next. Many of the Chileans who had wandered to the area found it difficult to believe that Pinochet had actually lost his own one-man presidential election. When I walked through the crowds wearing my press credential, several people approached me to ask if it were true that Pinochet had fled to Paraguay, or when the helicopter to take him to the airport would arrive. After a while the crowds grew bolder, with some shouting for Pinochet to resign. Occasionally a government official ventured to look out one of the windows, as if trying to estimate the size of the crowds, which remained around La Moneda until nightfall.

That evening Pinochet appeared on television, wearing not one of the civilian suits that he wore during the campaign but a white dress army uniform. He announced that he would continue as commander in chief of the Chilean army, and that the military would continue to play a key role in government. Pinochet had reinstated the cabinet ministers whose resignations he had demanded the previous night, and Interior Minister Sergio Fernandez said the regime would hold talks with opposition groups "if it is necessary," giving the impression that authorities would maintain a hard-line approach during their final year in power.

Security around Pinochet's residence in eastern Santiago was stepped up, as celebrating "No" voters held a massive car caravan throughout the city. Not everyone was celebrating, however, and a U.S. embassy official living near Pinochet's residence reported that "a large group of thugs" was stopping cars, demanding to know how the occupants had voted, and damaging the vehicles of suspected "No" voters. The group continued to menace passing motorists for at least an hour, "despite the presence of large numbers of security forces assigned to protect the president."[1] Carabineros also attacked a group of foreign journalists covering the opposition celebrations in downtown Santiago, some of whom were left with broken bones, concussions, and bruises. "Now it's our turn!" several of the policemen shouted during the attack, confiscating and damaging cameras and film.

Over the next two weeks there were signs that Pinochet, and some regime officials, had not yet accepted his electoral defeat. Interior Minister Fernandez said in a speech October 8 that Pinochet continued to be the "number one political force in the country," since the "No" vote's support was really divided sixteen ways for each of the political organizations in the multipartisan coalition. Progovernment radio stations began broadcasting calls to regime supporters to rally around Pinochet, while a tiny political group, the Independent Pro-Pinochet Movement, printed posters with the dictator's picture and the words, "1989: Year of Decision." A group of more than one hundred proregime demonstrators congregated near the home of the leader of the Christian Democratic party, Andrés Zaldívar, and as carabineros looked on impassively, hurled bottles and rocks at his house, shouting "¡Viva Pinochet!" and "¡Viva Fernandez!" Another mysterious group calling itself "Pinochet's missionaries" began a short-lived campaign to make Lucía Hiriart de Pinochet the regime's presidential candidate in the December 1989 election.

The regime's security forces almost certainly had organized, or at least helped to organize, these demonstrations of support for Pinochet, but there was backing for the dictator in less extremist circles as well. Hernán Felipe Errázuriz, a former regime cabinet minister who was serving as Chile's ambassador to Washington at the time, appeared on Cable News Network's public affairs program *Crossfire* and said that Pinochet could be a presidential candidate, noting that he had received a "substantial 44 percent of the vote" in the plebiscite.[2]

Less than three weeks after the vote, Pinochet spoke to a pro-regime women's organization and said that the regime had been beaten in the plebiscite, but not vanquished. "Remember," he told his audience, that "in the history of the world there was another plebiscite, in which Christ and Barabbas were judged, and the people voted for Barabbas. . . . We have fought in these times over the fifth of October, with Russia, with the United States, with the European countries, with the Church," he said. "And with Cuba!" some of the women shouted back.[3]

Comparing his regime with Jesus Christ and his opponents to Barabbas may have disgusted many observers who read about Pinochet's remarks the following day, yet the speech was typical of his improvised presentations and illustrated well Pinochet's own mindset: the embattled general engaged in a never-ending fight against outside forces. A few days later he told reporters that his electoral defeat had been "unjust" but that "it does not weaken us."[4]

Within the regime, and among its most hard-line backers, there were also embittered arguments over whom to blame for the opposition victory. These tensions came into public view a few weeks later when a scandal involving members of the military and intelligence community erupted and became front-page news for several weeks. According to press reports, on October 29, 1988, Manuel Contreras, Jr., son of the former DINA chief, shot and killed a top CNI official during an argument at a party.[5] The victim was Major Joaquín Molina, whose seventeen-year-old daughter Tania had been dating Contreras. There had been a birthday party for the teenage son of Molina's live-in girlfriend, and according to witnesses Contreras had arrived at Molina's house, located in an eastern Santiago neighborhood inhabited largely by military families, at about 9:30 P.M. Molina, it was said, liked the younger Contreras, and had been a great admirer of his father. In 1978, when the DINA chief and two other security agents were temporarily interned in the military hospital (following the U.S.

request for their extradition in the Letelier assassination), Molina had visited Contreras to pay his respects.

Molina's companion, María Alicia Saez, worked in the office of the military judge investigating the 1986 assassination attempt on Pinochet and the arms caches discovered that year in northern Chile. The younger Contreras worked in the same office, while Molina had been the CNI's point man with the military judge, delivering intelligence reports on the guerrilla organization, the Manuel Rodríguez Patriotic Front.

The other guests included many young adults from Chilean military families who had worked with Molina's daughter and son in Pinochet's campaign a few months earlier. One of the invited was Danko Derpich, the son of another high-ranking CNI official. At some point that night Contreras began fighting with Derpich, who was left semiconscious and with a concussion. According to Molina's friends, the CNI official intervened to stop the fight and ordered Contreras, Jr., to leave the party. Another argument ensued, and the former DINA chief's son fired twelve bullets into Molina with a Browning pistol. The CNI official died several days later in the military hospital in Santiago, while Contreras, Jr., claimed he had acted in self-defense.

Tania Molina and her brother defended their father's killer at a press conference held at the offices of Alfa-Omega, Contreras, Sr.'s private security agency, stating that Molina had been drunk and had fired the first shots at Contreras. Chilean officials attempting to investigate the case encountered an obstructive intelligence community: CNI agents prevented carabineros arriving at the scene from entering Molina's house, and the younger Contreras eluded a judge assigned to the case by checking into the military hospital, claiming to be suffering from hepatitis. (The judge interrogated him there anyway and found him in good health.)

As supporters of Molina and Contreras began lining up and angrily trading accusations in public, the private lives of the regime's security forces were suddenly on display. It was not a pretty sight. Chile's opposition press had a field day as witnesses, family friends, and associates came forward with charges and accusations against both parties.

The former DINA chief's son was depicted as a brutal and dangerous spoiled brat who had lived for a time after the 1973 coup in the notorious German settlement Colonia Dignidad in southern Chile, where his father was a frequent visitor. The late Major Molina had been linked by human rights organizations to executions of political prisoners during this same period. The scandal also weakened the elder Contreras, who was still feared in Chile and whose agents at the Alfa-Omega security agency were suspected of doing dirty work for the army on a freelance basis. The killing of a high-ranking CNI official and the injuries suffered by another CNI official's son by Contreras's son was like an axe blow splitting the regime's intelligence community.[5]

The former DINA chief's problems were compounded several weeks later when José Miguel Barros, a former career diplomat who had once served as the regime's ambassador to the United States, revealed that senior Chilean officials had been aware for years of Contreras's involvement in the Letelier assassination, despite public denials. Barros said he had attended a meeting in the offices of the regime's deputy interior minister, retired admiral Enrique Montero Marx, on April 27, 1978, and that Montero had said that "this intelligence genius mounted an operation to assassinate Letelier." Asked to whom he was referring, Montero answered that it was Manuel Contreras, former head of the DINA. According to Barros, the deputy interior minister then described how Contreras had attempted to cover up DINA's involvement. Montero hastily issued a statement saying his remarks to Barros were only personal opinions. Like many Chileans, Montero probably feared Contreras, who had compiled extensive dossiers on regime officials and supporters as well as on opposition figures.[6] Barros, meanwhile, received several death threats from anonymous callers undoubtedly linked to Contreras.

Yet the former DINA chief himself was feeling his position slip in wake of the charges against his son and in the changing political climate after the plebiscite. Barros's statements prompted the Letelier family to call for the case to be reopened. Sensing a need to publicly defend himself, Contreras contacted the Universidad Católica television station, whose news programs were less stridently proregime than those of other networks and enjoyed the highest viewer ratings in Chile. He gave a brief interview at the offices of his Alfa-Omega security agency, blandly denying any involvement in the Letelier assassination. The content of the interview was predictable, but Contreras's unexpected foray into the glare of a nightly news program after years of secrecy created yet another crack in the Pinochet regime's edifice.

On March 2, 1989, the U.S. embassy in Santiago received a call from what sounded like a poorly educated, middle-aged man. The caller spoke of hunger and economic hardship, and said that bombings and the killing of Chilean policemen had failed to get results. In order to get the attention of other countries, the caller said, Chilean fruit had been poisoned so that people in other countries would die. The embassy switchboard operator hastily scribbled down what was being said. The conversation was interrupted by a beeping sound characteristic of public telephones in Chile.

When the man telephoned again six days later, his call was recorded on tape. Poisoned fruit had been packed into boxes destined for export, he said, adding that "We have very specialized personnel; we have people everywhere."[7] Yet the caller named no group such as the Manuel Rodríguez Patriotic Front—which often telephoned the news media to claim responsibility for bombings and other acts of sabotage—as having poisoned the fruit. If this were some new group, it would have to have organized for months before attempting such an elaborate operation, and most likely would have undertaken some less ambitious actions before. In addition, low-paid Chilean fruit pickers and packaging plant workers would not have access to cyanide or other poisons, even if they were willing to risk arrest and loss of their jobs. Poisoning fruit was reminiscent of the 1982 Tylenol scare in the United States, the kind of action taken by extortionists or mentally unbalanced loners—not Chile's left-wing groups.

The U.S. embassy reported the telephone calls to Washington, and the Food and Drug Administration (FDA) was alerted. On March 14, 1989, FDA agents began a laborious inspection of Chilean fruit carried by the *Alméria Star*, a freighter that had left Chileo on February 27—three days before the U.S. embassy in Santiago received the first anonymous telephone call—and was now docked on the Delaware River in Philadelphia. Out of the thousands of crates of fruit, the FDA found two grapes with light-colored rings looking as if they had been perforated with a needle. Subsequent laboratory tests turned up traces of cyanide in the two grapes, in amounts too small even to cause illness. U.S. officials ordered an embargo on Chilean fruit arriving in the country, and a withdrawal of Chilean fruit from supermarket shelves in the United States. "This could be an isolated incident," the FDA commissioner, Frank Young, said. "But we don't want to run the risk." In Santiago, the Pinochet regime's interior minister, Carlos Cáceres, appeared on television and radio shortly after midnight to announce the government was studying the situation and blamed the Chilean Communist Party for the sabotage.[8]

The discovery of the cyanide-injected grapes, occurring at the height of the Chilean fruit harvest, eventually caused losses of at least $300 million to fruit growers and related businesses. Leaders of the Chilean Communist Party, however, publicly rejected the accusation that they were involved, and urged that a special prosecutor be named to investigate the sabotage.[9]

The knee-jerk anticommunist reaction among regime officials was predictable, but Chilean fruit growers, a group with largely pro-regime sympathies, began to direct their fury against the United States. The right-wing Unión Democrática Independiente (UDI) party, which had backed Pinochet in the plebiscite, organized anti-U.S. demonstrations, and growers transported busloads of their workers in from the countryside to fill the crowds. The demonstrations were held in front of the U.S. consulate in Santiago, which faced an open park, rather than the embassy, which was located in an office building on a narrow downtown sidestreet not easily accessible to such gatherings. The demonstrators waved placards and bunches of grapes, while proregime motorists formed automobile caravans reminiscent of the Pinochet campaign's final rally prior to the October 5 plebiscite. Some Chilean shipping executives charged that California fruit growers could have been behind the sabotage, while the navy commander, Admiral José Merino, said the ban on Chilean fruit was "yet another dirty trick by the United States against Chile, cooked up here by Communist scoundrels."[10]

Laboratory tests showed that the grapes found by the FDA on board the *Alméria Star* could not have been poisoned in Chile, for fruit injected with cyanide would have shriveled during the two-week trip to Philadelphia. Suspicions that the whole affair might indeed have originated in the United States were heightened when Ricardo

Claro, a prominent Chilean lawyer with business interests in shipping, wine, and agriculture, suggested that the United States might have deliberately sabotaged Chile's fruit exports to dissuade regime backers from undercutting the transition to democracy. Claro, who had served as director of the Chilean-American Cultural Institute in Santiago and who had had close ties to the U.S. embassy for two decades, recalled a conversation he had with the deputy chief of mission, George Jones, several weeks earlier. According to Claro, Jones had told him that the United States would impose sanctions against Chile if the regime or its supporters attempted to prolong Pinochet's rule. Jones denied having had such an encounter with Claro; and if it had taken place, it would not have constituted evidence of U.S. involvement in the affair.

Yet the theory of a U.S.-backed sabotage against Chilean fruit exports had a certain logic. The growers' parent organization, Chile's National Agricultural Society, had invited right-wing senator Jesse Helms to Santiago a few years earlier, a visit that rankled with the State Department. And hadn't the United States backed the opposition in the plebiscite, via funds for the opposition newspaper *La Época*, voter registration, and other related activities?[11] Chilean fruit exports had boomed during the previous five years, doubling to $585 million annually, and were considered one of the Pinochet regime's showcases (although fruit pickers and other seasonal agricultural workers received minimal earnings and benefits). After weeks of meetings with FDA and other U.S. officials, and promises to improve safeguards against possible health hazards, Chilean authorities managed to have the ban lifted. But for many proregime Chileans, the whole episode looked like a deliberate attempt by the United States to financially weaken an important part of Pinochet's constituency, although there would never be any way to conclusively prove responsibility.

On the morning of June 9, 1989, former air force lieutenant Roberto Fuentes Morrison stepped out of his house in southeastern Santiago and was hit by a burst of gunfire. His killers took the time to snatch his briefcase, but not the Browning pistol he habitually carried, before fleeing in an automobile that Chilean police later identified as having been stolen the previous week. Fuentes Morrison, who had been an active member of the right-wing extremist group Patria y Libertad during the Allende government, had joined the Chilean air force reserves in 1975 and been a key figure in the Comando Conjunto, the service's secret intelligence unit that was responsible for the arrest and killing of dozens of leftists. Two years earlier a civilian judge investigating the Comando Conjunto had issued an order for his arrest; the Chilean air force, anticipating such a move, announced that Fuentes Morrison had been assigned to a post in South Africa.

The air force offered their former reservist no service honors at his funeral, where Fuentes Morrison's brother darkly alluded to the security agent's "betrayal" by fellow operatives. Although an anonymous caller had telephoned the offices of the French news service Agence France Presse shortly after the killing, claiming to be a spokeswoman for the Manuel Rodríguez Patriotic Front, there were many signs that left-wing extremists might not have been behind the assassination. Why had his killers taken his briefcase, but not his pistol? According to some accounts, Fuentes Morrison knew too much about the Comando Conjunto for the comfort of his former associates, who were afraid he might make a deal with Chilean judicial officials still investigating the case. And some retired air force officials believed that Fuentes Morrison feared for his life as well.[12] The assassination and ensuing speculation over just who had been responsible were another sign of the tensions in the Chilean intelligence community, and as in the case of Joaquín Molina, drew public attention to one of the Pinochet regime's ugliest legacies.

Chile's first presidential election in nearly two decades was scheduled for December 14, 1989, and a few months after the plebiscite three candidates had emerged. For the opposition's sixteen-party coalition, which had indeed remained intact after the plebiscite, Patricio Aylwin, the former senate leader, Christian Democrat, and official president of the multiparty group, was running; so was Francisco Javier Errázuriz, an independent candidate who presented himself as a populist businessman. The regime's nominee was former finance minister Hernán Buchi, a youthful American-educated technocrat. Buchi, who sported longer hair and was known for his devotion to health and fitness, had been a leftist sympathizer during his student days in the sixties and, like so many of his generation, had steadily veered to the right. The epitome of the Chilean yuppie, he attracted the support of much of the country's business community, as well as of the right-wing political parties backing Pinochet in the plebiscite.

By the middle of that year, Pinochet seemed resigned to the fact that he would be vacating the La Moneda presidential palace. During a visit to the offices of the Banco del Estado, Pinochet told reporters, "One has to live with reality. I, at this moment, am not a good candidate," and indicated he would not try to run in the forthcoming presidential election.[13] However, he was adamant about not surrendering his post as army commander, which raised fears that Chile's future president would be little more than a puppet worked from behind by a military leader. This scenario was undoubtedly what Pinochet himself had in mind, and yet as the date for the elections approached his public statements revealed a growing hostile defensiveness.

"The day they touch any of my men will be the end of the state of law," he warned in a speech two months before the vote. He would remain commander of the Chilean army, he said, to protect "his" people. If Pinochet meant to threaten a military uprising in the event of an official inquiry into his regime's human rights record, Patricio Aylwin—who by now was the favored presidential candidate—remained unruffled. "What is one to understand by touching a man? Is it to apply the law and justice?" he asked. "I believe that phrase was an unfortunate one pronounced by this gentleman in an outburst, without really thinking."[14] Aylwin also pointed out that if Pinochet's statement was taken seriously, it would be tantamount to sedition.

On December 15, 1989, nearly six million Chileans went to the polls to elect a new president and congress. Aylwin won easily, with 55.2 percent of the votes. Buchi trailed behind with 29.3 percent, and Francisco Errázuriz finished with 14.4 percent. The returns also gave Aylwin's coalition a seventy-two to forty-eight majority in the Chilean congress; but in the senate, which the 1980 constitution stipulated would have nine members appointed by the military regime, the new government controlled twenty-two of forty-seven seats. Several tiny far-Right parties, such as the CNI-controlled Avanzada Nacional, failed to get any of their candidates elected, and thus according to the regime's own electoral rules could no longer legally operate as political parties. Pinochet gave a televised address the day after the election, urging Chileans to "face with hope the new horizon we ourselves have opened to our children," but conspicuously did not extend even the slightest congratulations to his impending successor as president.

March 11, 1990, was the last day of Pinochet's presidency. As his motorcade drove through the streets of Valparaiso, his hometown and the site of the new Chilean congress, Pinochet's open car was pelted with eggs, and he was confronted with cries of "Assassin! Assassin!" Grim-faced, the general removed the presidential sash and passed it to Aylwin, and the two men exchanged a perfunctory *abrazo*. For many Chileans it was a scene they thought they would never see. Among the foreign dignitaries at the inauguration was former U.S. ambassador Harry Barnes, whose term in Santiago had ended shortly after the 1988 plebiscite but who had been personally invited by Aylwin to attend the ceremonies. The diplomat whom Pinochet and his supporters had so detested was embraced by Chile's new president.

The next day Aylwin took a symbolic step toward healing some of the wounds of repression. As eighty thousand people gathered in Santiago's National Stadium, the most notorious site of mass detentions, torture, and executions after the coup, Aylwin gave his first major address to the nation. "From this spot, which in the sad days of blind and hateful dominance of force over reason was for many a place of prison and torture, we say to all Chileans and to the world that is watching us: Never again insults to human dignity! Never again hate between brothers! Never again fratricidal violence!" he said. Down on the field the mother of a *desaparecido* began to slowly perform the *cueca*, a Chilean folk dance, as an homage to the hundreds of Chileans missing and still unaccounted for following their arrest by the regime's security forces. Other Chilean public figures, including popular entertainers—some of whom had received death threats from a pro-regime extremist group two years earlier—joined in an emotional tribute to the country's new democracy.

Those Chileans still resistant to the notion that there had been gross violations of human rights during the military regime received a further jolt to their complacency later that month. Workers at Exxon's La Disputada copper mine north of Santiago discovered the bodies of three men buried on the site, which had formerly belonged to the Chilean army. The men were identified as leaders of the Communist

Party who had disappeared following their arrest in 1976. More bodies were uncovered at other clandestine burial sites around the country, including the remains of twenty men buried near Pisagua, a former prison camp in the Atacama desert. Officially, the prisoners had been "shot while trying to escape," but the condition of their remains, well preserved in the dry desert, told a different story. Most of the cadavers had been placed in bags, and several of the men had been tied up and blindfolded before being executed. In some cases, identity cards and personal letters to family and friends were found on the bodies, allowing quick identification. It was hardly the first time unidentified mass graves had been discovered: the Catholic Church had denounced the existence of a clandestine burial plot in Santiago's general cemetery as far back as 1979. But the discovery of the graves, coming on the heels of Aylwin's inauguration and speech at the National Stadium, moved even former regime officials to express shock. Sergio Diez, who had served as Pinochet's United Nations ambassador and who had defended the regime in the face of international criticism over Chile's human rights record, said that "no one had any idea of the extent of the abuses, and the truth must now be told about them."

Since leaving the junta in 1978, retired air force general Gustavo Leigh had operated a real-estate business, working with his son and another former air force general out of an office in eastern Santiago. On March 21, 1989, two masked gunmen burst into Leigh's private office and shot him and his associate, critically injuring both men before fleeing. A woman claiming to represent the Manuel Rodríguez Patriotic Front telephoned the Christian Democratic radio station, Radio Cooperativa, to announce that the left-wing guerrilla group was responsible for the attack, and warned that other former regime officials would be killed if Chile's new civilian government failed to bring to justice those responsible for human rights abuses. The Chilean left certainly had reason to hate the former air force commander, whose intelligence unit, the Comando Conjunto, had hunted down and killed suspected communists. But Chile's far Right also hated the dissident general, for his "disloyalty" to the regime and his increasing willingness over the years to make public his former comrades' secrets. Another group calling itself the Nationalist Resistance Front also claimed responsibility for the attack on Leigh, charging that he had betrayed the ideals of the September 11, 1973, coup.[15]

Leigh survived, but the attack shattered the all-too-brief atmosphere of reconciliation following Aylwin's inauguration. Pinochet, who now seemed a sinister observer from his offices at the Chilean defense ministry, grimly predicted that there would be a chain of attacks on former regime officials. President Aylwin immediately reacted by asking Pinochet to pass on any information the army might have regarding such a plan, and Pinochet backed down, denying he had ever made such a statement (which had in fact been printed in the pro-regime *El Mercurio* newspaper shortly after the attack).

On April 15, 1990, the Chilean Communist Party newspaper *El Siglo* published a list of nine hundred civilians who had worked for the CNI, the army-dominated intelligence organization that had replaced DINA in 1979. The list appeared to be accurate, and the individuals named—who included doctors, lawyers, and many relatively prominent Chileans—were aghast at and embarrassed by the revelations. More significant, the list of names appeared to have been leaked by a regime insider, indicating continuing ferment within Pinochet's intelligence community. Many suspected former DINA chief Manuel Contreras had been behind the leak, which would have served as a warning to any former collaborators that he could still damage them if he was not afforded sufficient protection.

Less than two months after taking office, the Aylwin government launched an official inquiry into the Pinochet regime's human rights record, announcing the appointment of a commission for truth and reconciliation. Led by Raúl Rettig, a former high court judge, the committee included two lawyers active in human rights groups, a respected Chilean historian, and even a member of a token human rights commission formed by the regime's interior ministry in 1987. The announcement enraged Pinochet, but his ensuing confrontations with the Aylwin government and even with many military officials only served to demonstrate how weak the former dictator had become. According to several accounts he tried at least five times to get Aylwin on the telephone the day the commission was officially formed, only to be told the president was too busy to speak with him. On May 3, the two men finally met at La Moneda, where Pinochet accused Aylwin of staging a witch-hunt against the military and his regime. Aylwin reportedly told him that his government was acting with far more decency than the military regime had shown to its predecessor, the socialist government of Salvador Allende. The Chilean armed forces were not going to be placed on trial, but the truth of what had happened to several hundred Chileans who disappeared during his regime must be established.[16]

Pinochet warned he would not attend a luncheon given by President Aylwin for Chile's military commanders the following day, but was told his absence would be interpreted as an act of insubordination. Army general Hugo Salas Wenzel, ex-director of the now-defunct CNI, turned up in Pinochet's stead. According to sources present at the luncheon, carabinero director General Rodolfo Stange, Admiral José Merino, and air force commander General Fernando Matthei shouted down Salas when he tried to attack the Aylwin government. The scene was reminiscent of the night of the October 5 plebiscite, when Pinochet failed to enlist the junta members' support for extending his powers.[17]

There were further confrontations between Pinochet and Aylwin, with the former dictator sometimes resorting to saber-rattling. In late May the army issued a communiqué charging that the Commission for Truth and Reconciliation would be used by those seeking to attack the Chilean army in general and Pinochet in particular. The communiqué prompted Aylwin to summon Pinochet to La Moneda, where his armored car was denied entrance at the palace gate. Forced to walk from the defense ministry across the street, Pinochet confronted demonstrators shouting "Murderer!" and other epithets as he made his way to the meeting. Inside La Moneda the army commander was reprimanded for "questioning or discussing decisions taken by the president," a government spokesman said. Aylwin also asked Pinochet to turn over all the CNI's records and files, in order to assist the new government with the human rights inquiry. Pinochet, who left the meeting through a private underground exit to avoid demonstrators and the press, told Aylwin of "the army's willingness to cooperate," according to a statement issued by the army.[18] But the files, which human rights investigators believed could contain clues as to the fate of several hundred missing people, never reached the new government, and Pinochet, when questioned by journalists about the promised cooperation, replied, "What archives? I don't have any."[19]

On September 4, 1990, exactly twenty years after he won a plurality of votes in Chile's presidential election, Salvador Allende's body was moved from the unmarked grave in Viña del Mar and given a symbolic state funeral. Thousands of people gathered along Santiago's main avenue as the vehicle carrying Allende's coffin passed; some wept, some shouted slogans of support, some tossed flowers at the open vehicle carrying the late president's remains. A funeral Mass held at Santiago's metropolitan cathedral was attended by Aylwin, his cabinet, and several foreign dignitaries such as Danielle Mitterrand, wife of the French president, and Lisbet Palme, the widow of the late Swedish prime minister. Allende was buried at Santiago's general cemetery in a new mausoleum built alongside the tombs of other former Chilean presidents.

The previous evening Hortensia Bussi de Allende had given an interview on Chilean television in which she came close to admitting that her husband had committed suicide. When asked if she wished Allende had surrendered to the military and left La Moneda alive, she said: "Never. What would Salvador have done in exile? He did the best he could do, which was to die in La Moneda."[20]

Pinochet, asked to comment on the Aylwin government's decision to have Allende reburied, called the funeral a political act, and replied with an abrupt "No" when asked if the Chilean armed forces would render the customary military honors befitting a deceased president. Four bombs exploded early on the morning of Allende's reburial, causing no injuries but damaging monuments, a shopping center, and an automobile dealership. Chilean police said the explosives were placed by a right-wing extremist group, the September 11 Command, which had taken its name from the date of the 1973 coup.[21]

The Chilean army still appeared solidly behind Pinochet, and yet even this institution was about to be shaken by a series of shock waves originating not from the Pinochet regime's opponents but from within the service's own ranks. An illegal money racket run by CNI officials came to light in the wake of the murder of one dissatisfied investor who demanded his money back. His widow began to make public accusations, and the ensuing criminal investigation by the newly convened congress was gleefully covered by the Chilean press. The racket, dubbed "La Cutufa" after one official's dog, offered investors— mostly military officers and those close to the regime—tax-free interest rates of up to 20 percent a month. The funds were used to finance a sordid network of cocaine and arms trafficking, as well as a bizarre sideline of smuggling aboriginal mummies from the Atacama desert.

Pinochet ordered an internal investigation of the affair, which resulted in four army generals taking early retirement, sixteen officers being cashiered, and two hundred more sanctioned. At the same time, he refused to divulge the full findings of the army inquiry and gave civilian officials only a list of 150 officers who had lost their savings in La Cutufa. Many of those whose names appeared on the list felt betrayed by Pinochet for revealing their involvement, while other officers were said to be discomfited by their commander's refusal to divulge the full army investigation into the scandal, feeling that this obvious attempt to protect certain high-ranking officials damaged the institution's honor. The Chilean army, supposedly so incorruptible, so disciplined, was looking decidedly dirty.

Then congressional investigators also turned up a questionable payment by the army to Pinochet's eldest son. Augusto Pinochet, Jr., had received a check for U.S. $3 million from the army in mid-1989 when the service purchased a small rifle company. His name did not appear on any list of the rifle company's owners, and no one seemed willing to explain why he should be the beneficiary of this questionable acquisition by the Chilean army. The case, which the local news media called the case of the "Pinocheques," brought renewed calls for Pinochet's removal as army commander. A close Pinochet adviser, General Jorge Ballerino, approached the Aylwin government, purportedly to discuss the terms for his commander's early retirement; otherwise, Pinochet would head the army until 1997 when he would be eighty-one. But on December 19, 1990, the day Ballerino was scheduled to meet with the Aylwin government's civilian defense minister, Pinochet stormed into the army headquarters and placed the 57,000-member force on alert. The next day the Aylwin government's civilian defense minister, visibly shaken, appeared on television to deny that there had been any negotiations for Pinochet's departure from the army.[22]

Significantly, the army protest was not backed up by the other branches of the Chilean military—the air force, navy, and carabineros. And even within the army there were rumblings of dissatisfaction with Pinochet. A few weeks after he ordered the army placed on alert, a left-wing newspaper, *Fortín Mapocho*, reported the confidential briefing of a retired army general, who had indicated that the CNI racketeering scandal and the Pinocheques affair had prompted a call within the service for Pinochet's removal. Pinochet, according to the newspaper's version of this report, was in the view of many officers hurting the army's relations with other branches of the armed forces. The retired general later said he had been quoted out of context but did not disclaim the newspaper account. There were signs that the army was negotiating for Pinochet's early retirement, to be timed in such a way as to make it appear that old age, rather than outside pressure, was the real motive for his departure.

The moral conscience of the nation requires the truth about the grave human rights violations committed in the country between September 11, 1973, and March 11, 1990. Only on the basis of truth will it be possible to satisfy the elemental demands of justice and to create the indispensable conditions for a real national reconciliation.

—From the report by the Aylwin government's inquiry into human rights abuses during the regime

For nine months the Commission for Truth and Reconciliation had been painstakingly gathering information on politically motivated killings, torture, and other violence during the military regime. Much of the data had already been compiled by the Catholic Church's Vicaría de la Solidaridad, the Chilean human rights commission, and related organizations over the years, but the Aylwin government investigative body also went to considerable lengths to seek out additional witnesses both in Chile and abroad. The commission documented 877 cases of persons missing following their detention by regime security agents, and at the time of writing still had one group of 133 cases under investigation and another group of 77 cases that had been received only recently. In many instances these incidents involved victims in isolated rural areas whose relatives had not dared to come forward until the Pinochet regime had ended. Another 815 persons had died under torture or were executed; an additional group of 101 victims had been killed "while trying to escape." The commission also turned up dozens of cases where the regime's security agents had committed murders on their own, motivated not by ideology but by revenge or personal vendetta. The final tally compiled by the commission came to 2,279 people: 2,115 at the hands of the regime, and the remaining 164 "victims of political violence," a figure that included police officers and others killed by left-wing extremists.[23]

Some families of Chileans still unaccounted for after their arrest by the regime security forces had clung to the fragile hope that the *desaparecidos* would still be alive, perhaps in some secret detention center, or at the very least, that the remains of those whose bodies had not been found would be located and given decent burials. These families were understandably left distraught by the commission's report, although Aylwin, speaking in a televised address to the country the day the six-volume report was delivered to his office, said that Chile's courts should continue investigating these cases.

Nevertheless, the commission's report was particularly critical of the Chilean judiciary under the Pinochet regime, which on countless occasions had refused to issue writs of habeas corpus in behalf of those arrested by security forces.[24] Aylwin noted that when regime officials committed abuses other branches of government failed to act and that there was not enough public outcry to prevent or halt these abuses. "For this reason, in the name of the entire country, I ask forgiveness from the families of these victims," he said.[25]

The report did not identify any particular individuals as responsible for the abuses, and Aylwin, in his speech, asked the armed forces for help in determining the fate of the missing. But despite the report's careful language, it was received in Pinochet's office at the Chilean defense ministry as a damning indictment of his sixteen-and-a-half years in power.

Addressing an assembly of senior military officers, Pinochet blasted the report as a one-sided version of events under his regime and called members of the Commission for Truth and Reconciliation unqualified to judge the actions of the Chilean army. "Its content reveals an unpardonable refusal to recognize the real causes that motivated the action to rescue the nation on September 11, 1973," he told the cheering officers.

In fact, the report included a historical summary of Chile's political changes over the past four decades, describing how the Cold War had affected the country and the role played by different political groups up to 1973. The Council of Retired Army generals, led by former DINA chief Manuel Contreras, published a lengthy statement in the press, arguing once again that the report was partial and did not give sufficient credit to the military for its "patriotic sacrifices" on behalf of the country under Pinochet. The statement said that while no members of the armed forces were named in the report, the long list of "supposed" victims of human rights abuses could incite a kind of mob violence against the military.[26] The statement, almost certainly drafted at Pinochet's behest, did not reflect the views of all retired Chilean army generals but did allow Pinochet, who had played a negligible role himself in the coup, to rouse some defensive reaction from the military, which he clearly intended to manipulate to support his own position as army commander. But times were changing, and even those officers bristling from the Aylwin government's human rights inquiry did not necessarily want the aging Pinochet to remain their commander for seven more years.

On one of the last days of the Chilean summer, a group of about twenty women walked down a street in the working class San Miguel section of Santiago toward a building housing some municipal government offices. Fifteen years earlier the building had been the site of the Tres and Cuatro Alamos detention centers run by the DINA. The women, each bearing a red carnation, walked slowly through the building, stopping often to recall the areas where they had been detained, interrogated, and tortured. It was a painful visit; several of the women wept aloud as they moved through the former DINA installation.

Among the women was Isabel Plaza, fifteen years old. Her mother, eight months pregnant at the time of her arrest, had given birth to

Isabel while a prisoner at the center. The mother and infant daughter had gone into exile when they were released months later, and Isabel had spent her entire childhood outside Chile, returning only three years earlier. Though many of her contemporaries considered her an outsider, she was still determined to make the country her own. And one step toward reclaiming Chile was to visit the grisly site of her own birth and her mother's suffering.

"I am Chilean," she told the newspaper *La Nación*. "And I want to study and work in my country." The former prisoners of Tres and Cuatro Alamos exchanged hugs and left their red carnations at the entrance to the building.[27]

No elected civilian government, inaugurated after sixteen years of a military dictatorship, can hope to redress all the pent-up grievances of its newly enfranchised electorate. One of the first measures undertaken by President Patricio Aylwin's government was a tax increase to finance a $2.35 billion public spending program. The new government managed to secure backing for the program in the Chilean senate, where regime appointees and rightist politicians held a majority. Yet it would have been difficult for this faction, now accountable to voters, to publicly oppose the measures Aylwin wanted: an increase in the minimum wage from $51 to $94 per month, plus improvements in the country's worn-out infrastructure.[28] Santiago, a city of over four million people, would finally get a sewage system, a project the regime's planning ministry had rejected years earlier as uneconomic. The new measures did not go far enough to satisfy the demands of labor unions and other groups whose expectations had been raised by Chile's return to democracy, while business groups remained skeptical of the new government's commitment to free enterprise. The Chilean economy grew by 2 percent in 1990, down from the 5 percent growth rate of previous years, but recovered the following year and in 1992 grew by 10.4 percent, the largest growth rate reported in twenty-seven years, according to the central bank. Inflation declined from 18.7 percent to 12.7 percent in 1992, while unemployment fell to 4.8 percent, the lowest level in nearly two decades.

The regime's presidential candidate and former finance minister, Hernán Buchi, frequently criticized the Aylwin government's eco-

nomic performance, accusing officials of having caused a "loss of dy-
namism" in the economy. Buchi, along with former regime labor minister José Piñera and debt negotiator Hernán Somerville, began
frequent trips abroad to advise other countries on privatization and
other economic reforms. The collapse of communism in Eastern Europe lent a new gloss to the Pinochet regime's economic policies.
Czechoslovakia sought Buchi's advice on privatization, and Poland
consulted him about the country's bankrupt state banks. A research
group headed by Buchi, the Institute for Liberty and Development,
hosted twenty-five economists from the former Soviet Union at a 1992
conference on the regime's economic model.[29]

Yet such visitors to Santiago have been confronted with an environ-
mental disaster at least as daunting as any left by the fallen communist
dictators of Eastern Europe. The Chilean capital has become one of
the world's most polluted cities, forcing authorities to order the temporary closing of schools and factories when smog reaches its worst
levels during the southern hemisphere's winter. An estimated two-
thirds of pollution comes from the city's bus system, which was dereg-
ulated by the regime's economic team. Some eleven thousand buses,
often poorly maintained, spew black clouds of diesel exhaust throughout Santiago. The number of buses, all in private hands, far exceeds
passenger demand, and even during rush hour many carry fewer than
ten people.

On June 28, 1992, Aylwin's center-Left political coalition won 53.3
percent of the votes in Chile's municipal election, while the right-
wing opposition alliance received 29.8 percent—four points below
their showing in the 1989 presidential election. If the municipal elections seemed a vote of confidence in the Aylwin government, the results only made Chile's political right wing harden its position in the
senate and announce it would oppose efforts to amend the Pinochet
regime's constitution.[30]

The aging former dictator had spent three weeks in the hospital
earlier that year and had been fitted with a pacemaker. Now nearly a
generation older than any of the Chilean army's corps of generals, he
planned to stay on as army commander until 1997, when he would be
eighty-one. Lifelong tenure for Pinochet and other military com-

manders was one of the constitutional provisions the Aylwin government wanted to change, along with the regime's nine appointed senators-for-life.

Pinochet had ambitious plans for reorganizing the Chilean army, and in a post-communist world he soon found a new external threat to the country—the United States. In a speech at Santiago's military academy, he warned of the "dangers generated by the hegemony of a superpower." He proposed expanding the Chilean military's role to include antidrug and antiterrorist operations.[31] The Aylwin government's civilian defense minister, Patricio Rojas, commented afterward that any reorganization of the Chilean military would be the president's job, not Pinochet's.

Pinochet's two predecessors as army commander, General René Schneider and General Carlos Prats, were murdered by right-wing extremists and the regime's security forces. If his predecessors' assassins posed no threat to him, Schneider's and Prats's violent deaths did not make the final years of his career any easier. "When I am finished here, they can come kill me as I expect," he had told a group of foreign journalists in 1984. "I'm a soldier and I'm ready." The spectre of an assassination still lingered in his mind years later, and in September 1992 he seemed to be almost boasting when he told the Chilean tabloid newspaper *La Tercera* that he still received death threats. "I'm in the first or second place in every list of people they have targeted to kill," he said. [32]

This old soldier did not want just to fade away, but despite the long shadow he cast over the country, Chile was no longer the ideological battleground it once was. Pinochet's influence was slowly dwindling. Even the country's right-wing parties did not want to cede any more power to Pinochet. "We are grateful for what he did, but we do not want a return to military rule," said Juan Antonio Coloma, a right-wing member of the chamber of deputies. "We believe in democracy."[33]

Notes

Prologue

1. Nathaniel Tarn, ed., *Pablo Neruda: Selected Poems*, Dell, New York, 1972, p. 201.
2. *Time*, Jan. 14, 1980, p. 46.
3. From a written statement issued by the Chilean bishops' conference, Jan. 1986.
4. See "Note from the Publisher," in Pinochet, *Crucial Day*, p.9.

Chapter One

1. Allende's family was not able to get a certificate of his death from Chilean authorities until 1977, his daughter Isabel told the Chilean newsmagazine *Hoy* (Oct. 19–25, 1983).
2. *APSI*, Aug. 29–Sept. 4, 1989.
3. For a summary of Chile's population makeup, see *Chile: A Country Study*, Area Handbook Series, U.S. Government Printing Office, Washington, D.C., 1982, pp. 57–72.
4. Isabel Allende, *The House of the Spirits*, Alfred A. Knopf, New York, 1985, p. 156.
5. "When you go back, tell people we are not all Indians here" is a remark made frequently to North American and European visitors to Chile.
6. See Nunn, pp. 72–79.
7. *APSI*, Aug. 29–Sept. 4, 1989.
8. Pinochet, *Crucial Day*, p. 17.
9. Ibid., p. 19.
10. Ibid., p. 29.
11. Pinochet, *La Guerra del Pacífico*.

12. Pinochet, *Geopolítica*. A Chilean scholar, who asked not to be identified, compared the book's text with Rodríguez's lectures.

13. Interview with retired General Horacio Toro, Santiago.

14. Pinochet, *Crucial Day*, p. 46.

15. U.S. Senate Intelligence Committee, *Covert Action in Chile*, Washington, 1975, p. 26.

16. Hersh, *Price of Power*, p. 289.

17. See Isabel Letelier and Michael Moffit, *Human Rights, Economic Aid, and Private Banks: The Case of Chile*, Institute for Policy Studies, Washington, D.C., 1978.

18. This account comes from a participant at the meeting with Pinochet, who asked that his name not be used.

19. Interview with Moy de Tohá, Santiago.

20. The account of this interservice meeting comes from participants at the gathering, who have requested anonymity.

21. According to Chile's national statistical bureau and figures from the central bank, annual consumer price inflation reached 508.1 percent from December 1972 to December 1973, with an 87 percent jump in October, the month following the coup. Regime defenders have often cited a figure of 1,000 percent during the Allende period, but the record shows that inflation, while extremely high, never reached such levels.

22. Interview with retired air force General Nicanor Díaz, Santiago.

23. Testimony by a chief petty officer in the Chilean navy, cited in *Evidence on the Terror in Chile*, a report compiled by Raúl Silva, Birgitta Leander, and Sun Axelsson (Ab Raben & Sjogren, Stockholm, 1974), p. 1. English trans. pub. by Merlin Press, London, 1974.

24. Many Chileans close to the Allende government were surprised by Pinochet's eventual compliance with the coup plotters. According to some accounts, Allende's widow, Hortensia Bussi, when advised of the military uprising on September 11, 1973, exclaimed, "And what will become of poor General Pinochet?" See, for example, Harrington and González, p. 148.

25. Prats, pp. 480–81.

26. Pinochet, *Crucial Day*, p. 108.

27. Moy de Tohá interview.

28. Colonel René Cantuarias was brought to the Chilean military academy the day after the coup, but there is little information available about what went on at the army mountaineering school on September 11, 1973. Cantuarias died in detention; his death was described by military authorities as a suicide.

29. The Pinochet family later tried to cover up this damaging incident. Lucía, his eldest daughter, gave an interview to the Chilean women's magazine *Caras* (April 19, 1989) in which she claimed that her mother and siblings

had gone skiing in Portillo, a resort in the same area. She granted the interview on condition that the magazine let her see the article before it was published, arguing that "I am so sincere I might say bothersome things."

30. Sergio Arellano Iturriaga, *Mas Allá del Abismo*, Editorial Proyección, Santiago, 1985, p. 47. Arellano's father, General Sergio Arellano Stark, was one of the chief coup plotters in the Chilean army and served as a principal source for his son's book.

31. Pinochet, *Crucial Day*, p. 123.

32. Ibid.

33. Chileans residing near Avenida Colón described this scene to me.

34. Díaz interview.

35. Interview with Dr. Patricio Guijón in Santiago.

36. On the first anniversary of the coup, the regime broadcast a tape recording of Carvajal's telephone conversation with Allende, omitting Allende's response. Allende supporters circulated a different version, in which he supposedly told Carvajal to tell the Chilean air force general who had offered him the plane, "Tell General Von Showen that the president of Chile does not flee in a plane. As he knows how a soldier should act, I will know how to fulfill my duty as president of the republic."

37. Guijón interview.

38. Interview with Sergio Arellano Iturriaga in Santiago.

39. Guijón interview.

40. Miria Contreras, who received political asylum in Cuba, caused a stir in early 1988 when she told guests at a dinner party in Havana that Allende had committed suicide, and embellished her version of events by claiming that Augusto Olivares—who in fact died before Allende—brought her to the room where Allende had killed himself. Her remarks were printed in an article by an Italian journalist present at the gathering and reprinted in *El Mercurio*, Chile's right-wing daily newspaper. Contreras did not deny making the remarks, which outraged and embarrassed those Allende supporters who continued to believe that he had been killed by the military.

41. Guijón interview.

42. Sergio Badiola later became a trusted ally of Pinochet's, and like his commander tried to downplay his former association with Allende. On May 10, 1988, Badiola met with the foreign press association in Santiago, of which I was a member, and he was asked about his recollections of his time as Allende's aide-de-camp. "It was a posting of about nine or ten months' duration, er, seven or eight, let's say six months' duration. The treatment was correct, but I did not get to know Allende personally."

43. Arellano interview.

44. Pinochet, *Crucial Day*, p. 135.

45. Interview with Guillermo Norambuena, Santiago.

46. General Díaz made this statement in an interview with Chilean journalist Sergio Marras, author of *Confesiones,* a collection of accounts by former regime officials, p. 111.

47. Pinochet, *Crucial Day*, p. 137.

48. Interview with Silvia Alessandri, Santiago.

49. Prats, p. 513.

50. Pinochet, *Crucial Day*, pp. 141–42.

51. Harrington and González, p. 30.

52. Quoted in Harrington and González, p. 37.

53. This account comes from Chilean army sources who requested anonymity.

Chapter Two

1. Marta Gabriela Cortés Reyes described her experiences for me in an interview in Santiago.

2. Moy de Tohá's account can be found in the book *Miedo en Chile,* by Patricia Politzer. She elaborated further on her experiences for me in two extended interviews in her home.

3. *New York Times,* Sept. 16, 1973, p. 1.

4. *New York Times,* Sept. 17, 1973, p. 12.

5. *New York Times,* Sept. 20, 1973, p. 13.

6. Neruda, *Memoirs,* pp. 349–50.

7. Nemesio Antunez was interviewed in his home in Santiago.

8. Patricio Guijón recounted his experiences in two separate interviews at his office in Santiago.

9. Pinochet, *Crucial Day*, p. 146.

10. Interview with Nelson Morales Leal in his attorney's office in Santiago. The Tacna regiment, to which he was assigned, was one of three army units whose troops stormed La Moneda the day of the coup.

11. Interview with Jorge Edwards at his home in Santiago.

12. These claims are documented in *El Estadio Nacional,* a pamphlet of eyewitness accounts put together by the Agrupación de Familiares de Ejecutádos Políticos (AFEP), 1988.

13. Interview with María Cristina González at her home in Santiago.

14. For an account of Charles Horman's arrest, see Thomas Hauser's book *Missing,* originally published as *The Execution of Charles Horman: An American Sacrifice* (Harcourt Brace Jovanovich, New York, 1978). I disagree with the author's contention that U.S. officials set up Horman for arrest by Chilean authorities because he supposedly happened upon evidence of American involvement in the coup during a visit to Viña del Mar; it seems extremely improbable that the U.S. military officers he met would have so carelessly spilled such information. Although allegations of U.S. efforts to undermine

Allende had circulated for years, hard evidence did not come to light until years later in Washington. Given the scale of the repression following the coup, Horman could have been arrested simply because as a foreigner he looked suspicious to a zealous procoup Chilean. Hauser, who did not visit Chile while researching the book (he contracted freelance writers living in Santiago to supply the descriptions of the Chilean capital and of Viña del Mar and Valparaiso), also left out certain circumstances surrounding Horman's arrest for reasons of personal privacy. Nevertheless, the book raises disturbing questions about U.S. officials' actions toward detained American citizens in Chile during this period.

15. Statement of Adam and Patricia Garrett-Schesch to the Senate, Sept. 26, 1973, p. 17. U.S. Government Printing Office, Washington, D.C., 1973.

16. Ibid.

17. Nathaniel Davis, *The Last Two Years of Salvador Allende*, Cornell Univ. Press, Ithaca, N.Y., 1985, p. 378. Davis has convincingly answered accusations that he and other U.S. embassy officials were involved in Charles Horman's arrest and murder, and sued Universal Pictures, which made the Costa Gavras film *Missing*, for libel. The suit was unsuccessful; Davis and the other plaintiffs were unable to prove malice.

18. *El Estadio Nacional*, pp. 43–44.

19. "Report of the Comptroller General of the United States: An Assessment of Selected U.S. Embassy Consular Efforts to Assist and Protect Americans Overseas During Crises and Emergencies," United States General Accounting Office, Washington, Dec. 4, 1975, p. 23.

20. Ibid., p. 26.

21. *El Valle de las Viudas*, Agrupación de Familiares de Ejecutádos Políticos (AFEP), Santiago, 1988.

22. A complete account of this particular case can be found in Máximo Pacheco's book *Lonquén* (Editorial Aconcagua, Santiago, 1980).

23. Verdugo, *Tiempo de Días Claras*, p. 35.

24. *Revista Análisis*, Mar. 7–13, 1988, p. 12.

25. The story that follows is from my interview with Moy de Tohá.

26. Interview with Lincoyán Zepeda at his office in Santiago. He has also recounted part of his experience in *Los Zarpazos del Puma*, by Patricia Verdugo (pp. 136–37 and 147–48) and in a newsmagazine article, "Dramático Relato de Sobreviviente," *Revista Análisis*, Santiago, Nov. 19–25, 1985, pp. 7–8.

27. One of those executed was a lawyer, Roberto Guzmán, whose case illustrates the brutal capriciousness of military justice at the time. According to documents released in 1987 by the Chilean lawyers' guild, Guzmán had already been tried and sentenced to prison twice before General Arellano's visit. On September 25, 1973, a military judge in La Serena ordered him to spend two hundred days in prison; two days later a higher military court in-

creased this sentence to five years. On June 26, 1975, almost two years after Guzmán had been executed, his sentence was reduced to 541 days. Finally, on January 6, 1976, the court dismissed all charges against him.

28. The Truth and Reconciliation Commission, a special committee appointed by President Patricio Aylwin to investigate human rights abuses under the military regime, reported that the thirteen Copiapó prisoners' bodies were finally uncovered on July 31, 1990, after the group filed suit. According to the commission's report, published in *La Nación*, Mar. 5, 1991, some of the bodies "were mutilated, with bullet wounds, and bearing evident signs of knife slashes" (p. 62).

29. Zepeda interview.

30. *Diario Atacama*, Copiapó, Oct. 18, 1973, p. 1.

31. Pinochet, *Crucial Day*, p. 122.

32. Interview with Eugenio Rivera at the home of another retired military officer in Santiago. His account also appears in Verdugo, *Los Zarpazos del Puma*, pp. 189–205.

33. "Informe de la Comisión de Verdad y Reconciliación," complete text, p. 57. Published as a special supplement by the Chilean government newspaper, *La Nación*, Mar. 5, 1991. The group said it found no evidence of sabotage by leftists in the area (including rumored thefts of explosives at the state-owned Empresa Nacional de Explosivos and damage to mining installations), and that this desert region of Chile had in fact seen almost no resistance to the coup.

34. "Ejecuciones del Norte: Versiones de una Massacre," *APSI*, Santiago, May 25–30, 1987, pp. 11–12.

35. Rivera interview.

36. Sergio Arredondo later joined the regime's secret police organization, the DINA, as did two other members of Arellano's committee, Major Pedro Espinoza and Lieutenant Armando Fernandez Larios. Espinoza and Fernandez Larios were sought by the U.S. Department of Justice for their part in the 1976 car-bomb assassination in Washington of Orlando Letelier, the Chilean exile leader.

37. Rivera interview.

38. Notarized statement signed by General Joaquín Lagos Osorio, reprinted in *APSI*, Dec. 15–28, pp. 18–21. This statement also substantiates my description of the meeting.

39. Morales interview.

40. According to the report of the Aylwin government's Truth and Reconciliation Commission, Denrio Max Álvarez Olivares was a seventeen-year-old university student and a member of the Chilean communist party who was detained on December 3, 1973. He was taken from the jail to the Buin army regiment just outside Santiago, and his cadaver was later recovered at the Instituto Médico Legal, Chile's coroner's office. The cause of death, according

to the report, was a bullet wound; the commission concluded that Álvarez and another young prisoner "were executed by agents of the State, in grave violation of their human rights" (*La Nación*, Mar. 5, 1991, p. 49).

41. This account of General Bachelet's death comes from the commission, which concluded that although he died in his cell of a heart attack, the brutal treatment he had received earlier certainly aggravated his condition, and therefore his death was the responsibility of his captors (ibid., p. 113).

42. Morales interview.

43. Guijón interview.

44. Ibid.

45. Ibid.

46. Moy de Tohá interview.

47. Ibid.

48. Ibid.

49. The commission investigated Tohá's death, noting that the former Allende cabinet minister was "in a grave state of malnutrition," and concluded that the circumstances surrounding his death constituted a clear case of abuse at the hands of his captors (*La Nación*, Mar. 5, 1991, p. 113).

Chapter Three

1. Excerpts from the junta's speeches of Sept. 11, 1973, were taken from Pinochet, *Crucial Day*, which reprinted the complete texts (pp. 247–48).

2. The Soviet Union and other communist countries, except Romania and the People's Republic of China, broke relations with Chile shortly after the coup.

3. Cavallo, Salazar, and Sepúlveda, p. 8.

4. Ibid.

5. The regime's multiple cabinet changes were reprinted in a graph in *El Mercurio*, Oct. 23, 1988, p. D1.

6. Interview with retired air force general Nicanor Díaz at his home in Santiago.

7. Interview with Frederico Willoughby, Santiago.

8. *Revista Qué Pasa*, Nov. 19, 1987, cited in Cavallo, Salazar, and Sepúlveda, p. 24.

9. *Libro Blanco del Cambio de Gobierno en Chile*, Editorial Lord Cochrane, Santiago, 1973, pp. 54–57.

10. Millas, pp. 9, 23.

11. Interview with Edgardo Boeninger at his office in Santiago.

12. For a comparison of U.S. and multilateral aid to Chile under the governments of Eduardo Frei, Salvador Allende, and the military regime through 1978, see Isabel Letelier and Michael Moffit, *Human Rights, Eco-*

nomic Aid and Private Banks: The Case of Chile, Institute for Policy Studies, Washington, D.C., monograph, 1978.

13. "Kennedy Proposes 'No Rush' to Aid New Chilean Regime," *Miami Herald*, Sept. 30, 1973.

14. Interview with Orlando Saenz at his office in Santiago.

15. "Private U.S. Loans to Chile Up Sharply," *New York Times*, Nov. 12, 1973; "New Chilean Regime Gets $12 Million in U.S. Grain Aid," *Miami Herald*, Nov. 26, 1973.

16. "Chile Gets Loan After 3-Year Ban," *Washington Post*, Apr. 26, 1974.

17. *Wall Street Journal*, July 25, 1974; *Journal of Commerce*, Oct. 25, 1974; "Chile Reportedly to Pay ITT $100 Million," *Los Angeles Times*, Dec. 20, 1974; "Cerro Corp. Says Chile Agrees to Repay At Least $41.9 Million for Seized Mine," *Wall Street Journal*, Mar. 13, 1974; "Chile to Repay Firm," *Miami Herald*, Mar. 14, 1974.

18. Interview with retired general Horacio Toro, Santiago.

19. Quoted in Thomas Hauser, *Missing*, Harcourt Brace Jovanovich, New York, 1978, pp. 181–82.

20. "Black Attaché to Chile Barred by U.S. Military Aide in Chile," *Washington Post*, Dec. 1, 1973. Ray Davis, the U.S. Milgroup head cited in this article, is also discussed in Hauser.

21. Lars Schoultz, *Human Rights and United States Policy Toward Latin America*, Princeton Univ. Press, Princeton, N.J., 1981, p. 53.

22. "U.S. Suit Asserts Campaign Was for Military Regime, Full Information Is Asked," *Wall Street Journal*, Dec. 19, 1978; "Chile Lobbied Illegally, U.S. Charges," *Miami Herald*, Dec. 19, 1978.

23. Quoted in "Informe de la Comisión de Verdad y Reconciliación," p. 31, published as a supplement to the Chilean government newspaper, *La Nación*, Mar. 5, 1991.

24. Interview with Alvaro Zuñiga at his home in Santiago. He, along with three other foreign-service officers, was fired in 1988 and later reincorporated into the Chilean foreign service by President Patricio Aylwin. At the time of writing he was Chilean ambassador to Norway.

25. Heraldo Muñoz, *Las Relaciones Exteriores del Gobierno Militar Chileno*, Ediciones del Ornitorrinco, Santiago, 1986, p. 21. Muñoz was the Chilean ambassador to the Organization of American States at the time of writing.

26. Cavallo, Salazar, and Sepúlveda, p. 20.

27. *El Mercurio*, Mar. 12, 1974.

28. Ibid.

29. This information comes from sources present at the ceremony, who did not wish to be identified.

30. Cavallo, Salazar, and Sepúlveda, p. 23.

31. *El Mercurio*, June 28, 1974.

32. *Revista Qué Pasa*, Sept. 16, 1981.

33. Correa, Sierra, and Subercaseaux, *Los Generales del Régimen*, Editorial Aconcagua, Santiago, 1983, p. 13.

34. For a detailed and nonpolemical analysis of Chilean economic troubles during the Allende government, see Felipe Larrain and Patricio Meller, "The Socialist-Populist Chilean Experience, 1970–1973," in *The Macroeconomics of Populism in Latin America*, Rudiger Dornbusch and Sebastian Edwards, eds., Univ. of Chicago Press, 1992.

35. Text of Finance Minister Jorge Cauas's speech, reprinted in *Chilean Economic Policy*, Juan Carlos Méndez, ed. Central Bank of Chile, Santiago, Nov. 1979, pp. 157–63.

36. From Frieden, p. 155.

37. Lavin, *Miguel Kast*, p. 42.

38. Ibid., p. 47.

39. Nicanor Díaz interview.

40. See *Covert Action in Chile, 1963–1973*, staff report of the Senate Select Committee to Study Governmental Operations with Respect to Intelligence Activities (U.S. Senate), U.S. Government Printing Office, Washington, D.C., Dec. 18, 1975.

41. "$4.4 Billion Bill Barring Chile Aid Passed by Senate," *Los Angeles Times*, Feb. 19, 1976.

42. From a State Department telegram sent by the U.S. embassy in Santiago Feb. 21, 1976, declassified under the Freedom of Information Act.

43. "Chile Arms Pledge Called 'Shoddy Deal,' " *Washington Post*, June 25, 1976.

44. "Chilean Military Stays Out in the Cold," *Financial Times*, Dec. 21, 1983.

Chapter Four

1. Interview with Guillermo Norambuena, Santiago.

2. Interview with Germán Campos, who at the time of writing headed the security department of the Sheraton Hotel in Santiago.

3. Cavallo, Salazar, and Sepúlveda, p. 33.

4. *¿Dónde Están?*, vol. 3, pp. 547–49.

5. Interview with Aedo's wife, María Cristina González, in Santiago.

6. For good accounts of the Contreras-Pinochet relationship, see Dinges and Landau, and Branch and Propper.

7. Toro interview.

8. Quoted in Verdugo, *Tiempo de Dias Claras*, p. 35.

9. Colonia Dignidad has been the subject of many newspaper articles in Chile and abroad. See for example *Financial Times*, May 19, 1988, p. 4. On Feb. 1, 1991, President Patricio Aylwin issued a decree stripping the colony

of its status as a charitable organization, thus allowing officials to investigate it. Reuters dispatch, Santiago, Feb. 2, 1991.

10. "Confesiones de un agente de seguridad," pamphlet published by the Agrupación de Familiares de Detenidos-Desaparecidos, Santiago, Dec. 1984. Valenzuela's descriptions are also from this source.

11. Willoughby interview. Other sources credit him with helping several Chilean journalists avoid arrest by the DINA.

12. From a copy of a letter in the Vicaría's Centro de Documentación, Santiago.

13. Quoted in Marras, pp. 21, 23.

14. Cavallo, Salazar, and Sepúlveda, p. 51.

15. Ibid., p. 53.

16. Arellano Iturriaga, pp. 64–65.

17. The DINA's overseas operations, killings, and attempted assassinations have been the subject of several books, including Dinges and Landau's *Assassination on Embassy Row* and Branch and Propper's *Labyrinth*. Propper, formerly an assistant U.S. attorney general for the District of Columbia, was one of the chief investigators in the Letelier case and questioned Michael Townley, whose testimony revealed a great deal about the DINA's operations.

18. Dinges and Landau, p. 174.

19. Interview with Ines Callejas de Townley, now Mariana Callejas, Santiago. At the time of our interview she was still residing in the house in eastern Santiago that the DINA had provided for her and Townley. According to the authors of *Labyrinth*, Townley agreed to help CNI chief Odlanier Mena, who succeeded Manuel Contreras, in locating some of Contreras's bank accounts in return for a stipend of U.S. $1,500 per month to Mariana Callejas, $165 per month for himself while in prison, upkeep and repairs on their house in Santiago, plus payment of his $20,000 in lawyers' bills (*Labyrinth*, pp. 596–97).

20. Cavallo, Salazar, and Sepúlveda, p. 117.

21. Dinges and Landau, p. 277.

22. Ibid., p. 231.

23. Germán Campos's account of robberies and killings committed by the DINA is confirmed in the report by the Aylwin government's Truth and Reconciliation Commission. The commission said that it had studied "numerous cases of deaths caused by agents of government, without any political motive, for reasons of vengeance or other motives." *La Época*, Mar. 5, 1991.

24. Interview with Jaime Troncoso, Santiago.

25. Callejas interview.

26. Branch and Propper, p. 577.

27. Cavallo, Salazar, and Sepúlveda, p. 170.

28. Campos interview.

29. *Ercilla*, May 16, 1979. The Chilean Supreme Court rejected Townley's testimony on the ground that it was the result of a plea bargaining agreement, although many Chilean criminal statutes recognize the validity of plea bargaining. For a discussion of how the Chilean Supreme Court reached its ruling, see Branch and Propper, p. 597.

30. *El Mercurio*, Dec. 22, 1978.

31. Cavallo, Salazar, and Sepúlveda, pp. 141–42.

32. From a declassified State Department telegram dated Dec. 20, 1977.

33. Excerpts from Pinochet's speech of Jan. 4, 1978, were taken from *Revista Qué Pasa*, pp. 12–13. The periodical published a special edition on Jan. 6, 1978, with a cover photograph of Pinochet.

34. Cavallo, Salazar, and Sepúlveda, pp. 175–76.

35. Interview with retired general Gustavo Leigh at his home in Santiago.

36. The text of Leigh's interview with *Il Corriere della Sera* was reprinted in *Hoy*, July 26–Aug. 1, 1978, pp. 8–9.

37. Cavallo, Salazar, and Sepúlveda, pp. 179–80.

Chapter Five

1. Interview with Hernán Cubillos, Santiago.

2. Cavallo, Salazar, and Sepúlveda, p. 215.

3. *Hoy*, Mar. 26, 1980.

4. Cavallo, Salazar, and Sepúlveda, pp. 218–19.

5. The Marcos government managed to avoid a complete break by dispatching a senior diplomat to Santiago to explain that authorities in Manila had discovered a terrorist plot against Pinochet. This explanation, while not exactly convincing, was face-saving enough to satisfy the regime.

6. *Time*, Jan. 14, 1980.

7. *Chile: Economic Outlook Report*, U.S. embassy, Santiago, p. 2.

8. *Chile: Economic Trends Report, 1981*, U.S. embassy, Santiago, p. 11.

9. Huneeus, pp. 26–27.

10. *Textos comparados de la Constitución Política de la República de Chile—1980, de la Constitución Política de la República de Chile—1925*, Instituto de Estudios Generales, Santiago, 1980, pp. 151, 155, 158.

11. Frieden, pp. 150–51.

12. For a description of Pinochet's handling of the Chilean army, see Arriagada, *La Política Militar de Pinochet*.

13. *Textos comparados*, p. 108.

14. Interview with Floreal Recabárren, Antofagasta.

15. From a State Department telegram, Sept. 1980, released to me under the Freedom of Information Act.

16. Reprinted in *APSI*, Feb. 8–14, 1988.

17. I covered the Sept. 11, 1980, plebiscite for the *Financial Times,* the *Economist,* and other media.

18. *El Mercurio,* Sept. 13, 1980.

19. Cavallo, Salazar, and Sepúlveda, p. 258. At a foreign press luncheon I attended in 1984, Cardinal Silva also recounted this exchange with Pinochet.

20. I covered David Rockefeller's press conference.

21. *Financial Times,* Nov. 26 and Dec. 2, 1980.

22. I covered this ceremony at the Diego Portales building.

Chapter Six

1. *Newsweek,* international ed., July 13, 1981.

2. *Cosas,* June 3, 1982.

3. *Newsweek,* international ed., July 13, 1981.

4. Cavallo, Salazar, and Sepúlveda, p. 267.

5. Fernando Dahse, *Mápa de la Extrema Riquéza,* Editorial Aconcágua, Santiago, 1979, pp. 27–46.

6. Quoted in the *Financial Times,* Mar. 9, 1983.

7. *Financial Times,* Nov. 10, 1981.

8. From a tape recording of Jeane Kirkpatrick's press conference in Santiago on August 3, 1981, which I attended.

9. Interview with Fabiola Letelier, Santiago.

10. Jaime Castillo described his expulsion in an interview at the Human Rights Commission in Santiago. Following his deportation Castillo spent two years in exile in Caracas, Venezuela.

11. I covered the Frei funeral and witnessed the incidents described.

12. *Financial Times,* Feb. 18, 1982, and *Chile: Economic Trends Report,* p. 3.

13. Interview with Hernol Flores at the public employees' union offices in Santiago.

14. For a discussion of the regime's social security system in the context of turning state programs over to the private sector, see Paul Sigmund, "Chile: Privatization, Reprivatization, Hyperprivatization," *Estudios Sociales* 62, trimester 4, Santiago, 1989, pp. 101–2. A later study by the International Labor Organization (ILO), published in Sept. 1992 in the *International Labor Review,* calls into question just how cost-effective and profitable Chile's private pension fund system will prove over the years. The article noted that the operating costs of the companies that administer the private pension funds have increased to the point where the firms now consume a quarter of members' contributions. While between 1981 and 1991 the returns averaged 15 percent annually, the article predicted that the private pension companies are unlikely to repeat this performance in the nineties, and said they were already struggling to find investment homes for the $10–12 billion under manage-

ment and the $200 million entering the system each month. The ILO predicted that in the future Chilean retirees will be receiving pensions worth well below half their previous earnings and that the government will have to expend considerable resources to honor its commitment to supplement inadequate pensions as well as those pension funds lost to mismanagement, fraud, and bankruptcy of private pension-fund companies. The ILO concluded that a state-run system, if properly administered, would probably be cheaper and offer more benefits in the long run.

15. Signorelli and Tápia, ¿*Quién Mató a Tucapél?* p. 43.

16. Ibid., pp. 471–80.

17. Ibid., pp. 469–70.

18. There is much to suggest that Kast did not view unemployment as a pressing economic problem. During a meeting with foreign journalists, he was asked about the persistently high unemployment rate in Chile. Kast shrugged, indicating he thought the problem was overemphasized, and added that "at my family's farm in the south we have a lot of trouble finding workers."

19. Lavin, *Miguel Kast,* p. 27.

20. *Latin American Weekly Report,* July 22, 1982, and *Financial Times,* Aug. 10, 1982.

21. *Financial Times,* Jan. 5, 1983.

22. *Financial Times,* Nov. 9, 1983.

23. Frieden, pp. 170–71.

24. Barbara Stallings, "Politics and Economic Crisis: A Comparative Study of Chile, Peru and Colombia," pp. 130–31, in Joan M. Nelson, *Economic Crisis and Policy Choice: The Politics of Adjustment in the Third World,* Princeton Univ. Press, Princeton, N.J., 1990.

25. Interview with Carlos Cáceres when he was Chile's central bank president.

26. Interview with Fernando Dahse, Santiago.

27. Claudia Rosett, "The Free Market and Chile: An Aborted Economic Test," *New York Times,* July 3, 1983.

Chapter Seven

1. *Financial Times,* Jan. 5, 1983.

2. *Latin American Weekly Report,* Feb. 11, 1983.

3. This account is based on the various press conferences held by PRODEN and the Alianza Democrática I attended in 1983.

4. Interview with Rodolfo Seguel for *Newsweek,* international ed., Aug. 15, 1983.

5. *Hoy,* May 18–24, 1983.

6. *El Mercurio,* May 17, 1983.

7. Cavallo, Salazar, and Sepúlveda, p. 310.

8. Seguel interview.

9. James Theberge was the director of Latin American studies at George-town's Center for Strategic and International Studies and the author of two books on the influence of the Soviet Union in Latin America and the Caribbean. A regime-backed publishing company, Editora Nacional Gabriela Mistral, had first published a Spanish translation of his *Soviet Presence in Latin America* in 1974. Soon after his arrival in Santiago copies of this book began appearing at newsstands and among the offerings of the street booksellers. Notwithstanding the regime's attempts to use the ambassador's book as a Red Scare propaganda tool, the work itself was a serious analysis that viewed the number of MIR guerrillas active in Chile in 1973 as "insignificant" (see app., p. 136).

10. Cavallo, Salazar, and Sepúlveda, p. 310.

11. "Breve Reseño de la Creación del MIR," internal carabinero report I obtained in 1985. Three members of the MIR arrested in connection with the Urzua assassination later told the Chilean newsmagazine *Cauce* (Apr. 1986) that the CNI had been following them closely for weeks before the attack, which if true suggests that the security forces could either have intervened to prevent the murder or else bumbled their surveillance.

12. Cavallo, Salazar, and Sepúlveda, pp. 318–19.

13. "Breve Reseño de la Creación del MIR."

14. I spoke to several government employees obliged to participate in the parade under the threat of dismissal.

15. *El Mercurio*, Oct. 3, 1983.

16. *La Segunda*, May 1, 1984.

17. Julio Ponce Lerou had held directorships or other executive positions in the Chilean telephone company (1979–1983), the state development company, Corfo, which oversaw the regime's privatization programs (Apr.-Aug. 1983), the state nitrate company, Soquimich (1980–1983), and the state energy company, ENDESA (1982–1983), among others.

18. *Revista Análisis*, Oct. 22–28, 1985. CODELCO issued a statement denying any wrongdoing on its part but stopped short of denying the involvement of Augusto Pinochet, Jr., in the transaction.

19. *Newsweek*, Mar. 19, 1984.

20. *Hoy*, Aug. 11–17, 1984; *Cauce* special supplement, "Porque Atacaron a Lavandero," undated. I spoke to several Chileans who claimed to have heard from good sources that Lavandero's personal life had been the real motive for the brutal attack.

21. For a summary of the regime's crackdown on the press during this period, see "Chile: No News Allowed," a report by the Committee to Protect Journalists, New York, May 1985.

22. I visited the Raúl Silva Henriquez settlement the day of the army raid and on several other occasions from 1983 to 1985.

23. *Hoy,* Oct. 15–21, 1984.

24. Cited in the U.S. State Department human rights report on Chile, released in Feb. 1985.

25. I covered the La Victoria raid for ABC News that day. The Chilean government television station, Channel 7, deliberately stalled at transmitting ABC's footage of the view inside the San Eugenio soccer stadium from a multistory apartment building nearby, claiming that it had not received the necessary authorization.

26. State Department Human Rights Report on Chile, Feb. 1985.

27. *New York Times,* Dec. 16, 1984.

28. *Washington Post,* Dec. 28, 1984.

29. *El Mercurio,* Feb. 24, 1986.

30. I covered Langhorne Motley's visit to Santiago, including an off-the-record session at Ambassador James Theberge's residence and his airport press conference.

31. *New York Times,* May 16, 1986.

32. Interview with Francisco Javier Cuadra, *Newsweek,* international ed., Apr. 1, 1985.

33. For a complete account of the crime and the investigation, see Monckeberg, Camus, and Jiles.

34. The report of the Aylwin government's Truth and Reconciliation Commission said that under the military regime the Chilean judiciary system failed to act "with sufficient energy in the face of human rights violations," and noted that writs of habeas corpus filed in behalf of political detainees "were invariably rejected until the last part of the 80s" (Informe de la Comisión Nacional de Verdad y Reconciliación, supplement printed by the government newspaper, *La Nación,* Mar. 5, 1991, p. 21).

35. *Financial Times,* Aug. 5, 1985.

Chapter Eight

1. According to some critics, a certain amount of U.S. military aid continued to arrive in Chile after the 1976 arms embargo (see Cynthia Aronson and Michael Klare, "U.S. Still Equips Chile's Military," reprint from the Institute for Policy Studies, Washington, D.C., 1978). Even if this is true, it hardly diminished the hostility of regime officials and supporters toward Senator Kennedy. General Vernon Walters's visit to Santiago on Dec. 11 and 12, 1983, was officially to "exchange points of view with the Chilean government about global affairs," but in reality was aimed at soothing the regime's injured feelings over the U.S. decision to lift the arms embargo against Argentina.

According to some diplomatic sources, Pinochet flew into a rage against the United States during the second of his two meetings with Walters. A partially declassified State Department cable nine pages long contains several blacked-out passages that may describe such an incident; after one lengthy deleted passage the cable states, "Ambassador Walters pointed out that his own presence showed that the U.S. government was interested in Chile, and wished to maintain good relations." Another passage refers to Walters "persuasively defending" the U.S. actions. A subsequent cable to Walters from then-ambassador James Theberge thanks him for his help "in avoiding serious erosion of U.S. relations with Chile."

2. Cavallo, Salazar, and Sepúlveda, pp. 381–82.

3. From a U.S. embassy cable to the State Department, Jan. 16, 1986. In Washington, a State Department spokesman sidestepped questions as to whether the regime had organized the anti-Kennedy demonstration.

4. Cavallo, Salazar, and Sepúlveda, p. 383.

5. From a cable written by U.S. ambassador Harry Barnes to the State Department, following a visit by Máximo Pacheco, his wife, and his housekeeper to his residence Jan. 19, 1986, to discuss the kidnapping. The ambassador's cable says that the "Pinochet government's displeasure with both Senator Kennedy's visit and with human rights groups in Chile may have been the motive behind the abduction and interrogation."

6. Council on Hemispheric Affairs (COHA) *Report on the Hemisphere,* Washington, D.C., Dec. 25, 1984, pp. 4–5.

7. The loan figures are from a Center for International Policy Aid memo, Mar. 17, 1986.

8. *Financial Times,* Mar. 21, 1986.

9. Sources at the Catholic Church's human rights department, the Vicaría de la Solidaridad, said that persons detained by the carabineros were reporting far fewer instances of mistreatment in the wake of Stange's promotion.

10. Cavallo, Salazar, and Sepúlveda, pp. 376–77.

11. Arriagada, p. 195.

12. Interview with Sergio Molina for *Newsweek,* international ed.; the article appeared Apr. 14, 1986.

13. Interview with Marcelo Montecinos at Santiago's general cemetery on the second anniversary of Rodrigo Rojas's death.

14. Interview with Tore Austad during the conference.

15. Quoted in the *Times on Sunday* (Sydney, Australia) Oct. 4, 1987. Other details of the incident come from Verdugo, *Rodrigo y Carmen Gloria.* Although this book is mostly a compilation of material that previously appeared in the press, it caused sufficient concern within the Chilean army for the military to call Verdugo before a military judge early in 1987.

16. *El Mercurio,* June 3, 1986.

17. The Chilean Communist Party subsequently used Rojas's picture on at least two different posters, including one that listed well-known communist figures such as Pablo Neruda and Mikhail Gorbachev as a kind of advertisement. However, it is difficult to see how he could have been accepted into the organization—which presumably had strict screening procedures and would have been suspicious of a youth raised in the United States—within the two months he was in Santiago.

18. Verdugo, *Rodrigo y Carmen Gloria*, p. 72.

19. Interview with Carmen Quintana at her parents' home, Santiago, 1987.

20. Verdugo, *Rodrigo y Carmen Gloria*, p. 188.

21. *El Mercurio*, July 11, 1986.

22. *El Mercurio*, July 12, 1986.

23. From ABC's *This Week with David Brinkley*, July 20, 1986.

24. The *Journal of the American Chamber of Commerce in Chile*, no. 36 (June 1986), p. 6.

25. The Economist Intelligence Unit, "Chile Country Profile 1989–90," p. 39; and "Subsidizing Pinochet: Aid and Comfort for the Chilean Dictatorship," Sept. 1985, pp. 6–7, Center for International Policy, Washington, D.C.

26. *Financial Times*, Feb. 10, 1987. Chile's privatization program had many critics even within the regime, such as its advisory body, the Economic and Social Council, which expressed concern over the secretiveness surrounding some of the transactions and warned against exchanging a state monopoly for a private one in some areas.

27. I obtained a copy of the Channel 7 footage of General Ojeda's presentation. A station employee made a point of shutting off the recording equipment when the official abruptly stood up and left the room without allowing questions.

28. *Times on Sunday*, Sydney, Australia Oct. 4, 1987.

29. *Hoy*, no. 474 (1986), pp. 18–24.

30. Cavallo, Salazar, and Sepúlveda, pp. 389–90.

31. This account comes from my notes of the government television broadcasts the night of Sept. 7, 1986.

32. *Newsweek*, international ed., Aug. 18, 1986.

Chapter Nine

1. *El Mercurio*, July 11, 1986.

2. Fernandez Larios and his lawyer Axel Kleinboimer were interviewed in *APSI*, Feb. 9–22, 1987.

3. Fernandez Larios testified in U.S. Federal Court in Washington, D.C., on Feb. 2, 1987.

4. Fernandez Larios's letter to Chilean army vice commander Santiago Sinclair was published in *APSI*, Feb. 17–22, 1987, among other publications.

5. *Negro en el Blanco*, Mar. 9–15, 1987.

6. *Financial Times*, Jan. 5, 1988.

7. I covered the actors' activities, as well as the visit of Christopher Reeve, for ABC News and the *Financial Times*.

8. Interview with Javier Díaz, Santiago.

9. Marras, p. 36.

10. *La Época*, Sept. 18, 1988.

11. Willoughby interview.

12. *Financial Times*, Sept. 1, 1988.

13. Interview with Patricio Bañados, Santiago.

14. I watched this and most of the opposition and pro-Pinochet broadcasts, and obtained a videocassette containing excerpts of the "No" campaign's fifteen-minute broadcasts, from which this quote and the descriptions of the program are taken.

15. Interview with Florcita Motuda, Santiago.

16. Bañados interview.

17. The figures are from a study by Sergio Bitar, "Chile: Experiments in Democracy," Institute for the Study of Human Issues, 1986, and quoted in Dornbusch and Edwards, p. 177.

18. Lavin, *Chile: A Quiet Revolution*, p. 94.

19. Hepatitis and typhoid fever, as well as parasites and other intestinal ailments, are widespread in Chile. They are usually caused by eating contaminated food or produce that has not been disinfected. Most Santiago supermarkets sell a food disinfectant in the fruits and vegetable section.

20. The coordinator of the "No" campaign, Genaro Arriagada, told me that his group calculated that Volodia Teitelboim's statements cost the "No" side about 6 percent of the vote.

21. From a partially declassified U.S. embassy cable to the State Department, Oct. 1, 1988.

22. Interview with Bruce Babbitt at a press conference at the Hotel Carrera in Santiago, Oct. 6, 1988.

23. The military parade was held in Santiago's O'Higgins Park on Sept. 19, 1988.

24. Cavallo, Salazar, and Sepúlveda, p. 442. The account of events of Oct. 5, 1988, was compiled from my coverage of the plebiscite for ABC News and the *Financial Times*, and includes Chilean television and radio broadcasts too numerous to recount. General Matthei later described the junta members' meeting with Pinochet for *Revista Qué Pasa*, Oct. 13, 1988.

25. From a partially declassified U.S. embassy cable to the State Department, Oct. 5, 1988.

26. General Matthei's statement that the "No" vote was winning was quickly broadcast on Radio Cooperativa, a Christian Democratic radio station in Santiago.

Chapter Ten

1. From a declassified U.S. embassy cable to the State Department, Oct. 7, 1988.

2. *La Época*, Oct. 10, 1988.

3. *La Época*, Oct. 26, 1989.

4. *La Época*, Oct. 30, 1989.

5. The Molina-Contreras case received almost daily coverage in the Chilean press at the time, and the reports—in virtually every newspaper and newsmagazine—are too numerous to cite here. Among the accounts I have used are *La Época*, Nov. 22, 1988, Nov. 23, 1988, and Feb. 15, 1989; *Revista Qué Pasa*, Dec. 5–11, 1988; *Hoy*, Nov. 28-Dec. 4 and Dec. 5–11, 1988; and *Revista Análisis*, Dec. 5–11, 1988.

6. *APSI*, Jan. 30-Feb. 5, 1989.

7. From a transcript of the calls to the U.S. embassy in Santiago, published by *La Época*, Mar. 30, 1989.

8. *La Época*, Mar. 14, 1989.

9. *La Época*, Mar. 15, 1989.

10. Ibid.

11. The National Endowment for Democracy, created by the U.S. Congress in 1983 to foster democracy in foreign countries, channeled $1 million to "support advocates of Chilean democracy," with about half of that amount administered by Democratic party officials. See "How U.S. Political Pros Get Out the Vote in Chile," *New York Times*, Nov. 16, 1988, p. 16.

12. *La Época*, June 10, 1989.

13. *La Época*, June 21, 1989.

14. Quoted in *Latin American Weekly Report*, Oct. 26, 1989.

15. *Financial Times*, Mar. 21, 1990, and *Latin American Weekly Report*, Apr. 5, 1990.

16. *Financial Times*, May 22, 1990.

17. Ibid.

18. Associated Press dispatch, Santiago, May 28, 1990.

19. *Financial Times*, May 30, 1990.

20. *Financial Times*, Sept. 5, 1990.

21. Reuters dispatch from Santiago, Sept. 4, 1990.

22. *Financial Times*, Jan. 17, 1991.

23. From the text of the Commission for Truth and Reconciliation's 120-page report, published in *La Nación*, Mar. 5, 1991.

24. The Chilean supreme court justices called the commission report "impassioned, reckless, and biased," and protested the criticism of the judiciary in a twenty-four-page statement issued ten weeks later (Latin American Weekly Report, May 20, 1991). Two of the commission's eight members were former Pinochet regime officials, so the charge of bias seems unfounded.

25. *La Época*, Mar. 5, 1991.

26. Newspaper insert by the Council of Retired Army Generals, printed in *El Mercurio*, Mar. 17, 1991.

27. *La Nación*, Mar. 5, 1991.

28. The *Economist*, Sept. 28, 1991.

29. *Financial Times*, Feb. 4, 1992.

30. *Financial Times*, July 1, 1992.

31. Associated Press dispatch from Santiago, Aug. 21, 1992.

32. *La Tercera*, Sept. 20, 1992.

33. Quoted in the *New York Times*, July 12, 1992.

Select Bibliography

Archdiocese of Santiago. *¿Dónde Están?* Vols. 1–7, Santiago: Archdiocese of Santiago, 1979.

Arriagada, Genaro. *La Política Militar de Pinochet*. Santiago: Ediciones Fernando Silva, 1985.

Branch, Taylor, and Eugene Propper. *Labyrinth*. New York: Viking, 1982.

Canetti, Elias. *Crowds and Power*. New York: Farrar, Straus, and Giroux, 1984.

Cavallo, Ascanio, Manuel Salazar, and Oscar Sepúlveda. *Historia Oculta del Régimen Militar*. Santiago: Ediciones La Época, 1988.

Correa, Raquel, Malú Sierra, and Elizabeth Subercaseaux. *Los Generales del Régimen*. Santiago: Editorial Aconcagua, 1983.

Dinges, John, and Saul Landau. *Assassination on Embassy Row*. New York: Pantheon, 1980.

Frieden, Jeffry. *Debt, Development, and Democracy: Modern Political Economy and Latin America, 1965–1985*. Princeton, N.J.: Princeton Univ. Press, 1991.

Government of Chile. *Libro Blanco del Cambio de Gobierno en Chile*. Santiago: Editorial Lord Cochrane, 1973.

Harrington, Edwin, and Monica González. *Bomba en una Calle de Palermo*. Santiago: Editorial Emisión, 1987.

Hersh, Seymour. *The Price of Power: Kissinger in the Nixon White House*. New York: Summit, 1983.

Huneeus, Pablo. *Nuestra Mentalidad Económica*. Santiago: Editora Nueva Generación Ltda., 1979.

Lavin, Joaquín. *Chile: A Quiet Revolution*. Santiago: Editorial Zig-Zag, 1987.

———. *Miguel Kast: Pasión de Vivir*. Santiago: Editorial Zig-Zag, 1986.

Magnon, C. R. O. *Humanos y Humanoides*. Santiago: Editorial Aconcagua, 1988.

Marras, Sergio. *Confesiones.* Santiago: Editorial Ornitorrinco, 1988.

Mendez, Juan Carlos, ed. *Chilean Economic Policy.* Santiago: Banco Central de Chile, 1979.

Merrill, Andrea T., ed. *Chile: A Country Study.* Washington: U.S. Government Printing Office, 1982.

Millas, Hernán. *Los Señores Censores.* Santiago: Editorial Antártica, 1985.

Monckeberg, María Olivia, María Eugenia Camus, and Pamela Jiles. *Crimen Bajo Estado de Sitio.* Santiago: Editorial Emisión, 1986.

Muñoz, Heraldo. *Las Relaciones Exteriores del Gobierno Militar.* Santiago: Prospel-Cerc, 1985.

Neruda, Pablo. *Memoirs: Confieso Que He Vivido.* New York: Penguin, 1978.

Nunn, Frederick. *The Military in Chilean History.* Albuquerque: Univ. of New Mexico Press, 1976.

Pinochet Ugarte, Augusto. *The Crucial Day.* Santiago: Editorial Renacimiento, 1982.

———. *Geopolítica.* Santiago: Editorial Andrés Bello, 1977.

———. *La Guerra del Pacífico: Campaña de Tarapacá.* Santiago: Editorial Andrés Bello, 1980.

———. *Textos Comparados de la Constitución Política de la República de Chile 1925, 1980.* Santiago: Instituto de Estudios Generales, 1980.

Politzer, Patricia. *Miedo en Chile.* Santiago: Editorial CESOC, 1985.

Prats, Carlos. *Memorias: Testimonio de un Soldado.* Santiago: Editorial Pehuén, 1985.

Santibañez, Abraham. *El Plebiscito de Pinochet—Cazado en su Propio Trampa.* Santiago: Editorial Atenas, 1988.

Signorelli, Aldo, and Wilson Tápia. *¿Quién Mató a Tucapél?* Santiago: Editorial Ariete, 1986.

Varas, Augusto. *Los Militares en el Poder.* Santiago: Pehuén, 1987.

Verdugo, Patricia. *Los Zarpazos del Puma.* Santiago: Ediciones Chile y America, 1989.

———. *Rodrigo y Carmen Gloria: Quemados Vivos.* Santiago: Editorial Aconcagua, 1986.

———. *Tiempo de Días Claras.* Santiago: Ediciones Chile y America, 1990.

Verdugo, Patricia, and Claudio Orrego. *Detenidos-Desaparecidos: Una Herida Abierta.* Santiago: Editorial Aconcagua, 1980.

Index

Compositor:	BookMasters, Inc.
Text:	10.5/13.5 Caledonia
Display:	Caledonia
Printer and Binder:	BookCrafters, Inc.